SURVIVING THE HOLOCAUST WITH THE RUSSIAN JEWISH PARTISANS

SURVIVING THE HOLOCAUST WITH THE RUSSIAN JEWISH PARTISANS

JACK KAGAN
and
DOV COHEN

Foreword by Sir Martin Gilbert

VALLENTINE MITCHELL
LONDON • PORTLAND, OR

First published in 1998 in Great Britain by
VALLENTINE MITCHELL & CO. LTD
Newbury House
900 Eastern Avenue
London IG2 7HH

and in the United States of America by
VALLENTINE MITCHELL
c/o ISBS
5804 N.E. Hassalo Street
Portland, Oregon 97213-3644

British Library Cataloguing in Publication Data

Kagan, Jack
Surviving the Holocaust with the Russian Jewish Partisans
1. World War, 1939–1945 – Jewish resistance – Belarus –
Novogrodek 2. World War, 1939–1945 – Belarus – Novogrodek –
Personal narratives
I. Title   II. Cohen, Dov
940.5′486′478

ISBN 0853033366 (cloth)
ISBN 0853033358 (paper)

Library of Congress Cataloging in Publication Data

A catalog record of this book is available
from the Library of Congress

Typeset by Footnote Graphics, Warminster, Wilts.
Printed in Great Britain by
Bookcraft (Bath) Ltd, Midsomer Norton, Avon

IN LOVING MEMORY OF OUR LOVED ONES KILLED BY THE NAZIS AND THEIR COLLABORATORS

Mass grave in Skridlevo

Grandma **Hannah Gitel Gurevitz**, from Karelitz, killed in Novogrodek,
7 August 1942
Jack's Father **Yankel Kagan**, aged 43, killed while escaping from Koldichevo
Concentration Camp, February 1944
Jack's Mother **Dvore Kagan**, aged 40, killed in Novogrodek, 7 May 1943
Jack's Sister **Nachama Kagan**, aged 17, killed in Novogrodek, 7 May 1943
Dov's Father **Moshe Kagan**, aged 43, killed in Novogrodek, 8 December 1941
Dov's Mother **Shoshke Kagan**, aged 41, killed in Novogrodek, 8 December 1941
Dov's Brother **Leizer Kagan**, aged 14, killed in Novogrodek, 8 December 1941
Aunt **Haike Sucharski**, killed in Novogrodek, 7 May 1943
Cousin **Srolik Sucharski**, aged 17, killed in Novogrodek, 6 August 1942
Cousin **Sheindel Sucharski**, aged 19, killed in prison, March/April 1943
Uncle **Yosef Gurevitz**, from Karelitz, killed in Novogrodek, 7 August 1942
Aunt **Breine Feigel Gurevitz**, from Karelitz, killed in Novogrodek,
7 August 1942
Cousin **Nachama Gurevitz**, aged 17, from Karelitz, killed in Novogrodek,
7 August 1942
Cousin **Hassia Gurevitz**, aged 12, from Karelitz, killed in Novogrodek,
7 August 1942
Uncle **Haim Kapushevski**, from Karelitz, killed in Dvoretz while building
airport, 1943
Aunt **Malke Kapushevski**, from Karelitz, killed in Novogrodek, 7 August 1942
Cousin **Berele Kapushevski**, from Karelitz, aged 10, killed in Novogrodek,
8 December 1941
Cousin **Nochim Kapushevski**, from Karelitz, aged 8, killed in Novogrodek,
7 August 1942

NOT TO FORGIVE AND NOT TO FORGET

Contents

Foreword

by Sir Martin Gilbert

The fighting Jewish partisans of White Russia were a remarkable Jewish phenomenon. Under the leadership of the Bielski brothers, these partisans harassed German military convoys and installations throughout the Novogrodek area of White Russia (now Belarus), and protected hundreds of Jewish families. In setting out their recollections, two of those partisans, the cousins Berl and Jack Kagan, have written a book which recalls many aspects of the Jewish life and fate in their home town, Novogrodek, both before and during the war.

The grandparents and great-grandparents of many of the Jewish readers of this book will have left this part of the former Tsarist Empire a hundred years ago, when it was part of the heartland of eastern European Jewish life. In a mere three years, following the German invasion of the Soviet Union in the summer of 1941, that life was wiped out.

This book has many pages devoted to the Jewish world that existed in Novogrodek in the two decades before the Holocaust: the vigorous life of the six thousand Jews of the town, only a hundred of whom survived. It was a Jewish community that had existed for five hundred years. It is important that its memory should be preserved.

The partisan sections of this book are inspiring. As many as 1,200 Jews managed to find refuge with the Bielski brothers. As many as 360 managed to take up arms: a veritable regiment. The hell from which those partisans escaped is graphically described: 'unimaginable horrors' is the phrase used by Berl Kagan. His cousin Idel (Jack Kagan), whose memoirs form the second part of the book, and whose escape from Novogrodek and life with the Bielski partisans is both a harrowing and an inspiring story – as indeed is his life after liberation – has assembled many documents relating to those horrors, and to the work of the Bielski partisans.

One of the documents published here in full is the German

district court verdict on Johann Artmann, a German army lieutenant who had been appointed the 'Town Major' of Novogrodek. Although the case against Artmann was dismissed, the transcript makes chilling reading. Like this book, it ought to become one of the basic texts of Holocaust study.

London, 1997

Acknowledgements

The authors would like to express their gratitude for the valuable time and generous assistance during the preparation of this book given by Dr Martin C. Dean, Metropolitan Police War Crimes Unit, Tamara Vershitskaya, Curator of Novogrodek Museum, and the Directors of the Imperial War Museum, London, where the exhibition on Novogrodek, 'Surviving the Holocaust with the Russian Jewish Partisans', was held in November 1997.

Preface

Hundreds of thousands of Jews were imprisoned in more than 100 ghettos and camps in Belorussia. The largest ghetto was in Minsk (100,000 people); others were in Brest (34,000), Bobruisk (20,000), Vitebsk (20,000), Borisov (10,000), Baranovitz Lida Grodno (2,000), Slonim (24,000), Novogrodek (6,500) and so on. During the years of occupation about 400,000 Jews perished.

Anti-fascist movements started in the ghettos in very difficult conditions. They established contacts with the underground anti-fascist groups outside the ghettos; they took part in sabotage in factories which served the army, spoiled machine-tools, equipment and raw materials; they repaired or constructed weapons and explosive devices, and collected medicines and clothes.

In many ghettos, there were uprisings before the massacres and armed resistance to the enemy was organised by the prisoners. Contacts were established between ghettos and partisan units, and thousands of the prisoners of the ghettos joined the partisans. Jews from the Minsk ghetto formed, or enlarged to a great degree, nine partisan detachments and one battalion.

In 1992 the Belorussian association of Jews for former prisoners of ghettos and Nazi concentration camps was registered.

Part One

MY LIFE

by

Dov Cohen (Berl Kagan)

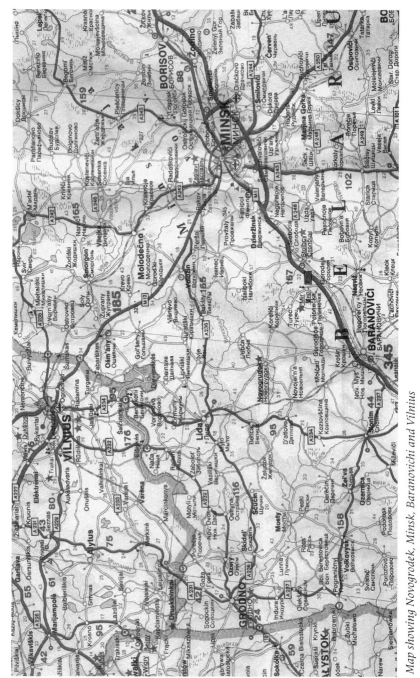

Map showing Novogrodek, Minsk, Baranovichi and Vilnius
© *Mairs Geographischer Verlag Ostfildern*

1 *Novogrodek – the Town where I was Born*

THE SETTLEMENT at Novogrodek was apparently founded in the twelfth century by Prince Yaroslav the Clever of the Kingdom of Kiev. The site was chosen to serve as a fortress, guarding the Russian border against the attacks of nomadic tribes and Teutonic Christians.

The site was well chosen, both strategically and topographically. The town is located about 140 kilometres south of Vilnius (Vilna), the present day capital of Lithuania, and 150 kilometres west of Minsk, capital of today's Belarus (formerly Belorussia). It was built on a plateau, commanding the surrounding countryside and major roads.

The fortress, with its massive walls, towers, deep moats and drawbridges, was almost impenetrable. The local people found refuge within its walls in times of trouble.

The importance of Novogrodek increased during the reign of the Lithuanian princes, and in the united kingdom of Poland-Lithuania, in the fifteenth century. By this time it had a population of 12,000, and was developing into an important cultural centre. During the reign of the Lithuanian princes, the supreme court, or Tribunal, convened there regularly and official events, such as royal weddings, victory marches and conventions of the aristocracy, were held there. The people of Novogrodek had been granted special trade and tax privileges.

We hear of Jews living in Novogrodek as early as the fifteenth century. The majority probably came there from Poland and Russia. By the early twentieth century, as many as 70 per cent of the town's inhabitants were Jews, mostly craftsmen and merchants.

In the Polish Republic established after the First World War, Novogrodek served as a district capital even though it was neither a commercial centre, nor the largest town in its district. It was chosen because of its glorious past, uniqueness and rare beauty.

3

The fortress, Novogrodek

Castle in Novogrodek, from a nineteenth-century painting

Market place, Novogrodek. Yankel, the water carrier

The great Polish poet, Adam Mickiewicz, who was born in Novogrodek, describes its beauty in his work. Living in exile in Italy, he expressed his longing for his native town in wonderful poems, likening the place to life and health and declaring that only he who resides far away can truly appreciate its rare charm, and regret the fact that he doesn't live there. Mickiewicz, who knew the Jews of Novogrodek, admired them and praised their merits: their scholarship, family values and faithfulness. He found many talented Jews in Novogrodek. One of these was Yankel the musician, the cymbal player described in the poet's great work, *Pan Tadeusz*. Yankel was a professional artist, whose music penetrated the hearts of his listeners. When Yankel played, his music spoke of the glorious past of the town and state, of bygone tragedies and suffering, as well as hope for a better future and the blossoming of spring. Mickiewicz wrote this great poem while living in Poland, under the cruel Russian regime.

5

Adam Mickiewicz, the great Polish poet

Novogrodek also had its musicians, choir and cantors – both soloists and amateurs – expert Scripture readers, Hasidim with their tunes, a fireman's band, a children's choir and yeshiva youths who chanted the eternal song of the *gemara*. The Jewish community of Novogrodek took pride in its writers, thinkers and world famous rabbis as well as its leaders, its cultural and welfare institutions, and the special atmosphere of its community. The simple folk, craftsmen and shopkeepers who were often quite poor, sometimes even hungry, did all they could to give their children an education, that is, a Jewish, Hebrew education full of feeling for Zionism and the homeland in Palestine. Even though they were far from wealthy, the Jews of Novogrodek managed to establish dozens of cultural, financial and public institutions, which enriched their spiritual life.

Novogrodek's Beit-Yosef Yeshiva, founded in 1906, was famous throughout the Jewish world. Headed for many years by Rabbi (Ba'al Hamusar) Yosef Yozel Horwitz, this yeshiva was known for its Doctrine of Morality and the high morality practised by its students. The doctrine, based upon profound religious faith, deals with the issues of the eternity of man's existence on earth and the purpose of life. At the time, this Doctrine of Morality appealed to many young Jews, all over Belorussia and the Ukraine. Yeshivas like Novogrodek's Beit-Yosef were founded in other cities, attracting young students, as well as older men who felt drawn to the Doctrine. Many students educated and inspired by Beit-Yosef later became great rabbis and scholars, writers and poets. Their works commemorate the yeshiva, and emphasise the importance of morality for the Jewish nation.

Shortly after the First World War and the Balfour Declaration, as the Zionist movement gained influence in the Jewish Diaspora, and the third Aliyah began, a Hebrew school was established in Novogrodek, the H. N. Bialik Jewish Hebrew School, Tarbut. The curriculum resembled that of schools in Palestine, and all subjects, in all classes, were taught in Hebrew. The school was characterised by a positive educational atmosphere, Jewish consciousness and Zionist ideals. Indeed, most of its graduates ultimately went to Israel and took part in the national effort of settlement and the establishment of the state.

There were several other Jewish schools, including small yeshivas, a religious Hebrew school of the Mizrahi movement and private *cheders*, or elementary schools, where *melammeds*, tutors for the young, taught children from an early age. Five-year-olds

The Old Synagogue, Novogrodek

learned Hebrew, prayers and the Torah. At 13, they were prepared for the Bar-Mitzvah.

Jewish children also attended Novogrodek's Polish elementary and secondary schools. All children attended one school or another. The Jews of Novogrodek believed that by educating their children, they would guarantee the nation's future. The town's synagogues, most of which were located in Synagogue Square, were especially famous. There was the Great Synagogue, with its unique architectural beauty and exquisitely carved Holy Ark, and the Great Beit Midrash, or house of learning, where many Jews came to study the Torah. There were also smaller synagogues, each serving craftsmen of a particular profession – synagogues of the Hasidim, Mitnaggedim and Mitaskim.

Among the welfare institutions, there was an orphanage, supervised by a public committee, which provided the town's orphans with all their needs.

Inside the Old Synagogue

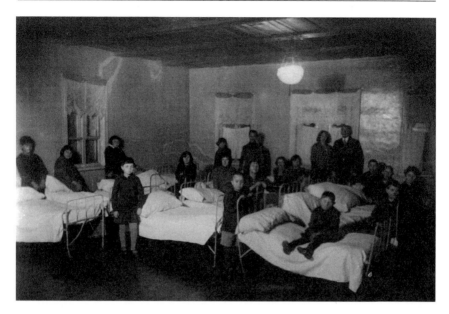

The Orphanage

The Orphanage

Doctors and nurses of the Jewish hospital

This orphanage housed all of the young Jewish orphans in Novogrodek. Associated with it was the Shokdei Mlacha, a type of professional school. When they grew up, the children of the orphanage attended this institution, which taught them a profession and prepared them for the future. Placed by the public committee in the workshop of a professional craftsman, each of the orphans was able to master a trade, and later practise it independently.

The old folks home, Moshav Skanim, took care of all the old people who could no longer stay with their families.

The hospital treated the Jewish population of Novogrodek. The doctors were Jewish and the hospital was well-equipped. It was primarily concerned with treating poor Jews from welfare institutions, and it had its own maternity ward. This Jewish hospital, renowned for its staff's professional excellence and kindliness, attracted needy patients from the whole surrounding region.

Hashomer Hatzair Scouts, Novogrodek, 1935

All Zionist movements and parties had active branches in Novogrodek. The most prominent among the youth movement was Hashomer Hatzair, which conducted educational activities in all the town's schools. Hehaluz held Hachshara camps, in which members acquired agricultural skills and prepared themselves for Aliyah to Palestine. Members of all Zionist youth movements were required to learn the Hebrew language.

The financial institutions active in the town included the merchants' bank and the craftsmen's bank.

A number of other Jewish institutions were active. The Jewish weekly, edited by comrade Boselevitz, published everything that happened in the public life of the Jewish community.

There was a municipal library, where books in Hebrew, Yiddish, Polish and Russian could be taken out twice a week. The Maccabi Athletic Union held gymnastic classes for all ages in a well-equipped gym. Various sports teams trained there as well. The union also had a sports field for soccer and volleyball matches and athletic competitions. The Maccabi's soccer team won many

Jewish weekly newspaper

matches against Jewish and Polish teams from nearby cities. An amateur theatre staged plays, mostly in Yiddish and occasionally in Hebrew, which attracted large, enthusiastic audiences.

For over 500 years, many generations of Jews, with many different life-styles had lived in Novogrodek: Torah scholars, simple folk, labourers, Mitnaggedim and Hasidim, men of morality from Beit-Yosef Yeshiva, educated men of science, Zionists and revolutionaries. They built places of learning and yeshivas, Hebrew and Yiddish schools and other educational institutions, all full of young children and Torah scholars. The Jews of Novo-grodek contributed to the growth and development of the town in all areas.

The Holocaust destroyed this excellent Jewish community. Only a few hundred of Novogrodek's 6,000 Jews survived, having somehow managed to escape the Nazi murderers. Many of these joined the partisans and fought heroically against the Germans and their collaborators. Acts of exceptional heroism were performed by the Jews of Novogrodek, for instance by the 1,200 Jews of the Bielski partisan regiment who took up arms to avenge the deaths of their brethren. Most now live in Israel and have

Members of the Old Folks Home

raised their families there. They have established their own organisation to 'remember and never forget' the Nazis and the horrors of the Holocaust, and to commemorate our outstanding community, our murdered loved ones, our families, parents, brothers and sisters.

2 *Our Family*

My Father's Family

MY PATERNAL grandfather, Leizer Kagan, was a saddler. His workshop, inherited from his father, was located on Racelo Street in Novogrodek, next to his home. My grandfather was an excellent craftsman. Landowners came from far and wide to order harnesses and saddles for their horses. The local peasants knew and respected him. He was an honest, well-liked man, nicknamed 'Lizerko'. His wife Idele was a charitable woman and first-class housewife.

Leizer and Idele had five children. Three sons, Moshe (my father), Yizhak and Yankel and two daughters, Haike and Zvia-Bella. When the boys grew up, they entered the family business, which flourished despite the difficult times, the political instability, the First World War and frequently alternating regimes (the region was conquered by one army after another: the troops of the Russian tsars, the Germans, Bolsheviks, Poles and various gangs, including White Russians and Mensheviks). In an ever-changing world, the family remained united, devoted and industrious.

My uncle Yizhak died young, of typhoid. His picture, which hung in our dining room, showed a great resemblance to my aunt Haike. My aunt Haike married Notke Sucharski, a tinsmith. They had three children: the eldest daughter Sheindel, a son, Srolik, and the youngest, Idele, named after my grandmother.

The beloved little girl Idele died of appendicitis in 1934, at the age of three. At the time, in Novogrodek, there were no doctors skilled enough to perform the necessary operation. My uncle Yankel took the child to specialists in Vilnius, but by then it was too late, complications had occurred and the operation could not save her life.

My other aunt, Zvia-Bella, married Kalman Sanderovski and moved to the town of Zdzienciol, about 30 kilometres from Novo-

My father, Moshe Kagan, as volunteer in the Fire Brigade

grodek. The couple had one son, Leizer, my cousin who now lives in Kvutzat Kineret, Israel. My aunt died in childbirth, or a short while later. The child, Leizer, grew up in our home, in Novogrodek.

I never knew my grandfather Leizer. He died of blood poisoning before I was born; he probably contracted it at his workshop. My grandmother, Idele, was a God-fearing woman. She was quiet and gentle, a good wife and an excellent housekeeper. I remember her from the age of three or four. Paralysed and confined to a chair, she would sit at the dining-room table for days on end, reading the Scriptures and prayer books. Her eldest son, Moshe (my father) took care of her with endless patience and devotion. He would take her out of bed, dress her every morning, feed her, put her to bed and help her with her biological functions. She died in the summer of 1927. I remember that Friday morning, when my father came to get her out of bed and found her lifeless, in a sitting position, leaning back on her pillows and still holding a glass of water.

After the death of my grandfather Leizer – I do not remember precisely when this happened – the family business was run by the two brothers, Moshe (my father) and Yankel. Moshe was the expert craftsman. The saddles and harnesses he made were of the finest quality. He had a special touch and was patient and thorough. The man was an artist. My father could fix a clock or a sewing machine, sew a football by hand and knit. He could do almost anything. He was quiet and kindly, a good husband and wonderful family man. His brother Yankel, on the other hand, was better educated. Though no great craftsman, he was a gifted businessman. The brothers' partnership was very successful, and their business flourished and grew. Over the years, additional

Market day in Novogrodek

shops were opened, where various products were sold: leather articles, harnesses, shoes and boots made of leather and felt. Eventually the brothers opened another workshop, where they manufactured shoes and sandals, especially footwear with crepe-soles which was in great demand in those days.

My Mother's Family

I never knew my maternal grandfather Berl Gurevitz, who died before I was born. My grandmother told me that he had been a teacher, well-versed in the Scriptures, a man of culture and a poet.

My grandmother, Hannah Gitel Gurevitz, ran the family home in Karelitz, a small town about 21 kilometres from Novogrodek. I remember my grandmother's house very well as I spent many summer vacations there. The wooden country house stood on a river bank and had a large vegetable patch with mostly cucumbers. The produce, sent to the market at Novogrodek, added to the family's income.

My grandmother had four children: three daughters, Shoshke (my mother), Dvore and Malke, and a son, Yosef.

My uncle, Yosef Gurevitz, married Breine Feigel London who came from a prominent family of rabbis and Torah scholars. The couple lived in Karelitz and had three daughters, Rachel, Nachama and Hassia. The family had a leather shop, but was quite poor. My uncle Yosef was not a healthy man and apparently suffered from diabetes. His wife Breine Feigel had a brother in England, Shlomo Haim London, a highly respected and very wealthy fur merchant.

In 1937 the rich uncle, Shlomo, visited Karelitz and took his niece, the 13-year-old Rachel back to England with him. Rachel left her family, was educated in England, and later married Sam Konigsberg in London where she and her family still live today. The Konigsbergs had three children, a son, David, and two daughters, Jennifer and Deborah (Debby). My late aunt Breine Feigel had a sister living in Palestine, Tovah Rogovin of Kfar-Sava. My uncle Yosef Gurevitz, his wife Breine Feigel and their daughters Nachama and Hassia all died in the Holocaust.

My other aunt on my mother's side, her younger sister Malke, married Haim Kapushevski in Karelitz, and had two sons, Berele and Nochim. They all died in the Holocaust.

(Standing): *my father Moshe Kagan, my aunt Dvore Kagan, friend Gitel London and a friend of the family.* (Front row): *myself, my uncle and aunt Yoshke and Breine Feigel Gurevitz and grandmother Hannah Gitel Gurevitz, 1923*

Our Family

I don't have many details about the period when my father and his brother were still unmarried. It seems they both had some youthful love affairs (especially Yankel), but none that got out of hand, so to speak, in those conservative times. During the First World War my father served in the Russian army, was captured by the Germans and spent several years in Germany, as a prisoner of war.

My father apparently met my mother, Shoshke Gurevitz, through a matchmaker. The wedding took place in the family home in Novogrodek. The marriage was a great success. My mother was a tall and beautiful woman, with many virtues. She was kind, devoted, gentle and honest, an excellent housewife, very house-proud and authoritative. She was also a wonderful wife and dedicated mother.

When she came to the Kagan home, she immediately took charge of the household, in which my grandmother Idele and her children Yankel and Haike continued to reside. My mother took care of my paralysed grandmother devotedly, for she liked and ad-

My uncle Notke Sucharski

20

mired her. She soon realised that she had joined a good and special family, which was also quite well-off.

Her brother-in-law Yankel, who was several years younger than my father, and still unmarried, was an excellent young man. My mother had a fantastic plan: to arrange a marriage between Yankel and her younger sister Dvore. It wasn't easy. Yankel was considered a good match, and many young women were trying to win his heart. But my mother's persistence paid off. Dvore was very beautiful, and it seems that Yankel was attracted to her. They were married. So the Kagan brothers, Moshe and Yankel, married the Gurevitz sisters, Shoshke and Dvore.

The two families lived together in my grandfather's large house, which was renovated and enlarged over the years. And they managed the family business together.

Later on, my father's sister Haike married Notke Sucharski the tinsmith, and their dowry was a house nearby. The other sister, Zvia-Bella, also got married, and went to live with her husband, Kalman Sanderovski, in Zdzienciol.

In our house, my mother managed the household, while Aunt Dvore, who had a taste for business, started working in the family leather and shoe shops. Our home was a perfect example of tranquillity, love and friendship. Even though two families lived there, I don't recall a single row or quarrel, or even a word of dissatisfaction. The unity and devotion which prevailed were amazing. Over the years, children were born to both families, but even that did not disrupt the harmony. All children were equally cared for, loved and educated.

The business was jointly managed and funds were shared, openly and willingly. When I think of this arrangement today, it seems almost too good to be true. How did this unusual partnership persist so ideally for so many years? Part of the explanation lies in the fact that two brothers had married two sisters. But brothers and sisters can argue or disagree at times. Not so in our family. I never heard a quarrel, argument or harsh word. Not even an expression of discontent. There was no jealousy in this partnership. Everyone contributed his or her share to the united family as a whole.

When my cousin, the late Nachama, was ten years old she contracted a lung disease. For a long time, she required special care

Novogrodek, 9 June 1936. (From left): *Sheindel Sucharski, her brother Srolik, Leizer Sanderovski, in front of him my brother Leizerke Kagan, next to him Idel Kagan, with his sister Nachama in front and Berl Kagan on the right. Three survived.*

and medical attention. My mother took care of her night and day with endless devotion, and was extremely relieved and happy when the child began to recover.

Our Home

I was born on 5 May 1922, not long after the end of the First World War. I was named Berl (Dov) after my maternal grandfather, the late Berl Gurevitz. I was my parents' first-born. I've been told that I was often ill, suffering from severe stomach aches, a bad case of whooping cough and unusually severe cases of various childhood diseases. My parents and the whole family were very worried about me. My early development was slow and problematic.

I was a very thin child and so every summer, my aunt Dvore

Nachama Kagan, Nachama Gurevitz and Berele
Kapushevski, 1938

would take me to the holiday resort of Novoyelna. There, for a full month, she would feed me up, making me eat calorie-rich foods, butter, cream and cake. Every weekend the family would come to visit, and everyone was very pleased when I had gained a few kilos. However, once back home, I would soon shed those precious kilos and return to my normal weight. To make matters worse, right after one of these vacations I began to throw up every morning. When the local doctors couldn't cure me, my Uncle Yankel would take me to see specialists in Vilnius. Fortunately, I soon grew out of this phase.

My late brother Leizer, five years my junior, on the other hand, was a strong and healthy baby, who became a handsome child, tall and blond. The family nicknamed him 'Lalke' (doll). Later in his teens, my brother developed into a fine athlete. He had many friends, and everybody liked him.

Leizerke Kagan (front right) *with his football team*

Yankel and Dvore's first child was Nachama, born in 1926, I believe. She was a beautiful girl, who looked like her mother. In 1929 their son Idel was born and was named after my grandmother Idele. This is my cousin Idel (now called Jack) Kagan, co-author of this book, who now lives in London and is married to Barbara Steinfeld.

Our large, spacious house was made of wood and had a tiled roof. It was located on Racelo Street, a Jewish neighbourhood at the centre of Novogrodek. It was a poor neighbourhood, built in a ravine. The wooden houses were very crowded and haphazardly thrown together. Most of the inhabitants were poor artisans with large families. Our family and my aunt Haike Sucharski's family were considered wealthy and respectable, not only in Racelo Street, but by all of Novogrodek.

I remember Racelo Street when it was still unpaved. The thawing snows of spring and the rains of autumn turned it into a muddy mess. In the winter, its snow-covered slopes became a

Nachama Kagan, Rachel Gurevitz (Konigsberg) and Sheindel Sucharski

playground, where hordes of children would compete noisily with each other on their home-made skis and sleds.

Racelo Street bordered on the Mickiewicz estate, which had formerly belonged to the great poet. Its five-metre-high stone wall ran the whole length of our street. Some chestnut trees grew on the estate, bearing fruit every year in the early autumn. As children, we would gather the fallen chestnuts, sometimes in cratefuls, and also 'help' them fall by throwing sticks and stones at the trees. With the collected chestnuts, we would play conkers, each type of chestnut having a price.

Every summer, especially when school was out, the children of Racelo Street would play the popular games of those times, such as 'Pigra', in which you throw sticks at a target, usually a tin can set on a pile of stones, at a distance of about 30 metres, and 'Palant', which is similar to today's rugby, and many other games. Racelo

Street was always bustling with children. It was a centre of games and activities.

Right next to our house there were several small, two-room apartments. The families that lived there were very poor, sometimes even suffering from hunger. I remember that our family used to donate clothes and food to these people. As each holiday approached, my mother would tidy our closets and pass some clothes on to our neighbours, especially the Schlachtmans who were the poorest family in the area.

The Schlachtmans lived in one small room with their three children, Yosef, Bella and Moishele. Bella died in her childhood of diphtheria. The mother, Sorke, was a native of Racelo Street. Her mother, Batiah, her brother, Eli, and her sister, Hassia, also lived there. I still remember old Batiah, lively, small and talkative. Sorke was a simple woman, quiet and shy. She married a man from distant Siedlitz, a town near Warsaw. Haim Schlachtman was lively, outgoing and talkative, very different from his wife. Haim would tell amazing stories, not all of which were strictly true. These fabricated tales, so easily invented, were responsible for his nickname: 'Haim the liar'. As I said, the family was very poor. They had a small store where they sold pottery, oil for wagons and kerosene. Sorke ran the shop, while Haim had various 'occupations' which brought him very little income. Actually, he was often out of work, and Sorke was forced to provide for her family. When we opened the footwear workshop, Haim started working there, and this helped his family somewhat.

Haim's parents lived in Siedlitz, but they didn't keep in touch or visit each other. His parents showed little interest in him and his family, and hardly ever wrote. But they did come on one occasion, and here's the story:

Once, when Haim Schlachtman's financial situation was even more desperate than usual, he sent his parents a telegram: 'Your dear son Haim is very ill. He is dying. His last wish is to see his parents before his death. Please hurry, if you wish to find him alive.' Haim's parents arrived two days later. They found him lying on the floor, under a sheet, with candles behind his head, pretending to be dead. When his parents saw the 'body' they began to cry and wail. Suddenly, a miracle occurred: Haim was resurrected. He got up and announced that he had not been admitted to the Kingdom of Heaven, but rather had been sent back to earth to provide for his family, save his children from starvation and deliver a message to his parents: if they wanted to live to a ripe old age, they must help and support Haim and his family. His mother fainted and his father took out a sum of 100 zlotys and gave it to Sorke. They left without saying goodbye, returned to Siedlitz and never came back.

Sorke Schlachtman's sister, Hassia, married Shalom Pilevski and lived next door in two small rooms, with their old mother Batiah. The Pilevskis had four children. Three sons, Yitzhak, Yisrael and Yosef, and a daughter Golda. They had a haberdashery stall which barely supported the family. Later on, the grandmother Batiah had a stroke and required special nursing. She lay in bed for several years in the Pilevski home and died in 1934. Hassia's husband, Shalom, left the family in the early 1930s and disappeared. Years later, a letter arrived from Buenos Aires, Argentina, saying that he was there, working as a baker and asking his family to join him. And so, several years before the Second World War, our good neighbours the Pilevskis joined their father Shalom in Argentina. I met their children Yitzhak, Yisrael and Golda when they visited Israel. Their mother Hassia is still alive and alert. She often speaks of Novogrodek, Racelo Street and the neighbours. Her sons have a large factory in Buenos Aires which manufactures women's clothes, and are quite well-off. They told me that when they arrived in Argentina, they found their father homeless, without a penny to his name. The family went through some very difficult times, before finally achieving financial stability.

Our house bordered on the vegetable patch of our neighbour, Hannah Mirke. For years she complained that we were breaking down the fence, trespassing and stealing her vegetables. The truth of it was that Hannah Mirke had raspberry bushes in her garden, and children from all over the neighbourhood would go in every night and eat the sweet raspberries. I never knew Hannah Mirke's husband, who died before I was born. But I do remember her three sons, Arke (Aharon), Koshke and Yankel. Arke, the eldest, was well-educated. He studied the theory of socialism and the works of Marx and Engels. Later on he joined the Communist Party, which was illegal in Poland at the time. When Arke felt that the authorities were getting suspicious, he escaped to Russia. The border between Poland and Russia ran about 50 kilometres east of Novogrodek. Arke was never heard from again. There were rumours that the Russians arrested him upon arrival, and that, suspected of Trotskyism, he was executed in the great political purges. His brothers Koshke and Yankel never married. They went on living with their mother. Yankel was a barber, though not one of the best. He supplemented his meagre salary by cutting children's hair in the neighbourhood. Koshke never worked, and I have no idea how that family managed to survive. The small income from the vegetable patch probably helped.

When the Second World War broke out, and the area was occupied by the Russians, Koshke inquired about his brother Arke. He was sent to the secret police, the NKVD. They took down his testimony, and told him to come back in a week's time. By then they would surely have the information he was looking for. Koshke was very excited that week. He could hardly wait for his next meeting with the NKVD officer. He went to the meeting, and was not seen again for six months. When he came back, he said that he had been in prison, where he was questioned at length about his brother, and that he, too, had been suspected of Trotskyism. Luckily, he hadn't been tried or exiled to Siberia. The whole family later died in the Holocaust.

My aunt Haike and her family also lived nearby. They had a wooden house on Racelo Street. Eventually my uncle Notke added a red brick structure, which housed our shoe and sandal factory. My aunt had a small garden, at the centre of which was an old apple tree. Its fruit, of the Anton variety, tasted much like the Grand Alexander variety. The apples were rather sour, and often had worms in them as well but, as children, we loved to climb the tree and pick the fruit from the top branches. Special gooseberry bushes also grew in the garden. They bore a green and thorny but very juicy fruit, from which a delicious jam could be made. And there were raspberries and beautiful flower beds as well. My aunt Haike's garden was a place of rest. A table and some benches stood around the tree, and on summer evenings and Saturdays, the family would gather there, drink tea and coffee, and talk about the latest news, economic and political problems, or the evil winds blowing in from the west from Germany.

The Sucharskis were considered respectable and well-to-do in the town. The husband, Notke, was an expert tinsmith. He had a basement workshop in the market-place, and made a good living. My aunt Haike also helped, by mending umbrellas. She was a kind, industrious, gentle woman, who stood behind her husband. Their home was always open, and they had a great many friends. Notke Sucharski was a public figure, a member of charity institutions, workers' unions and the hospital.

The children, Sheindel and Srolik, were warmly loved by their mother, and strictly disciplined by their father, who was a hard, fastidious man. Fortunately, my aunt Haike had enough patience, understanding, tact and wisdom to put up with her husband's excessive demands and habits. Haike and her children, Sheindel and Srolik, died in the Holocaust.

Later, during the War, Sheindel and her friend, Michle Sosnovski, tried to escape from the professional ghetto the Nazis set up at the court-house in Novogrodek. They got through the fences, and almost as far as the market, but then a Polish woman recognised them and notified the police. Sheindel and Michle were arrested, tortured and put to death.

Notke survived and fought with the Bielski partisans. After the war, back in Novogrodek, he died of an intestinal inflammation. Our relative Sarah-Elka lived with her relation Pessiah and Pessiah's husband Gavriel Chesli, in a one-room apartment in the synagogue area of Novogrodek. Sarah-Elka was my grandfather Leizer's sister. I never knew her husband, Mr Leveton. Her children lived in America and France, and she would bring me stamps from their letters. I remember her as a kind, pleasant, well-educated old woman, well versed in the Scriptures.

Sarah-Elka was known in and around Novogrodek for her healing powers. She could even help those whom modern medicine had given up on. Jews and Gentiles from Novogrodek and nearby villages would come to Sarah-Elka for help. She never took money or gifts for her services. To her, it was a sacred good deed, a *mitzvah*. Sarah-Elka could exorcise evil spirits and undo the evil eye. When called upon to treat cases of depression or anxiety, she would heat lead and pour the molten substance into a pot of water which she held over the patient's head. The lead would immediately harden into various shapes, and Sarah-Elka, carefully examining the strange forms, would discern the cause of the patient's fear or depression: a wild beast, a particular person or an evil spirit. After the lead treatment, Sarah-Elka would whisper certain verses and prayers, and that was it. Her patients said afterwards that the procedure had helped them. Sarah-Elka also used cupping glasses and various herbs with healing properties. Sarah-Elka's relation, Pessiah, who lived with her for many years, died in the 1930s. After Pessiah's death, Sarah-Elka married Gavriel Chesli, and stayed in the same apartment.

Sarah-Elka and Gavriel died in the Holocaust.

3 *The Time before the Germans Came*

THE FAMOUS *cheder* at which the *melammed* Alter Menaker taught was located in our street. Children began to attend this *cheder* at the age of five, and studied there for several years. The school year and the payments were divided into *zmanim* or semesters. The children learned to read Hebrew, and studied the prayers and the Torah. Alter Menaker was known as a good, strict teacher. His *cheder* was always full of young children, who studied there from early morning to sunset, lighting their way home every night with kerosene lanterns. I remember how Alter Menaker sat patiently with each and every student, scolding or praising, as the case merited. He had a wooden stick, with which he would tap the hands of children when their progress was unsatisfactory.

I went to Menaker's school for several years. He treated me well, because we were neighbours, and also because of my family's respectable position. I still remember Menaker, my first rabbi, a tall, pale Jew with a thick black beard, stern, nervous and senti-mental. He was a God-fearing man, who studied the Scriptures night and day. He stammered a little, but was also a reader at the Todres Synagogue in Novogrodek. Amazingly, when he read the Torah, Alter Menaker never stammered. He read fluently and correctly, with the proper *nigun* (melody). I remember that every year, on Purim eve, Alter Menaker would read the Megillat Esther (Scroll of Esther) in his home, to all the people who lived in our street. It was a merry occasion, especially for the children, who would shake their rattles, fire their toy guns and make a racket with all sorts of home-made contraptions such as a key and nail tied together with a wire: the hole in the key would be stuffed with sulphur, the nail would be pressed against it, and the whole device, when hurled at the wall, would produce a very loud explosion.

Menaker's wife, Rivka, died of a stroke. The treatment, which included bleeding and leeches, didn't help. Alter, his daughter Esther and his son Avraham Shmuel all died in the Holocaust. His

31

youngest son Ishie joined the Partisans and was killed in action, by German guards.

After a few years in Menaker's *cheder* I was sent to more advanced *cheders*: to the *melammed* Leibel, nicknamed 'Leibel the cheek', because of the lump on his cheek, to Parnas's *cheder* and to Mirski's *cheder*. In these *cheders* I acquired a basic knowledge of Hebrew and the Torah, and began to study the Talmud. My mother believed it was very important that I, her eldest son, should attend the Polish state secondary school, named after the poet Adam Mickiewicz. In preparation for this school, it was decided that, after the *cheders*, I must spend four years at the Polish elementary school to learn the Polish language and the secular subjects included in the high school entrance exams. Getting into the government secondary school at Novogrodek was no easy task, especially for Jews. Very few Jewish children were admitted, particularly in the 1930s, which was a very anti-Semitic era in Poland.

While attending the Polish elementary school, I was also tutored by private Hebrew teachers, so as not to forget my language and other Hebrew studies. In particular, I have favourable memories of my teacher Ovsiavitz who had a thorough knowledge of Hebrew literature and history, and of Mirski, a wise, well-educated Zionist. Sarah Shkolnik tutored me for a whole year, helping me prepare for the entrance examinations for the secondary school; she was considered one of the best tutors for this purpose and I passed. My family was very happy, and my mother was extremely proud that her son had been admitted to the secondary school. Thirty Jewish students had taken the entrance exams and only five were accepted. Many parents envied my mother.

Studying at the Polish secondary school in the years 1936–39 was difficult and complicated, especially for the Jews, whose command of the Polish tongue wasn't perfect. The teachers and professors often mistreated the Jewish students and demanded a great deal more than was required of the Christians. I did not enjoy my years at the Polish secondary school, and although I graduated successfully and got my diploma in 1939, a few months before the beginning of the Second World War, my memories of the time are not altogether pleasant. However, I was popular and made many friends.

Towards the end of the 1930s, Poland grew increasingly anti-

Semitic. The Poles, especially young people and university students, were influenced by the Germans' Nazi theories. The 'Endeks' or Free Poles party was formed, advocating active anti-Semitic measures: a boycott on Jewish trade, limiting admission of Jews to universities, banning Jews from public office, and various campaigns of racist propaganda. The government began to limit the civil rights of Jews and otherwise harass them. Physical injury, beatings and even pogroms became more common towards the end of 1938. I remember the rumour that spread through Novogrodek just before Passover of 1939: that the Poles were planning a pogrom for the night of the Seder. And sure enough, large numbers of young Poles in uniform arrived in the town with anti-Semitic slogans and threats, telling the local Jews they were about to die. Peasants from surrounding villages flocked to the town in their carts or on foot, carrying large sacks for the expected plunder. The Jews were terrified. That night we didn't celebrate the Seder. The women and children of my family and my uncle Notke's family all hid in the cellar, while the men prepared to defend us with iron rods, axes and pitchforks. But the pogrom never took place. It was prevented by the local police. Rumour had it that the chief of police had been bribed with a large sum of money and it worked.

It was quite clear to us that the poorly armed, old-fashioned Polish army wouldn't be able to defend the country in the event of war which we now expected. Our fear of the Germans grew very real indeed. The rumours about what the Nazis had done to the Jews elsewhere were alarming, but we had no place to run.

In August 1939, Russia and Germany signed a non-aggression treaty. The Second World War broke out at the beginning of September 1939. The German armoured divisions wiped out everything that stood in their way, and the cities of Poland were destroyed by the German air force. The Polish army retreated and left the front wide open. The Poles fought bravely, but even the Polish cavalry's suicide attacks were clearly no match for the German tanks and mighty forces.

The Russian–German treaty, signed by the foreign ministers, Molotov and Ribbentrop, had divided the land of Poland between her two powerful neighbours. The western parts of White Russia and the Ukraine, which had belonged to Poland, now became part of the Soviet Union. The advancing German armies stopped on the eastern border of these territories, marked by the River Bug. The Red Army liberated the area, and Novogrodek came under Soviet rule. The Jews of Novogrodek rejoiced. Russian rule was certainly better than German rule despite deep apprehensions, felt mostly by the wealthier Jewish families.

The city's Jews, especially the youths and children, swarmed through the streets, admiring the Red Army troops, their weapons, tanks and armoured vehicles. Battalions of Cossacks, cavalry and infantry marched through the town for days on end. We were greatly impressed. The Soviet authorities ordered the citizens to go on with their normal lives, open the shops and workshops, and follow orders closely. There were some arrests, mostly of high Polish officials and police officers. So we opened our shops, which were full of leather products and footwear, and made a lot of money. Our businesses boomed. Swarms of customers, mostly Russian soldiers, bought just about everything. They didn't even try to bring down prices, and they paid in rubles (according to an exchange rate of one ruble for one Polish zloty). Demand was so great that we raised the prices, but the customers just kept on coming. Within a few weeks the store had been emptied, but there was no source for renewing the stock. At home we had bagfuls of money, but we soon realised that its value was decreasing. Fearing difficult times ahead, the family decided to hide some of the fine leather and shoe soles, which were in great demand.

In October 1939 the Soviet authorities nationalised all shops, warehouses, banks, large houses, and so on. Most of the Jews were left with no source of income. Later on, the authorities established co-operative factories and workshops, where various craftsmen were employed. The pay was quite poor, but our family had everything it needed. Once in a while we would secretly sell some of our hidden goods, and buy necessary supplies, mostly food. My father and his brother Yankel worked in the co-operative leather workshop, and seemed well satisfied. We stayed in our large house, and life went on as usual. Every once in a while we were ordered to let some rooms to Soviet officials, and a Red Army officer also lived in our home, but that was quite tolerable. We were glad that the War and its horrors remained far away. We grew accustomed to the regime, and were reasonably happy.

I was admitted to the ninth grade at the Russian secondary school and graduated from the tenth grade in June 1941, receiving a Russian matriculation diploma. My brother Leizer and cousins Nachama and Idel attended the Yiddish secondary school.

After a while, the Soviets began to sort out the population. We were ordered to fill out forms and apply for Soviet identification cards. Many of the Jews had 'Clause 11' stamped in their documents, and at the beginning we didn't know what it meant. Later on it turned out that this indicated a disloyal element, a former rich merchant or high official in the Polish regime. Those who had been so designated were apprehensive about the future. Our family, however, had no 'Clause 11' stamps on its documents, and at the time, this made us very happy. My cousin Leizer Sanderovski was drafted by the Polish army when the War broke out and fought against the German invaders. When the Polish army took to its heels Leizer was taken prisoner, then escaped, crossed the border and came back to Novogrodek. We were very glad to see him. We all liked Leizer. As children we had called him Big Leizer, in order to distinguish him from my brother, Little Leizer. In Novogrodek, Leizer started working for the Russians, supervising a leather workshop. He was an outstanding worker and, as a reward, he was sent to a holiday resort in Minsk district. This happened just a few days before the war between Russia and Germany broke out.

Dark clouds were fast approaching our region. Persistent rumours circulated that Germany was getting ready to attack the Soviet Union. We trusted in the great Red Army, believing Soviet propaganda about its power, weapons and capabilities. And yet there was considerable anxiety, because the Germans had won many victories and marched through many European countries, including France. It seemed as though the Germans were simply unstoppable. Even those fortifications considered impenetrable such as the French defensive Maginot line hadn't been able to hold them back. The German armed forces simply went around the fortifications, never hesitating to trample and conquer neutral lands, for no reason, and without so much as a declaration of war.

In 1940–41, Jewish refugees who had escaped from territories held by the Germans in Poland, Czechoslovakia and other lands arrived in Novogrodek. They told tales of German atrocities:

arrests, concentration camps, executions and massacres. We heard these accounts, but refused to believe them. The horror stories simply didn't make sense. We went on with our lives, deluding ourselves that it was impossible for such murderous atrocities actually to be approved and perpetrated by the authorities. The Germans were considered a civilised nation. Many people remembered the German army of the First World War, which wasn't too terrible. The Jewish nation had known much suffering in its long history, and had learned to adapt and survive. And the Russian authorities had announced in May 1941, about a month and a half before the German invasion, that refugees who wanted to go back to the German part of Poland should register, and arrangements would be made. Some of them actually did register, and later on the Russians rounded them up and sent them to Siberia. But the fact that some refugees wanted to return indicated that the stories about the Germans might indeed be exaggerated.

Throughout the month of June 1941, the Russians made arrests in Novogrodek. For the most part, they arrested Jews who had the dreaded 'Clause 11' stamped on their identification cards. These people were stripped of all their possessions and deported to Siberia with their families as undesirable and unproductive elements. They were permitted to take only ten kilos of luggage per person. We felt sorry for the members of our community who were sent away in this fashion. But later it turned out that the Russians had done these people a 'favour', saving them from death and the horrors of the Holocaust. Most of them survived the war.

On the morning of Sunday, 22 June 1941, we heard that the German air force had bombed Russian cities without warning or even a declaration of war, and that German divisions had crossed the border at many points all along the Russian frontier. Listening to the radio that morning, we heard Molotov, the Soviet Foreign Minister, promise his people that the Red Army was indeed great and powerful, that it was fighting the fascist invaders relentlessly and would triumph in the end.

The Jews of Novogrodek were anxious and fearful. We tried to convince ourselves that the Red Army was invincible and the Germans would never reach our town. With every passing hour, our doubts and apprehension grew. We heard rumours that some government offices in the town had been ordered to get ready for evacuation, and were burning documents and preparing their vehicles. We didn't want to believe it, but the following morning we had to face reality. Red Army soldiers, unorganised, in small groups or one by one, began to pass through the town on their way east, to the former international border between Poland and Russia. Most of them were exhausted and frightened. Many had lost their guns. They told horrifying tales of a burning hell, devastating fire and thousands of casualties. The front line had collapsed, and the Germans were crushing all resistance and advancing ruthlessly.

The Jews were terrified. The town was in a state of panic. The Soviets were obviously leaving. The Jews ran about, sought advice, trying to decide what to do. It was a difficult decision. Escaping into Russia was one possibility, but it wasn't easy. According to rumour, young men in particular were in great danger, and they should save themselves. Many of Novogrodek's young men, especially the bachelors and those who had been involved with the Soviet regime, left town, heading eastward towards the old border, on foot or riding their bicycles. For husbands and fathers, the problem was more complicated. Most of them decided to stay with their families and endure whatever the future might bring. We had heard rumours of atrocities and concentration camps, but nothing about mass murder and executions. And so, most of Novogrodek's Jews stayed in the town, and waited. Those who tried to escape were surprised to discover that the Russian guards wouldn't let them cross the border into Russia. They had received orders that anyone who had been a citizen of Poland prior to 1 September 1939 must be refused entry and sent back home. Many of those who had run away were forced to return to Novogrodek. They told terrifying stories about German bombs, commandos and paratroopers behind the lines, thousands of casualties, human corpses scattered along the roads, and complete chaos and confusion in the retreating Red Army. Whole divisions of Soviet soldiers were surrendering with their weapons and supplies. The German army was advancing rapidly, making its way into Russia and towards its major cities and centres. At home, we were frightened.

One thing was certain, our men were not about to run away and abandon their families. I, like my schoolfriends, decided to run. On the third day of the war my family helped me get ready. I put on suitable clothes and took supplies and money, intending to ride my bicycle towards the border, through Karelitz where my grandmother and uncle lived, then on to Turetz, Mir and Stolpci, which was on the border, about 50 kilometres away from Novogrodek. But by then, many people had already come back, reporting that the border was tightly sealed, and Russian guards were shooting anyone who tried to cross. So I stayed with my family. Later on I found out that many of those who had reached the border were determined not to turn back and indeed managed to cross it a few days later. The border was simply abandoned, the guards left. Many of those who crossed over and escaped into the Russian interior survived the war.

On Tuesday, 24 June 1941, Novogrodek was bombed. The German planes came and dropped a few bombs which damaged some buildings and killed several people. But the damage was not extensive. Our home remained intact. That Tuesday, as increasing numbers of retreating Red Army troops passed through the town, it became clear that the front lines had collapsed and the Germans would soon arrive. Several days later, the town was abandoned by its government officials, police force and firemen. The civil guard, established by volunteers, maintained some degree of order and prevented robbery and looting. Peasants from nearby villages had come to the town, hoping for easy plunder. The looters broke into several clothing and food warehouses, but still feared the Russian soldiers passing through. The soldiers did in fact shoot a few looters, and their bodies served as a warning to others. On the afternoon of Saturday, 28 June 1941, German planes re-appeared in the sky. The town, heavily bombarded, was ablaze because many of its houses were made of wood. It was a terrible whirlwind of smoke and fire. The planes, with their ghastly sirens, flew over at low altitude, spraying everything with bombs and machine-gun fire. Hundreds of people were killed in this attack, most of them Jews who lived in the centre of town.

When the air raid began, we took refuge in the basement of our shoe factory, which was made of stone. A bomb destroyed the building, but fortunately it did not penetrate the cellar. We got out through the window and ran in the direction of Peresika, a suburb of Novogrodek. The whole town was on fire. A Christian woman named Novakovska whom we knew in Peresika let us wait out the fire in her barn. Our family hid there with the Sucharskis and several other Jewish families.

That evening we prayed Ma'ariv, and many wept and cried. The Sabbath ended, and we stood facing the burning town, with fear and sorrow in our hearts. The next day, my father, my uncle Yankel and I went back to see the extent of the damage. Our home had been reduced to ashes. We had lost all our possessions. All we had were the clothes we were wearing and a few dozen gold coins of ten Russian rubles each, which my uncle had on him. We thanked the Lord that our whole family was still alive. We saw some people removing food supplies from warehouses. We also took a sack of sugar and two sacks of toasted bread, and brought these precious goods to our family. We stayed in Mrs Novakovska's barn for a few more days.

Large portions of Novogrodek, particularly the Jewish areas in the centre of town, had burned down. We went to look for a house, and decided to reside at the Delatitski family home, near the fire station. The Delatitskis were deported by the Russians a few days before the German attack, because they had been wealthy and well-connected under the Polish regime. And so we settled at the Delatitskis: my family, the Sucharskis, our friends the Sosnovskis and two unmarried brothers named Kantorovitz. We found some utensils and clothing there, and began to settle in. On 2 July 1941 we heard a rumour that the Germans would be marching into town the next day. Groups of young Polish and Belorussian hoods got together and formed a militia which immediately began harassing, threatening and humiliating Jews. In the early morning of 3 July 1941, all Jewish men, myself among them, were ordered to start clearing the wreckage from the streets, preparing the town for the arrival of the German troops.

German patrolmen on their motorcycles were the first to enter Novogrodek, via Slonim Street. The armoured units followed. Brutalities against the Jews began on the very first day. The next day's decrees deprived the Jews of basic rights: they were not allowed to walk on the sidewalks and were compelled to wear a yellow circle which later became a Star of David sewn onto the back and front of their coats. And the trouble began.

4 *The First Massacre*

S EVERAL DAYS later 20 of the town's dignitaries were ordered to report to the local German military headquarters. Each of them was told to bring along ten more men. The pretext was electing a Jewish committee, or Judenrat. When they arrived, the 200 Jews were cruelly brutalised. They were ordered to carry water in pails from the well down in the courtyard up to the third floor without spilling a drop, while German soldiers standing on either side beat them with rifles, clubs and iron rods. The Jews who fell along the way were killed on the spot, and their bodies thrown into the courtyard. These atrocities went on all night, with the Germans thinking up all kinds of sadistic cruelties. Fifty Jews were killed. Out of those that remained, the Germans appointed the Judenrat. Their job was to make sure that the Jews would always carry out all orders issued by the German authorities, fully and promptly.

That same day, the Jews were deprived of all civil rights: they must only work as ordered by the authorities, they must not be found outside after dark, they must wear the yellow Star of David at all times, and obey each and every decree issued by the Germans. The penalty for the slightest disobedience was death. We soon realised that this was only the beginning, and that the future would bring unimaginable horrors. We talked things over and, assuming that young men were in greater danger than others and that small towns might be safer, decided that my uncle Yankel and I should try to reach my grandmother's home in Karelitz. We left at night with several other Jews. Karelitz lies 21 kilometres from Novogrodek. We didn't use the main road, in order to avoid German troops. We walked through the fields all night, and reached my grandmother's house at dawn. My cousin Idel Kagan was already there. He had arrived a week earlier, bringing my grandmother a sum of money from the family. Karelitz was relatively quiet. We helped our grandmother and hoped for calmer times.

A few days later, the local German authorities at Karelitz issued an order: all men over 16 must report to the town square within one hour. Anyone who disobeyed would be shot immediately. I reported to the market-place with my uncle Yankel. All the town's men were there. We formed straight lines and waited anxiously. We were told that a list would be prepared, in which the residents of Karelitz would be identified by their verified names, and classified according to profession and place of work. I was terrified. I wasn't a resident of Karelitz, and I knew that if the Germans found out, I would be questioned, tortured and finally shot. A short while later, the SS and gendarmerie men arrived. They brought Rabbi Vernik, the head of the town's congregation. He was given a list and told to read out the names. The Jews whose names were called out were ordered to line up separately. I will never forget this scene. The venerable Rabbi Vernik, with his well-combed beard, stood between two SS officers, bareheaded and without a coat, in a torn shirt. His belt had been removed, and once in a while he pulled up his trousers. With tears streaming down his face, the rabbi read out 105 names. The men whose names had been called, mostly the dignitaries of the congregation, were locked up in the cellar of the synagogue. Rabbi Vernik was one of them. Those who remained in the square were sent away with blows and gunshots. The 105 men imprisoned in the cellar were taken to Novogrodek the next day, and shot in pits prepared ahead of time next to the military barracks at Skridlevo, near Novogrodek. This horrid event convinced us that Karelitz was as unsafe as Novogrodek, and we decided to go back to our families. We left Karelitz early in the morning, taking the main road this time, and reached Novogrodek a few hours later. We encountered German troops on the way, but they suspected nothing because we were dressed as peasants, and we got safely back to our families. The Jewish men of Novogrodek had to report to the Judenrat courtyard in Grodno Street every morning, to be sent to work in different places. In return, they received half a loaf of bread and a few potatoes. My father worked in a German military camp, making leather suitcases for the officers. After I got back from Karelitz, he took me with him, as his assistant, and we worked there for several weeks, until the unit left the area. While we worked there the situation was tolerable. The German soldiers would sometimes give us some

41

left-over food, which helped the family. When the German unit left I joined the group of labourers who cleared the rubble from the streets. I worked with my uncle Yankel, my uncle Notke and our friends Efraim Shelubski and Neach Sosnovski. We became experts at the job and improvised special tools.

On Saturday, 26 July 1941, I was working, clearing the ruins of a stone building in the market square. Suddenly a commotion attracted my attention. The Germans were demanding 100 Jews within one hour, allegedly for a street cleaning job. The Jews were to report to the market square, and the Judenrat was responsible for meeting this demand. The members of the Judenrat and their assistants ran through the streets, burst into houses and grabbed every man they could find. Rounding up 100 men was not an easy task. Our group hid in the cellar of the building, where we had been working. Two hours later we heard gunshots: the Germans shot 52 Jews in the market square, while the town's Christians looked on. A German orchestra played music in the market-place while the killing took place. The teacher, Solomon, tried to escape. He managed to run about 100 metres, before he too was shot and killed. The remaining Jews were ordered to load the bodies and cart them away to the Jewish cemetery. One 'body', who had only been wounded, whispered to the man who was loading him onto the cart, asking him to try and lay him on top of the others. A Belorussian policeman overheard the whisper and told a German soldier. The German pulled out his pistol and killed the man. Jewish women were ordered to wash the pavement clean of the martyrs' blood. When we emerged from the cellar, we asked a Pole who happened to be passing by about the gunshots we had heard. His answer was that the Germans had shot some stray dogs.

The Judenrat, following German orders, organised some work-shops, and had craftsmen saddlers, shoemakers, tailors, car-penters, and so on working there for the military government, and sometimes for the local Christians. My father and my uncle Yankel worked in a saddle-making workshop and my uncle Notke was employed as a tinsmith. Our family lived tolerably well at that time. The craftsmen were able to trade with peasants who needed their services and who paid with agricultural produce. We ran the kitchen jointly, and everyone chipped in. Obtaining the supplies was quite dangerous. Contact with the Christian population was strictly forbidden. We spent the days at our places of work, and came home exhausted every night, with terrible tales about dreadful events. At night we had to stay at home and maintain a complete blackout. Usually we didn't turn on the lights. We'd go to bed as early as possible, to gather strength for the next exhausting day. The nights were also frightening. We'd wake up at the slightest sound or knock. Belorussian policemen and German soldiers would sometimes raid Jewish homes, raping and plundering. We heard rumours of a German soldier who, posing as a doctor, helped his mates enter Jewish homes, take out young women and later rape them. In our house, we sent the young girls, my cousin Sheindel Sucharksi and Michle Sosnovski, to sleep in the attic. One night a tall, red-headed German soldier came. He was looking for a Jewish girl, and was disappointed not to find one. He expressed his frustration by beating us up, but that was all. We were thankful.

One rainy autumn night, we heard knocks at the front door. It was still early, and we hadn't gone to bed. My uncle Notke immediately ran out of the back door. Mrs Sosnovski opened the door and three Belorussian policemen came in, wearing the black uniforms that had given these troops the nickname 'crow'. They started yelling that the blackout wasn't good enough, and asked who had just left the house. They must have heard some noise when my uncle Notke went out. We replied that everyone was present, and they ordered me and my aunt Haike to come with them. We were taken to a prison cell in a back alley of Bazilenska Street, and locked up with several drunkards. We were certain that in the morning we would be handed over to the Germans, questioned, tortured and sent to prison from which there was only one way out for Jews: execution and the pits of Skridlevo. Several hours went by. The cell was extremely cold. My aunt and I planned suicide, but no means were available. We accepted our fate. There was no way out.

Suddenly a police sergeant came in, and I recognised him. He was a friend of mine from the Polish secondary school, a fellow named Tsinar. He recognised me and asked what I was doing there. I told him what had happened, and he left without a word. About 30 minutes later two Belorussian policemen came in, and told me and my aunt to follow them. They led us back home, to our family. It was a miracle. The resurrection of the dead. We were welcomed with endless hugs and kisses.

Our rubble-clearing team was broken up, and we were placed in new jobs. My father Moshe and uncle Yankel went on working at the saddlery. The local German chief of staff valued my father's professional expertise, and ordered various leather products from him – saddles, briefcases and suitcases. My uncle Notke did body-work on German vehicles. I was placed in the Orlovski mechanical shop. This was a relatively good job. The shop belonged to the German authorities, so we were fairly safe all day, at work.

The local military government was replaced by a German civil government made up of Nazi party members and SS men. The governor was SS officer von Traub. The Jews believed that this might be an improvement: there would be no more kidnappings and executions of groups and individuals, well-defined rules would be set, and the Jews, knowing exactly what they were permitted to do, would no longer be anyone's easy prey.

The civil government immediately replaced the Judenrat. All the former Judenrat representatives were accused of disobeying orders and sabotaging the German war effort and were executed. A new Judenrat was appointed and instructed to follow all orders and decrees issued by the Germans.

Autumn brought horrifying rumours about massacres and mass executions carried out in Belorussia, the Ukraine, Russia, Lithuania, Latvia and Estonia, by special SS units called *Einsatzgruppen-SS*. Their mission was to rid these areas of all Jews, in the period before the Final Solution. We heard of a massacre in the town of Horodishze, not far from Novogrodek, where the whole Jewish community had been put to death. Other massacres had occurred in Slonim and other towns.

The Jews of Novogrodek were terrified. Some tried to bribe officials with gold, jewellery and other valuables, hoping to avoid this bitter fate, or at least to buy precious time. We heard rumours that the German advance had been halted, and that we might eventually be saved. Some Jews held spiritual seances, and told of clear signs that salvation was near, and the Messiah was coming. The Jews clutched at every favourable rumour, like drowning men.

One day in November 1941, at daybreak, as I was on my way to work at the Orlovski workshop, I slipped on the ice and fell, badly spraining my knee. I couldn't walk, and other Jews who saw me there took me home. According to German orders, every sick Jew had to be taken to the town hospital, allegedly in order to prevent disease from spreading. No sick Jew had ever come back from the hospital and we heard that they were all executed upon arrival. My uncle Yankel met with the manager of the Orlovski plant and bribed him, so that he wouldn't report my absence. After one week in bed, I went back to work at the same place.

A peasant brought us a message from Karelitz that my aunt Malke's husband, Haim Kapushevski, had been taken to work near the town of Dvoretz, where the Germans were constructing an airport, and that my aunt was desperate. She was alone with two small children, ten-year-old Berele and seven-year-old Nochim and my old, sick, bedridden grandmother, who lived with them. She asked for our help, begging us to take Berele into our home. So my aunt Dvore dressed up as a peasant woman, walked to Karelitz, and brought Berele over. Dvore said that she'd been lucky, and a farmer had given her a ride in his cart, all the way back to Novogrodek.

On Friday, 5 December 1941, a decree signed by the local governor, SS officer von Traub, was posted in the streets of Novogrodek: the Jews were ordered to go home at sunset, and stay there until further notice, awaiting instructions. They were not to report for work on Saturday. It was clear that the Germans were planning an 'Aktion'. That day my father and uncle Yankel risked their lives and went to see some Christian acquaintances who had formerly had business dealings with our family – a Kazik who lived in Peresika and a Tatar named Mikir who lived in Zalitucha, a suburb of Novogrodek. My father and uncle begged their former friends to hide our family until the danger was over, but they refused. They were scared.

On this terrible Friday night we tried to think of a hiding place. We decided to try the sewer that ran under Racelo Street. As children we had often played inside this large pipe, crossing it from one end to the other. Now, in the winter, it was dry and relatively warm. My cousin Srolik Sucharksi went out in the dark, risking his life, to check things out. He came back and reported that we couldn't possibly get there, because guards were patrolling everywhere, and shooting everyone without warning. So we stayed home and waited all night. Nobody slept. On Saturday, 6 December, a member of the Judenrat came to our house, accompanied by a Belorussian policeman and a German soldier. The Judenrat man read out our names from a list, and we were ordered to report to the court-house grounds, at the end of Karelitzer Street. Each of us was permitted to carry ten kilos of luggage. As it turned out, the court-house area was where the Germans gathered Jewish craftsmen with regular jobs, who were relatively protected. All other Jews, including old people and large families with many children, were concentrated in the yard of the convent on May 1st Street. About 6,000 of the town's Jews huddled together on the court-house grounds in the bitter cold. The Germans called out names and counted people but the confusion was too great; they couldn't get things organised. At dusk, the place was surrounded by soldiers and policemen who beat up the Jews. We stood out there until it was dark, and then we were ordered to go inside the court buildings and stay in the rooms.

On Sunday evening, one day before the massacre, I was taken to work with 100 other young men. We were ordered to take apart the wooden fence surrounding the market square at the end of Karelitzer Street, and carry it to the suburb of Peresika, where a Jewish ghetto would be built. The fence was made of thick logs and boards, which had absorbed a lot of moisture, and, were therefore very heavy. We broke the fence up into segments, and eight men carried each segment to Peresika a distance of two kilometres. I shall never forget this agonising march of terror. We were escorted by mounted *Wehrmacht*, Belorussian policemen and Lithuanian soldiers. They spurred us on with sticks, rifle butts and iron rods. Those who fell were immediately shot, and we were ordered to carry the bodies which we loaded onto the fence segments. And so we marched on to Peresika. We buried the dead in a field on the way to the village of Britzenko.

When I look back, I still wonder where we found the mental and physical strength to endure and survive this episode. We got back to the court-house at dawn, exhausted, weeping and mourning for the dead. The future appeared terrifying indeed.

On Sunday 7 December, we were certain that the Germans were making preparations for a massacre. We believed that the people at the convent would be killed while we would be spared, being productive Jews. On the morning of Black Monday, 8 December, some SS officers came to the court buildings, and a 'selection' began. Men, women and children, whole families whom the Germans disliked for some reason or another, were sent out to the *Umschlagplatz* in the court-house grounds and ordered to line up and wait for further announcements. Our family was in the same room as the Sucharskis, the Oppenheims, our friends the Sosnovskis and others.

My father, my brother Leizer, my mother and my little cousin Berele from Karelitz were sent out to the courtyard to their deaths. These poor unfortunates were loaded onto trucks and taken to the pits dug beforehand near the barracks at Skridlevo, three kilometres from Novogrodek. There they were cruelly beaten and finally shot to death.

I was one of the last people to remain in the room at the court-house. An SS officer asked me for my profession, and since I worked at the Orlovski mechanical shop, and had the official papers to prove it, I replied that I was a mechanic and metal-worker. The SS officer led me to his car, an open German military vehicle, parked beside the court-house. He told me he had some engine trouble, he couldn't start the car, and that I was to fix it within the next hour, using the tools in the trunk. He threatened me, saying that if he wasn't satisfied with my work, I would immediately join those awaiting their fate in the courtyard. I knew nothing about car repairs, and was well aware that I couldn't do what he had asked. So I said to him in German, which I had learned in secondary school, that the car couldn't possibly be fixed in one hour, the problem was serious, and I needed help. The German officer ordered me to go back to the building to get one of the Jews, whom I knew to be a professional mechanic, to help me. A German soldier escorted me back to our room in the court-house, and I pointed at Shmuel Oppenheim, who repaired type-writers for a living, and knew something about cars and engines. The German soldier told him to come with us. I explained everything to Oppenheim. Pale and shaking all over, he lifted the hood and fiddled with the engine, connecting wires and bolts, and finally starting the car. And it worked! We stood there, waiting for the SS officer.

The Jews were standing in long lines, in the open area next to the court buildings. Parents held their children, trying to reassure them. Every once in a while a truck would arrive, and take away 50 more Jews. German soldiers walked back and forth between the lines, demanding all valuables, money and jewellery. The Jews, who knew they were going to die, stood petrified, parents holding their children's hands, mothers with babies in their arms. They were perfectly silent. Even the children didn't cry. It was very cold, and the scene was frightening. The silence seemed unnatural. Oppenheim and I stood about 50 metres away from the rows of condemned Jews. My beloved family was no longer there. They had already been taken to the pits at Skridlevo. Standing there, I saw the local German chief of staff approach the line-up. And I heard him call out my father's name: 'Moshe Kagan, step forward and come to me! My horse's saddle isn't finished yet!' He called again, but there was no response. My father, mother, brother and little cousin had already been taken to the pits. The SS officer came back, exactly on time, got in the car and started it. As far as he was concerned, everything was fine. He ordered a German soldier to escort us back to the court-house. We were safe, for now.

I had suffered a great loss. It was a terrible day for the ancient Jewish community of Novogrodek, an illustrious Lithuanian community which had sent forth rabbis, poets, scientists and learned men of the Torah. More than 5,000 Jews died in the first great massacre. In one day, I lost my beloved parents, my dear brother Leizer and my little cousin Berele from Karelitz, who wasn't even supposed to be there.

That night a Jewish woman, frightened, deeply shocked and covered with blood, managed to get to the court-house. At first she couldn't talk, but the next day, she told us that she was one of those taken to the pits at Skridlevo. When they got there, all the Jews were ordered to get off the trucks, undress, run to the pits and line up at the edge. Then they were shot with machine guns and fell into the pits. She told us that in the pit she felt that she was alive and able to move. At night she managed to climb out, since she lay in the top layer of bodies, and reached the court-house. She was slightly wounded in the shoulder.

Later we heard from Belorussian policemen who had been

present at the scene of the massacre about heart-rending scenes and acts of courage. Some Jews tried to resist and attack the murderers. Others tried to escape and were shot on the spot. One Jewish barber attacked an SS officer with a razor and cut his face. He was beaten to death with rifle butts.

My uncle Yankel and aunt Haike Sucharski and their families had survived this massacre, but they grieved deeply for my beloved family.

5 *The Ghetto*

A FEW DAYS after the first great massacre, the remaining Jews of Novogrodek, about 1,300 in all, were herded into the ghetto established in the suburb of Peresika. The ghetto was surrounded by a wooden fence and barbed wire, and guarded by Belorussian policemen and German soldiers.

Our family, the Sucharskis and several other families settled in the home of the Zamkovi family, which was inside the enclosed ghetto area. It was terribly crowded. Twenty of us lived in one small room. At night we slept, pressed together, on three levels of bunks. In the ghetto, the Judenrat appointed a Jewish police force. Their job was to maintain order, prevent smuggling and help the Judenrat carry out German orders. A supervisor appointed to each house had to keep count of all the inhabitants. At night, the Germans and Belorussian police would often come into the ghetto and carry out head counts. Any discrepancy would result in the supervisor's arrest and probable execution.

Every morning the ghetto Jews, men, women and children from the age of 12 would leave the ghetto escorted by German and Belorussian policemen, to work at temporary or permanent jobs, as required. I continued to work at the Orlovski mechanical workshop, my uncle Yankel worked at the saddlery which had been opened in one of the buildings of the municipal court, together with several other workshops where clothes, shoes, furs and furniture were made. My cousin Idel worked at the military barracks at Skridlevo. Once in a while, after a day's work, we were ordered to labour some more, under the supervision of German and SS officers. We knew that this always involved beatings and other brutalities.

At about this time (February 1942), we heard rumours that there were partisans in the area. The partisans even managed to get into the town of Novogrodek several times, exchanging fire with the Germans. The German authorities were alarmed at this and ordered extra protective measures. They had set up their headquarters in the Polish governor's villa. This villa had a vast, beautiful garden, full of trees. The additional security consisted of cutting down all the trees that might conceal partisans. At the same time, they wanted to lay a water pipe from the local well to the villa, and construct suitable sewage facilities. This was in the winter time. The ground was frozen solid. For weeks on end, day and night, ghetto Jews worked in shifts to complete the task. We thanked God for every day that passed without major incidents. One night, three young Jewish men were laying the water line to the villa. The ground was frozen so solid that digging was impossible. In order to warm it up, the workers lit a fire. Suddenly the governor, SS officer von Traub, and some of his mates, came out of the villa and started shooting, using the Jews as live targets. The three labourers were hit, and the governor ordered the guards to put the bodies on the fire. One of the three was Hone Kushner, whom I knew well. He had been hit, but wasn't critically wounded, and he managed to crawl away from the fire un-observed. The next shift of Jewish labourers found him wounded, unconscious and half frozen, and smuggled him back into the ghetto. Hone was later killed escaping from the tunnel.

There was very little food in the ghetto. More and more Jews died of starvation. Every morning the dead bodies would be picked up and buried in a field on the way to the village of Britinke. Fortunately, our family had some food. My uncles Yankel and Notke worked in workshops and sometimes managed to trade with the farmers who came there. They'd give them clothes and jewellery and get food in return. Smuggling things in and out of the ghetto was another problem. German guards and Belorussian policemen stood at the gates and searched everybody. Those caught smuggling were usually arrested, interrogated and executed. My cousin Idel, who was only 12 years old, became an expert smuggler, displaying considerable courage and resource-fulness.

In the spring of 1942 the Germans started bringing Jews from nearby villages and towns to the ghetto of Novogrodek. The Jews of Lubcz, Vsielub and Karelitz were among them. I will never forget their arrival: 5,500 men, women, children and old folks, who had walked many miles and had been beaten and brutalised along the way. Wretched and exhausted, they lay down in the open plot near the Judenrat, weeping and wailing. The ghetto was terribly crowded already, and there was no place for the newcomers. They were housed in basements, attics and barns, in terrible conditions.

Our relatives from Karelitz also arrived. My 70-year-old grandmother Gitel, my uncle Yosef Gurevitz with his family, and my aunt Malke Kapushevski with her younger son Nahum (Malke's husband, taken to work on the construction of an airport near the town of Dvoretz, never came back, and her elder son Berele died in the first massacre at Novogrodek, with my parents and brother). We gave our bunk to our grandmother and we found some room in the attic and helped them as much as we could.

The newcomers were in terrible shape. They were depressed, penniless, away from home, forced to adjust to new surroundings. Their men were sent to work each morning, at the worst jobs. The starvation and poor sanitary conditions caused disease; many died. To make matters worse, the people of the ghetto felt certain that a second massacre was not far off.

Rumours of Russian partisans in the region reached the ghetto, and several young men managed to escape to join them. Despite the fact that nothing was heard from them and their fate remained unknown, their escape inspired others. Many wished to get away from the clutches of death. People whispered about young men planning to escape, but on the other hand they feared German retribution.

After a while we heard that those who had escaped had joined the Russian partisans and were fighting against the Germans. In one of their military operations they took the town of Naliboki and destroyed the German headquarters there. The Germans called for help, and several armoured units took the partisans by surprise. Most of the partisans managed to get away, abandoning the Jewish platoon. These 38 young Jews retreated to the local church and fought bravely. The Germans asked them to surrender, promising to treat them as prisoners of war, but the men didn't even reply. They all died fighting.

The ghetto's Judenrat was summoned to the German governor. The head of the Judenrat was arrested, accused of having contact with the partisans, and executed. The members of the Judenrat were warned that they would be the first to be executed if any Jews were found missing at the next head count. Every evening the Jewish police would take away the boots of those youths who, according to rumour, were planning to escape from the ghetto. Sometimes they were even arrested for the night. But some still managed to get away, disregarding the Germans' threats and the Judenrat's precautions. The problem was that once they were out, they had nowhere to go. The partisan movement was still very new. It happened that when young Jews eventually managed to find a Russian partisan group, they were shot as alleged German spies.

The summer of 1942 was a cruel, hopeless time for the Jews of the ghetto. It was clear to all of us that another massacre would take place very soon. At night, every house in the ghetto began to prepare a hiding place: some dug concealed holes in the ground, others constructed double walls and partitions in attics or basements.

On 6 August 1942 the Judenrat issued special permits for the craftsmen and other people whose work was considered important by the German authorities. They were ordered to move to the court buildings on Karelitzer Street. The rest of the Jews were not permitted to leave the ghetto or go to work. My uncle Yankel, his wife and Idel were among the 'lucky' ones sent to the court-house. So were my uncle Notke Sucharksi and his family, except for his son Srolik. Srolik remained at the military barracks at Skridlevo where he worked, and the Germans promised that he too would be sent to the court-house although he never was. It was clear that those sent to the court-house had a better chance of survival, because the Germans still required their professional services.

The ghetto guard was reinforced. We reached the court-house, which was surrounded by guards and barbed wire. Night came – a night of dread. We stayed in the workshops at the court-house, and waited.

Before noon, on 7 August 1942, German SS officers and Lithuanian soldiers gathered before the court-house. The Jews were ordered to muster in the courtyard. The Germans passed between the lines and took out the children. Babies were torn from their mothers' arms and thrown into a closed truck. The

Latvian soldiers searched the rooms, cellars and attics, and found babies who had been hidden there. In front of our very eyes they tossed the infants from the top floors of the building to the pavement below. Some had their heads smashed against the stone wall. The babies were thrown into sacks and loaded onto a truck. We stood there and watched in silence. Every sound was forbidden. The children in the trucks did not cry. Only some faint whimpering could be heard.

Miraculously, the soldiers did not get into one of the cellars where several infants had been hidden. Among these was our friend Shmuel Oppenheim's baby daughter. Unable to turn the lock, the soldiers called an expert locksmith – Mr Oppenheim himself. He tried and said that it was impossible, because the lock was very rusty and hadn't been opened for years. The soldiers believed him and left. The babies were saved.

On this day, over 5,000 Jews from the ghetto of Peresika were massacred. Among them was our whole family from Karelitz: my grandmother Gitel Gurevitz, my uncle Yosef Gurevitz, his wife Breine Feigel and their daughters Nachama and Hassia (as mentioned earlier, their eldest daughter Rachel whose name today is Rachel Konigsberg was sent to her uncle in England), and my aunt Malke Kapushevski with her little son Nahum. My cousin Srolik Sucharksi who worked at the military barracks didn't join us at the court-house. He was killed at the barracks while trying to escape.

Thus the Germans solved the problems of overcrowding in the ghetto. Only 500 Jews, mostly men, now remained, living in 15 houses. The Jews of Ghetto Peresika were massacred and buried in a common grave near the village of Litovka, not far from the town.

The day after the massacre I was taken with a group of Jews to the ghetto, to collect all the personal belongings left behind by the dead residents, and transfer them to the Germans' warehouses. When we got there we were warned by SS Officer Reuter not to take anything for ourselves. He said we would be thoroughly searched at the end of the day, and anyone found with suspicious items on his person would be killed.

Suddenly I remembered that I had some gold 10-ruble coins in my pocket, given to me by my uncle Yankel. I was terrified. What should I do? I didn't want to get rid of the coins: they were all that was left of our former fortune, and perhaps they could still buy us some food. On the other hand, keeping them meant risking my life. I decided to hide them, and tucked them into my long underwear, which was tied with strings to my ankles at the bottom. I tightened the strings, so as not to lose the coins, and went on working, although I was trembling with fear.

When the job was done we were ordered to line up and wait for SS Officer Reuter. He arrived on horseback, holding a whip, vicious and arrogant. SS Officer Reuter had the reputation of a real murderer, who never hesitated to kill a man for the slightest reason. He used to beat the Jewish workers and committed terrible atrocities. I was standing in line when suddenly, to my great horror, one of the coins somehow dropped through the strings and rolled down to the pavement. Without thinking, I stepped on it, bent down, and put it back in my pocket. I wondered how SS Officer Reuter, seated high on his horse right in front of me, didn't notice what had happened. It was a miracle. I was frightened, and regretted keeping the coins, but there was nothing I could do. However in the end, they didn't search us. Reuter probably felt certain that the Jews wouldn't have dared to risk taking anything. We were led back to the court buildings. I told my family about the incident. Once again I had been lucky.

The court-house buildings became a labour camp, and all the Jews there had to work in the various workshops. I worked with my uncle Yankel and cousin Idel in the saddlery section. The work camp was closely guarded by the Germans and the Belorussian police. Twenty of us lived in one small, terribly crowded room in one of the buildings. We lived with my uncle Sucharski's family, the Sosnovskis, the Oppenheims, our friend Efraim Shelubski, Yosef Shuster and his family, the Shabakovski brothers, and some others. Our condition deteriorated. The food ration was insufficient. We couldn't sleep at night. Our family, five people in all, lay on a wooden bunk near the ceiling. We could hardly breathe and the bedbugs bit us constantly, sucking our blood.

Somehow we carried on. Once in a while we managed to obtain some food by trading with farmers who came up to the camp fence, risking their lives out of sheer greed. But we felt certain that the next massacre wasn't far off, and that we would not survive it. We heard rumours about a Jewish group called Bielski's partisans.

This we heard from local farmers who were permitted by the Germans to enter the camp and buy products made by the work-shops. They told greatly exaggerated tales about hundreds of Jewish partisans who were fighting and attacking the Germans all over the area.

One day a member of this partisan group managed to sneak into the camp. He was a young Jew from our town who had escaped from the Peresika ghetto, and he told amazing stories about the Bielski group, their life in the woods, and the growing partisan movement. Eventually the young partisan left the camp, taking with him several other young men, including his brother and his friends. My friend Ishie Oppenheim, whose family had friends among the Bielskis, was one of those who had escaped from the camp.

The partisan's visit caused unrest in the camp, and fear of German reprisals once they discovered several Jews were missing. All the Jews in the camp wore a number stitched on their backs, in addition to the Star of David. Once in a while the Germans held head counts, and every missing Jew entailed severe punishment. But this did not stop those who decided to escape. Several other Jewish partisans also got into the labour camp and took out their relatives and friends.

The winter of 1942 approached. Most of the camp's residents did not want to risk escaping and joining the partisans, for several reasons: they doubted their ability to survive the coming winter out in the woods, they didn't want to leave their families and they feared the danger involved in the escape itself. But I decided to escape. My family was already dead, and I was sure that we would meet with the same fate.

6   *Escape to the Bielski Partisans*

O NE DAY, in November 1942, Ishie Oppenheim suddenly appeared in the camp. He had come from the Bielskis, to save his brother Ruvke. Ishie and I agreed that I would join them, and we set a date for the planned escape. I told my uncle's family of my decision. They did not try to stop me, though I knew that their hearts were heavy with sorrow. They wept, but they gave me their blessing.

On the appointed day, a little before noon, my co-worker Eli Zamoshchik and I removed the yellow stars and numbers sewn on our clothes. We intended to crawl out under the barbed wire at the northern end of the camp, near the living quarters. My cousin Idel Kagan was with us. We asked him to watch the guards and give us a signal when the patrol was on the other side of the camp. When Idel gave the signal, we began to crawl under the fence. It was broad daylight. And then we were outside. Slowly, so as not to attract attention, we walked away through the fields, towards the Horodzhilovka forest.

Some peasants spotted us; we must have looked suspicious, with our ragged clothes and starved, pale faces. But they said nothing. We got safely through the open field, reached the road, and finally, after what seemed an eternity, entered the forest, where we were supposed to wait until dark for Ishie Oppenheim and the others who had escaped with him. Ishie, his brother Ruvke and several others made it safely, and we waited for a few more people. When it was dark, we set off. There were six of us. We had mixed feelings. On the one hand, we were free. On the other, we had left our families behind, and knew that we might never see them again. The future seemed uncertain and frightening.

Escaping from the well-guarded camp, especially in broad daylight, was dangerous in itself. But since we felt certain that we would soon have been killed in a massacre had we stayed, we acted spontaneously, without much thought. We walked quickly through the snow-covered fields, skirted the town and its suburbs and made our way towards the village of Litovka, about four kilometres from Novogrodek. Ishie Oppenheim led the way. He knew the area well and promised us that everything would be all right. We reached the house of the Hicles (dogcatchers) at the end of the suburb of Peresika, on the way to Litovka. Ishie Oppenheim hoped to find one of the Bielski partisans, who used to visit the place, but they weren't there. The Hicles were Polish Gentiles whose job was to catch stray, unlicensed dogs found wandering in the surrounding woods and countryside. They lived in an isolated house, far from the town, which no one ever visited. But it was the Hicles who felt compassion for the Jews' bitter fate and helped as much as they could, smuggling food into the ghetto. The ghetto Jews knew about this humane behaviour. Every Jew who managed to escape from the ghetto and reach the Hicles was hidden for a day or two and supplied with food for the journey ahead. The Hicles kept in touch with the Bielski partisans, and they would tell runaway Jews where they might be found. When the Germans later found out about the activities of the Hicles, they killed them and burned their property.

After resting for about an hour in the Hicles' house, we went on through the fields to Boinski's farm. Boinski was a rich Polish farmer who raised and sold pigs. He had many friends among the Jews of Novogrodek, and he helped many Jews during the Holocaust. At midnight we knocked on Boinski's door. He came out, frightened, and told us that he lived in constant fear of the Germans, who paid him frequent visits. He agreed to hide us for one day. He led us into the barn and covered us with hay. At noon, the good man brought us some bread, potatoes and water, and when night fell we left the farm and made our way to the nearby road. Twelve kilometres down the road, and several hundred metres away from it, we reached the home of a Belorussian farmer named Kostik Kozlovsky, who used to bring messages and letters from the Bielski partisans to the ghetto Jews. We arrived at dawn, exhausted. Kozlovsky said that no partisans had been there for several days, but that they might very well come that night. He suggested that we should wait for them in a nearby grove. We spent the whole day in that grove, lying in a trench from which we could watch the road, bustling with German military vehicles. At

Konstantin Kozlovsky, the Righteous Gentile

nightfall, several young Jews from Bielski's partisans arrived at Kozlovsky's farm.

Our meeting with the partisans was a highly moving and astonishing experience. It was hard to believe that these armed, mounted partisans were actually Jews. We knew two of them, natives of Novogrodek who had escaped from the ghetto. But they seemed different. The fear and sadness had disappeared from their eyes. They had the appearance of tough, self-assured warriors. The partisans led us to a nearby village, where they took some horse-drawn sleighs from the farmers. We were on our way to the Bielskis' base. We passed several villages, travelling out in the open and unafraid. It was unbelievable. We entered an isolated farm, ate fine food and drank vodka to our heart's content, with the farmer serving us humbly, doing his best to make us happy. The partisans joked around and told tales about their brave feats.

I myself had mixed feelings: the sadness I felt for the relatives I had left in the ghetto, who would doubtless soon be dead, mingled with the ecstasy of freedom. I was finally free from terror, constant fear, barbed wire and torture. I was no longer awaiting my death.

We were taken to the Bielski camp deep in the woods. When we got there, we couldn't believe our eyes: armed Jewish men whom I knew well from Novogrodek, who had escaped from the ghetto. I stood there wondering if these could be the same people? They had changed so drastically. They were no longer pale, frightened and downtrodden. They stood tall and proud in their boots and breeches with their short coats made of sheepskins and fur hats bearing the red star of the Russian army. Some were wearing various articles taken from German uniforms. And most important of all: they were armed with pistols, rifles, sub-machine-guns and even machine-guns.

The place was bustling with activity: some women were cooking, other partisans were putting up tents, cleaning weapons, or standing guard. They all appeared to know their jobs very well. The whole scene was simply unbelievable. There were some children there too.

I couldn't get used to the idea that Jews, totally humiliated and doomed to die in the Final Solution, had found the courage to rebel, to take up arms against the Nazi beast, defend their lives and avenge the deaths of their loved ones. Such thoughts raced through my mind and I wondered how I would find my place among these partisans. Some approached me, asking about the fate of their families and friends, and I told them of the atrocities and growing terror I had left behind.

I was told to report to one of the Bielskis' commanders, Asael Bielski. He was a big, tall fellow, with a permanent smile and a kind, genuine expression. Asael welcomed me to the group, inquired about the ghetto, asked me about the fate of my family, expressed his sympathy and promised that I would make a good partisan. He said that very soon I too would get a gun and become a fighter. I would get the opportunity to fight the Nazi murderers and defend my life and, if I was fated to die, I would die honourably in battle. Asael wondered why so few Jews escaped from the ghetto, despite the message from the partisans that anyone who reached the Bielskis would be welcomed with open arms. One of the partisans whom I knew – a fellow from Karelitz named Bencie

Golkovitz, whose wife Yehudith was a distant relative of my late mother – approached Asael and said that I could join his group, the Elyushkis. Among the twenty or so members of this group, I was glad to find some familiar faces from Novogrodek.

It was midwinter. The bitter cold and heavy snow made any activity difficult. The Bielski partisans split up into groups, which moved to the winter bases prepared earlier. These were underground huts dug into the forest floor. I joined the Elyushkis, and our winter hut was in the Perelaz forest.

I found no peace of mind, knowing that my uncle Yankel's family was still in the labour camp. Ruvke, Ishie Oppenheim's brother, who had escaped with me, decided to go back to the ghetto and try to get his parents and little sister out. I asked him to help my uncle Yankel, his wife Dvore and their children, Nachama and Idel, to get out as well. I hoped that they would escape from the ghetto with the Oppenheims, who lived in the same room with us in the ghetto.

Ruvke Oppenheim managed to sneak into the ghetto and get his family out, together with my dear cousin Idel. It was a very cold winter night. On their way to the Bielskis' base the group of runaways crossed a frozen river. The ice broke, and several people, my cousin among them, slipped into the cold water. Idel's felt boots absorbed the water, and his feet froze. When his boots froze solid, Idel realised he would never make it to the partisan base. Heartbroken, he decided to go back to his parents in the ghetto. He crawled back to the road. At daybreak he spotted a peasant's sleigh heading back to Novogrodek and managed to hang onto it undetected. Fortunately for Idel, the sleigh reached the market near the ghetto, and he got off near the well, where the Jews came every morning to get water. He joined them and returned to the ghetto, exhausted and shivering. His toes couldn't be saved, and they were amputated secretly by a dentist, without the aid of anaesthetics.

The Bielski family came from the village of Stankiewicz, near Novogrodek. They owned a flour mill, and peasants from all the nearby villages used the services of Bielski the miller, whom they liked and respected. The miller had several sons and daughters, and some of them helped their father at the mill. The sons, Tuvia, Asael, Zush and Archik were tall and strong. They had been raised

61

in the country and resembled the local farmers in their looks and manner. They acquired their education from melammeds in Novogrodek.

Tuvia married and moved to the town of Lida, about 70 kilometres from Novogrodek. Asael and Zush continued to help their father at the mill and Archik lived in Novogrodek. The Bielskis and their relatives, who also lived in Stankiewicz and nearby villages, were popular and friendly with the local peasants. They knew the area well: the forests, the peasant families, the villages, isolated farms and huts, the roads and paths.

On 5 December 1941 the Germans raided the Bielski house and arrested the elderly couple. They were taken to the Novogrodek prison and from there to Skridlevo, where they were killed in the first big massacre of 8 December 1941. The other Bielskis and their relatives had left their homes in time and hidden in the nearby woods. The Germans, couldn't find them and burned down their home. The Bielskis remained in hiding, deep in the forest. At night they would visit their friends in the farms and villages, who provided them with food supplies. Gradually they grew accustomed to life in the forest.

The partisan movement was new at the time. Small groups were beginning to form, consisting mostly of former Russian soldiers, who hadn't made it to the border when the Germans came. They were joined by others, including criminals who liked the partisans' way of life, and men who didn't want to be sent to work in Germany. These were essentially the core of the partisan units. They got their weapons from stashes left behind and deliberately concealed by the retreating Red Army.

As for the Bielskis they gradually managed to obtain weapons for defensive purposes. At the beginning the Bielskis had no intention of actually fighting the Germans or raiding their territory, like the other partisan groups. They kept very much to themselves. The group was joined by friends and relations who had escaped from the ghetto of Novogrodek and Lida. It started out as a family-based unit, with no plan other than merely hiding out in the woods. By October 1942 the Bielski detachment numbered about 200 people. They named the detachment Zhukov, after the famous Russian General. The leader of the detachment was Tuvia.

Word of the Bielski partisans and their whereabouts reached the ghettos of Novogrodek and Lida. Members of the group were sent to slip into the ghetto and lead out the Bielskis' families and friends, and eventually others as well. At last, Jews escaping from the ghetto had a place to go. And even though rumour had it that the Bielskis wouldn't accept any more members, the fact was that those who reached them were never returned to the ghetto.

The Bielskis fought many battles to establish themselves and in order to be known in the territory. They punished informers, and won the respect of many villagers who were opposed to the Germans. The Germans responded by murdering those who helped the Bielskis or transporting them to Germany for slave labour.

Later on, the Bielskis began to debate the nature and purpose of their group. Some thought it should stay small and limited, because this would increase their chances of survival. By admitting more Jews and expanding, they would be risking their own lives. Others, mostly the armed young men, led by the 36-year-old Tuvia, and Asael and Zush Bielski, wanted the group to grow and become a fighting partisan brigade. They believed that this power was needed to protect the group.

Tuvia Bielski and his followers won this dispute, and Tuvia set the rules: any Jew who found his way to the group would be welcomed, regardless of age, sex or social position, so that those escaping from the ghettos would have a place to go. No Jew would ever be sent back to the hell he or she had fled from; mutual aid, responsibility and unity would be the guiding principles.

In 1942 Victor Panachenko, formerly a lieutenant in the Red Army, led a group of Partisans by the name of 'Octyabr'. Victor called on many villages and always heard the same story – that the Jews had been there and taken away from them everything they had. Victor, being young and naïve, believed them. Some were saying that the Russian partisans must be helped, that the Germans were taking everything by force but that the Jews were robbing them. Victor was furious.

News came to Bielski that Victor Panachenko wanted to liquidate the Bielskis. Bielski arranged to meet Victor to clarify the situation. They met and Bielski told him the places of his operation. The villages that Victor mentioned Bielski had never even been to. So Tuvia, with a group of men, joined up with Victor's men. They spent the night on a farmstead and the following day they went to the villages that had accused the Bielskis of robbing them. Victor knocked on the window of one farmhouse and asked for bread, to which the owner replied, 'So help me God, Comrade, the Jews were here at midnight and took everything away.' And his wife repeated that the Jews had been there and taken their bread, butter, eggs, onions and even some of their clothes. Victor knew that they were lying. He was furious and wanted to shoot the farmer. Tuvia stopped him. Victor introduced Tuvia to the farmer and told the farmer that he should thank Bielski for if it hadn't been for him, he, Victor, would have shot him. The two leaders became friends and joined together in many battles against the enemy.

Before the big manhunt in the summer of 1943 the partisan headquarters in Moscow restructured the partisan movement in Belorussia. They appointed General Chernyshev, pseudonym Platon, to head the partisan movement in the Baranovichi area. The Bielski detachment was officially attached to the Kirov brigade, and had a Russian deputy. It was named Kalinin, after the President of the USSR. Platon wanted to take away all the fighters from the Bielski family group. But after long negotiations with the help of Hersh Smolar who was known to the Russians as a reliable communist he avoided a catastrophe.

The General ordered the detachment to be split into two sections. The first was the fighting unit, called Ordzhonikidze, consisting of 180 fighting men led by a Russian commander, a Russian commissar and with Zush Bielski in charge of reconnaissance. The second unit retained the name Kalinin. This was the family group, led by Tuvia, with Asael as second-in-command with the same amount of fighting men. Tuvia and General Platon became friends.

The Kalinin family group grew to include, at its maximum, more than 1,200 Jews who had escaped from the ghettos of Novogrodek, Lida and smaller towns in the region. For Bielski, the problems of feeding and protecting the group were enormous. The group moved into the Naliboki forest. From there, groups of 10 to 15 young armed men would go out, leaving the safety of the forest and travelling up to 100 kilometres to bring back food for the group. The dangers they faced were huge. Most of the villages they took food from were located close to German garrisons.

At the liberation there were about 300,000 partisans in Belorussia, all that survived of a movement that at its peak numbered around 400,000. By contrast, the Bielskis lost just 50 people. And that was not as a result of luck but of clever leadership.

There was another large Jewish group led by Shimon Zorin. This group was mainly from Minsk. They suffered a lot of casualties, not only from the Germans but also from the Polish partisans, the fascist Narodowe Sily Zbrojne (NSZ), who were fighting the Germans, the Russians and the Jews. Zorin was wounded and lost a leg, but he succeeded in saving 800 Jews from the Minsk area.

The Bielskis were unique. There were Jews serving in other partisan units, but the Holocaust bred no other purely Jewish partisan unit of comparable size. The Bielskis and their commanders wrote a glorious page in the history of the Holocaust. The initial decision and ensuing actions of Tuvia Bielski, his brothers and his supporters, were of national importance, and will no doubt be regarded as such by our nation's chroniclers. The 1,200 souls saved by the Bielskis would probably have been lost but for them.

Tuvia Bielski was the leader, and he proved himself worthy of the task. He was charismatic, a natural leader who won the respect of his own men and the non-Jewish partisans alike. His opinions and criticisms carried weight at general staff meetings, and he firmly protected his own troops' essential interests. There were quite a few anti-Semites among the Russian partisans, who tried to harm us in various ways. In difficult times of hardship and danger, Tuvia's presence reassured us. He was our saviour and protector. He was a born leader, wise and resourceful, a good organiser, cautious, but capable of making quick decisions when necessary. His commands and instructions were carried out without question. Strict discipline was essential for our survival, and it certainly wasn't easy commanding the absolute obedience of our Jewish brethren. If Tuvia was the leader, his brother Asael was the operations officer. Everyone liked Asael. He was kind and easygoing, and always willing to listen to other people's troubles. Asael was a courageous fighter, and his men followed him willingly, often risking their lives. He always set a personal example, leading the way. I saw him in different circumstances, under fire, attacking or retreating, but always calm, never losing control. He had a thorough understanding of the battle in progress, and a unique ability to outwit the enemy, avoid traps and ambushes and attack where he was least expected. He knew the area well and led his men confidently. His deep hatred of the Nazis drove him to avenge the incessant murder of his Jewish brethren. He loved his people with all his heart and soul, and fought bravely on their behalf. When the area was retaken by the Russians, Asael joined the Red Army, and died heroically on the battlefield near Königsberg, in East Prussia.

Looking back, one may find some mistakes and misdeeds committed by Tuvia, Asael and the others. But these, and their human weaknesses, must detract nothing from their historical greatness and their contribution to the rescue of Jews. We must not forget that these were dreadful times, when Jewish lives had no value and no protector, and they were massacred and ex-terminated while their neighbours looked on, hostile or indifferent.

A day with the Bielskis was always full of acts of courage and resourcefulness, and large amounts of sheer luck. The partisans attacked German guards and police stations, sabotaged roads and railways, blew up bridges and destroyed telephone lines and post offices.

The environment in which the Bielski partisans operated was hostile. The Christian population, the peasants and villagers, were deeply anti-Semitic, and detested the Jewish partisans. Sometimes they would even turn in the partisans to the authorities. The Bielskis were forced to retaliate severely executing informers and burning their property. This was the only way to frighten the others, and teach them that Jewish blood wasn't cheap.

The problem of providing sufficient supplies for a camp of over 1,200 Jews was also complicated. Fewer and fewer provisions could be found in the villages: the partisans would often come and take what they needed in the way of clothing, footwear and food, and the German authorities also imposed ever-growing taxes. Villages suspected of helping the partisans were burned down, and their inhabitants killed. It wasn't easy, confiscating a farmer's last bit of property – his one remaining cow, horse or pig, or the stock of flour he had prepared. Sometimes they resisted violently, forcing us to retaliate in kind. The Belorussian farmers were willing to accept the notion of their own brothers, the Russian partisans, taking away their goods, realising that this was the price of war. But they refused to let the detested Jews rob them of their last possessions. Things got so bad, that we were forced to disregard the danger, and seek provisions in the outskirts of the cities. More and more frequently, our men encountered ambushes and a number were either killed in skirmishes or captured, tortured and executed in the Novogrodek prison. The Gestapo couldn't break their spirit, and they died in agony, but never revealed our whereabouts.

The existence of a purely Jewish partisan unit seemed insufferable to the Germans. It went against all their theories: the cowardly, hated Jews whom they had condemned to death, had become armed partisans, attacking and sabotaging the German forces. The very existence of the Bielskis greatly threatened the Germans, who were afraid that others might follow this example, take up arms and rebel. The Germans made great efforts to destroy the Bielski partisans. A very large reward was placed on the heads of Tuvia Bielski and his brothers. Special commando and SS units were sent to find the Bielski partisans and eliminate them, but they were unsuccessful. Our troops continued to grow and fight, avoiding the danger. Planes participated in the battle against the Jewish partisans, but to no avail. Every peasant who brought the Germans information about the location of the Bielskis' bases was exempted from tax payments. But those who informed on us, we punished severely. The peasants' reports about the size and operations of the Bielski group were often exaggerated. They spoke of thousands of well-armed partisans, who even had cannons at their disposal.

One interesting detail: the underground newspapers of the Warsaw Ghetto wrote of Jewish partisans near Novogrodek. Before the uprising in the Warsaw Ghetto, notices were distributed, urging the people to follow the example of the Jews of the Novogrodek Ghetto, who had rebelled against their oppressors, escaped to the woods and were heroically avenging the deaths of their loved ones. It appears that rumours of the Jewish partisans near Novogrodek were brought to the Warsaw Ghetto by Poles who were in touch with Polish partisans of the 'Homeland Army', whose units roamed the woods by the River Niemen not far from Novogrodek, and occasionally came across the Bielski partisans.

67

I spent the winter of 1942–43 with the Elyushki company of the Bielski partisans' Octyabr division, in an underground hut in the Perelaz forest. The hut had been prepared and concealed in the summer. We got used to life in the forest, which wasn't easy. It was a very cold, snowy winter, and fearing detection, we avoided lighting fires. But we never got sick. Hardship made us stronger, and our spirits were high.

We didn't do much fighting during the winter, unless defending ourselves when raiding villages to obtain supplies. There were 20 of us in the hut, and other groups spent the winter in similar huts, not far away. We would visit each other, guard the area and go out on raids together.

One night our boys went out, to get some medical supplies from a pharmacist who lived in a suburb of Novogrodek. We needed these supplies for two wounded men who were burning with fever. The party came back at dawn with the medication, as well as some carts loaded with provisions, sheep and cows. The day went by quietly. On the second day at dawn, we were awakened by the sound of gunfire, including machine-guns. We ran out of the hut towards the defence line that ran along the edge of the forest. There were 12 guards in each shift, and the man from our hut at this time was Shmuel Oppenheim, my friend Ishie's father. The armed men took up their positions, and the others, including women and old men, were sent to the rear. The gunfire grew louder, and we could now see our attackers, Belorussian police-men advancing and shooting in all directions. When we opened fire they stopped, then retreated. Apparently there weren't very many of them, and they must have feared a trap. Several women, who hadn't made it out of the huts in time, were killed.

A great miracle happened to Shmuel Oppenheim. When he spotted the policemen he fired several shots, to warn us. The Belorussian policemen saw him and opened fire. Hit in the face, he fell to the ground. The attackers found him there, his head and face covered with blood, and thought him dead. They took his gun and left him there, advancing towards the huts. When the policemen had retreated, we returned to our base and found Shmuel Oppenheim wounded and unconscious, but alive. The bullet had entered his face through one cheek, and gone out through the other. Our doctor, Dr Isler, treated Shmuel Oppenheim, and he recovered completely. That night, we left our relatively comfortable hut and moved to another forest, about ten kilometres away, where we dug ourselves another underground hut. It was hard work. The ground was frozen and we worked day and night, until the job was done.

Some time later we heard from our peasant friends that a few nights earlier, when the men who went to Novogrodek took a cow from one of the farms, one of its horns broke, and the dripping blood marked the way back to our hut. The Belorussian policemen followed this track and found us. Luckily, the attacking force was small, and our alert guard warned us in time. Several days later the whole area was searched by large forces of Germans and their collaborators, Ukrainians and Cossacks. But by that time we were long gone and far away.

On 4 February 1943, the day of the third massacre, all the Jews remaining in the ghetto of Novogrodek at Peresika were killed. The ghetto ceased to exist and only the labour camp in the court buildings remained, with a little over 500 Jews, all that was left of a community of 10,000 Jews from Novogrodek, Karelitz, Lubcz and surrounding areas.

The Bielski partisans were in the woods near the village of Izeba. One day, a few weeks after the massacre, our guards apprehended a Jew who claimed to be a survivor of the killing. His hand was wounded. He was taken to our headquarters. His name was Haim Lantzman. The Jews from the ghetto of Novogrodek knew Lantzman. But this man was not a native of Novogrodek. He and his wife had somehow managed to get into the ghetto, but no one had known them before. Gradually the people of the ghetto began to whisper that Lantzman was an informer sent by the Germans to find out what he could about those escaping from the ghetto to join the partisans. The ghetto Jews feared Haim Lantzman and tried to avoid him.

At the Bielski headquarters it was decided to hold the man and interrogate him about what he was doing, and how he had found his way to our hiding place. Haim Lantzman said he had been wounded in the massacre, pretended to be dead and escaped from the pit at night. He had wandered among the villages for two weeks, and the villagers had shown him the way to the partisans. Luckily, he found us.

Haim Lantzman's story didn't sound right, and his behaviour was strange and awkward. One night he tried to leave, but the alert guard stopped him. Finally he admitted that he had been sent by the Germans. He said that during the massacre, he and his wife had been taken back from the pits and locked up in the town jail. The German Gestapo had beaten them, then offered them a deal: in view of their good relationship with the Germans in the past, and if he carried out one more mission – that was, finding the Bielski partisans and letting the Germans know where they were – the Germans would spare the couple's lives. He agreed, and they let him go, keeping his wife in prison. To give him a cover story they shot him in the hand and instructed him to say he had escaped from the pits. Lantzman begged for our mercy, saying he never meant to go back and was willing to stay and be a good partisan. But the court set up by the partisans sentenced him to death, and Haim Lantzman was shot.

In March 1943 I was told by our commander Tuvia Bielski that the partisans' regional command had ordered the Bielskis (the Octyabr unit) to form a Komsomol (communist youth) chapter, and that this would be my job. Consequently, he said, I was being transferred to Victor's unit and would be trained by the Politruk communist political representative. Tuvia said he had chosen me because of my behaviour and personality, as well as my education and good knowledge of the Russian language. Together with this appointment I was ceremoniously given a gun. The next day I was taken by Asael to Victor's headquarters.

I stayed with Victor's troops for two months. At the beginning, these Russian partisans mocked me. I didn't seem to belong. I was obviously different. Most of Victor's partisans were Red Army men who had stayed behind German lines during the retreat. They had been joined by all sorts of rough Belorussians, even criminals, who adapted quite easily to their wild way of life. These men's heavy drinking caused many disasters. Victor's Russian partisans did not particularly love Jews, but generally the brigade behaved well. Many were antisemitic, and weren't at all sorry that the Germans had killed the Jews off. Sometimes Russian partisans even shot Jews who had escaped from the ghettos, saying that they must be German spies. I didn't hear of any such incidents in Victor's camp. On several occasions, Russian partisans mistreated Bielski's men and even took away their guns. Once two of our guards were attacked by a group of Russian partisans. Unsuspecting, they let the Russians approach, and the Russians murdered them.

I participated in some of Victor's military operations. We attacked German guard posts, ambushed vehicles and sabotaged railways. I knew that in order to win the respect and trust of my Russian comrades, I must strive to be more like them. I must adapt to my surroundings and prove that I was just as good a fighter. I constantly volunteered to go out on dangerous missions. Soon their attitude changed and I was seen as their good friend.

The town of Novoyelna, located 23 kilometres from Novo-grodek, was a very important railway intersection. In the spring of 1943 Victor's intelligence unit found out that a freight train loaded with weapons and ammunition had stopped at the station, and the partisans decided to attack the station and blow up the train. Several partisan divisions, including the Bielskis, were ordered to take part in this operation.

At nightfall, the partisans set out from their bases. The mission was carried out at midnight. The German guards retreated after a shoot-out and our men blew up the train. The explosion was huge, with flames lighting up the sky. German troops called in from Novogrodek and surrounding towns didn't arrive until it was all over. Ecstatic and triumphant, we made our way back to our bases, through the dark forest.

My communist training was a great success. I befriended the Politruk, comrade Shetzuras and, recommended by him, I was admitted into the Komsomol by the regional committee. My next mission was to organise a Komsomol chapter among the Bielski partisans, and so I went back to them.

The communist holiday on 1 May 1943 was drawing near. Bielski's troops celebrated the occasion with sabotage operations along the main roads leading from Baranovichi and Lida to Novo-grodek. We took saws and axes from nearby villages, then cut down telephone poles and blew up bridges along many kilometres of road. We did this for several consecutive nights, and it was a pleasant job. We did it enthusiastically, feeling that we were contributing to the war effort against the Nazi beast.

The Germans made great efforts to destroy us. Bielski's men set up base in the Zebleva forest and, one sunny day, towards the end of June 1943, we were suddenly attacked by German forces. The Bielski camp went into an organised retreat, well-planned and practised beforehand. We retreated, exchanging fire with the Germans, deep into the forest. We managed to lose the enemy, who was perhaps wary of traps in the forest. The gunfire ceased. We retreated slowly and cautiously, fearing an ambush. We had to cross some open spaces and I, as a Komsomol member who was supposed to set an example, was ordered to make sure that the coast was clear. I did my job, and was highly praised for it. I was told to report to the partisans' regional command, where I gave a full account of what I had done and received a commendation. We also had some casualties in this incident.

Being a member of the Komsomol, I was often forced to 'volunteer' for dangerous missions. One day our troop had visitors – a troop of sabotage experts from the 'Stalin' partisan regiment which operated near Minsk, in Belorussia. They asked for a guide who would lead them to the railway bridge of the Barano-vichi–Minsk line. Their mission was to blow it up. Asael asked me to go with them, and of course I agreed. We reached the bridge about two days later. That night I took part in laying the explosives and setting them off. The mission was a complete success. The railway line, which was very important to the Germans, was rendered useless for quite a while. The sabotage men asked me to join them, but I refused and went back to the Bielskis.

During another operation carried out by the Bielski troops, Asael led the men to Litovka, near Novogrodek, where the ghetto Jews had been shot and buried in a common grave. We planned to ambush German vehicles on the Vsielub–Novogrodek road. We got there at midnight, took up positions and waited.

Our first road-block stopped a Polish man on horseback, who was on his way to Novogrodek. The order was not to let him go until the mission was completed, so that he wouldn't report our presence to the Germans. But his careless guards didn't tie him up well enough and he escaped at dawn. Afraid that he would warn the Germans, we left the place and retreated quickly, in broad daylight, to our base – a distance of about 20 kilometres away. On the way we were attacked by German troops and some of our men were killed or wounded. Miraculously we managed to find refuge in the woods.

Finding provisions for the Bielski camp became increasingly difficult. The Germans had burned down the surrounding villages, and we were forced to seek supplies in the villages around the town, which was quite dangerous. The villagers had organised militias, trained by the Germans and armed with rifles, machine-guns and hand grenades. Their job was to chase the partisans away.

I remember one incident, in the spring of 1943. There were four of us – myself, my friend Ishie Oppenheim, Yudel Slutzki and Herzl Nokhimovski – and our destination was the village of Horodechno near Novogrodek. Before we left the camp, an elderly, sickly Jew named Zalman Koshtzinki came to us with a request: since he had heard that we were going to Horodechno, would we please stop by the house of a certain peasant whose name he gave us and bring back a fur coat the peasant was keeping for him? Zalman wanted the coat, because he suffered greatly from the cold at night.

We reached Horodechno, loaded a few carts with provisions, found the peasant, got Zalman's coat and started to go back. But as we were leaving the village we were ambushed by the local militia and found ourselves under heavy fire. We abandoned the carts and fled in different directions. A day later we got back to the Bielski camp, separately. We told Zalman what had happened, and that we were forced to leave his coat behind with everything else. Zalman got very depressed. He said he had sewn money and gold coins into the lining of the coat, everything he had in the world. We felt very bad. Some time later, Zalman died of a heart attack.

Large partisan forces were based in the forest of Lipichanski, between Slonim and Zdzienciol, on the banks of the River Bug. Some of these partisans were Jews, survivors of the ghettos of Slonim, Zdzienciol and the surrounding area. We heard of their great courage, under the leadership of the illustrious Dr Atlas. Dr Atlas was eventually killed in battle.

In the summer of 1943 I was ordered, together with two others, to go to the Lipichanski woods and make contact with some of these Jewish partisans. We got there safely, met the men, and were greatly impressed by their courageous spirit and fighting skills, as well as their fine weapons. Among them I met some men from Novogrodek, childhood friends who had gone to school with me – Elimelech Zamkovi, Yitzhak Rachkovski, and others (my friend Zamkovi was later killed by Polish partisans, and Rach-kovski died serving in the Red Army). We told them about the Bielski camp which included fighting men along with women, old men and children. We spoke of the importance of the Bielski group as a refuge for any Jew who had escaped from the Nazis. About 30 Jewish partisans from the Lipichanski woods decided to leave their units and join the Bielski partisans. I stayed with them for about a month, participating in their raids. When word came from the high command permitting them to join the Bielskis, we set out. A week later we reached the Bielski camp. These new partisans were a major reinforcement.

I was in the Ordzhonikidze force. We sabotaged railway lines and roads and attacked police stations and German government posts in nearby towns. One of our relatively big operations was an attack on the town of Vsielub, about 12 kilometres from Novo-grodek. Several policemen were killed in the attack on the local police station. The Germans fled, and the partisans held the town for two days. Our troop was one of several partisan units that destroyed the airfield built by the Germans near the town of Baranovichi. We blew up several enemy aeroplanes standing in the field.

The Bielski group continued to grow, constantly joined by survivors from ghettos all over the region, as well as Jews who had been hidden by peasants, and others who had been hiding out in the woods independently. In order to avoid detection, the Bielskis were forced to move frequently from one place to another, never staying at any one campsite for very long. This wasn't easy. Moving such a large base involved complex logistics. The troop travelled slowly, with all the old and weak people, the women and the children. Leading and protecting them was a grave respons-ibility. Providing for them wasn't easy either. A great deal of resourcefulness, planning, wisdom, acquaintance with the area, discipline and detailed intelligence were needed, if we were to outwit the Germans and survive.

Tuvia Bielski, his staff and commanders all displayed leadership, a sense of responsibility and efficiency. By July 1943 the woods around Novogrodek and Lida, where the Bielskis were based, grew dangerous. The Germans and their helpers raided and searched the forest and set up ambushes. Some of our men were killed in action, and the situation was growing worse. Our unit was attacked in the Zherovlenik forest and several men were killed. We were sustaining too many casualties. The unit's commanders and the regional partisan command decided to move the Bielski partisans in the early autumn to the densely wooded region of Naliboki.

The Naliboki woods, on the banks of the Niemen River, were very vast and dense. Some parts were impassable marshes. Quite a few partisan units, as well as the regional and district commands were based in these woods. A temporary airfield had been built, where Russian planes landed, bringing arms and ammunition. Red Army representatives and Politruks gave orders and instructions to the partisan forces. The importance of these forces behind enemy lines was inestimable. They sabotaged the enemy's transportation lines, and made it very difficult for them to supply their men at the front with provisions.

The fourth Novogrodek massacre took place on 7 May 1943. Two hundred of the 500 Jews living in the *Arbeitslager* (labour camp) were killed. Most of these were women. The killing was done near the forest of Horodzhilovka, quite close to the camp. Those remaining in the camp could hear their loved-ones being butchered with machine-guns. My dear aunt Dvore (my cousin Idel's mother), my aunt Haike Sucharski and my cousin Nachama, Idel's sister, were murdered that day.

As mentioned earlier, my cousin Idel had returned to the ghetto with frozen feet. During this massacre, when all the ghetto Jews were mustered in the courtyard, Idel stayed in his bunk, unable to walk. His toes had been amputated, and the wounds hadn't yet healed. His father Yankel Kagan and my uncle Notke Sucharski also survived this massacre. Several months later my uncle Yankel was sent to the work camp at Koldichevo.

My cousin Idel was left all alone. Friends of the family took care of him and brought him food. His most dedicated friend was Efroim Sielubski, who had worked in our shoe factory. Before he was sent to the Koldichevo camp, my uncle Yankel asked the ghetto supervisor, Daniel Ostashinski, to take pity on him and let him stay with his injured son. But it was no use.

The survivors who now remained in the labour camp had no illusions. They knew that the next, final massacre which would wipe out the ghetto completely, wasn't far off. The 300 remaining Jews began to plan an uprising. They intended to attack the guards and run to the forest. After some discussions and arguments, they agreed to dig an escape tunnel leading out of the ghetto.

7 *The Tunnel*

T HE STORY that follows and the information about the tunnel and the escape from the ghetto of Novogrodek was related to me by my friend Shaul Gorodinski.

After the second massacre, that of 7 August 1942, about 1,000 Jews remained in Novogrodek – 500 in the court-house and 500 in the ghetto. The Germans concentrated them all in the district court-house and the surrounding buildings. The area was fenced off with barbed wire, and later a high wooden fence was built so that the Jews wouldn't be able to see what was happening outside. A guard-room was built next to the entrance gate, and watch towers surrounded the camp. A searchlight installed in one of the towers lit up the camp at night, and the guards watched the inmates day and night.

Most of the people in this labour camp were craftsmen. Various workshops were set up in the buildings: tailors, shoemakers, metalworkers, carpenters, saddlers, and so on. They all worked for the German army. Conditions in the camp were difficult: hard labour from dawn to dusk, and very poor food, consisting of 150 grams of bread per day, and soup made of potato peelings.

The inmates began to organise an escape from the camp to the woods, planning to join the partisans. The idea was brought up by Dr Kagan, Berl Yoselevitz, Notke Sucharski and Aaron Oshman. Many inmates were opposed to the notion of attacking the guards and policemen. They said that now, after all the massacres, we probably had a few quiet months ahead of us, so why risk getting killed just yet? Life went on, in an almost 'normal' routine. Then we heard that on 4 February 1943, the last Jews remaining in the ghetto of Peresika, on the other side of town, had been massacred. The units guarding our camp were reinforced. The Germans started taking everyone out to be counted, then sending us back to work, several times a day. Two of Shaul's friends, Moshe Burstein and Ruvke Shabakovski, were arrested, taken to prison, and interrogated about the goings-on in the camp and if there were any kind of underground activities. They disclosed nothing, Moshe Burstein was tortured and killed, and Shabakovski was very badly beaten and returned to camp. Shabakovski had also risked his life a month before smuggling a radio into the camp.

One day in March 1943, the German SS officer in charge of Jewish affairs, Reuter, came to the camp, escorted by his assistants. They went from one workshop to the next, taking down the names of the best craftsmen. When we asked for an explanation, they said that all expert craftsmen would receive an additional 100 grams of bread every day, as suggested by the non-Jewish foreman. There were about 200 people on this list, including Shaul. Every ten days a truck loaded with bread would arrive, the inmates would gather in a large hall, the German supervisor would make a speech, saying that soon the war would end in German victory, there would be no more executions, and we would be transferred to a special concentration camp, 'where we would live happily'. When he finished his speech, the bread distribution would begin. All those entitled to an extra ration would receive a kilogram of bread for the next ten days. The other 300, who didn't get the extra bread, stayed where they were and went on with their work.

About a month later, in April 1943, several cars arrived, led by SS Officer Reuter. He ordered those with extra rations to line up in the courtyard, then go into the hall, to receive their bread rations. A week later, Reuter repeated this exercise. The inmates suspected malicious intentions behind all this, and they were right.

Early on the morning of 7 May 1943, the Germans came again with SS Officer Reuter in the lead, and said that they had brought bread as usual. This time all the inmates were ordered to muster outside: those who got bread rations on one side of the courtyard, and all the rest on the other side. Those entitled to extra rations were ordered to go to the workshops. A barbed wire fence separated the yard from the workshops. They passed through the gate and entered the building. At the same time, another gate opened at the other end of the fence. Hundreds of policemen swarmed in, surrounded the people there and ordered them to march towards the exit. People began to scream and cry. Some tried to escape, and even succeeded. The others were led to pits dug out beforehand, about one and a half kilometres away from the camp, and mown down with machine-gun fire. That day the Germans murdered 230 people. About 300 still remained in the camp.

These events had a deep effect on the survivors. People were intensely angry. The Germans had fooled them once again. That evening, after the massacre, it was decided to attempt a break-out. The plan was to throw hand grenades into the guardroom, then break out with everything we had: guns, iron rods, and so on. Some would make it, and the others would at least die heroically.

At nightfall the situation changed. The Germans brought in more guards, and the escape was postponed to the following day. The next day a committee was formed, and anyone who had ever been a soldier became a member: Yaremovski Izik who had been a corporal in the Polish army, Rakovski the electrician, Berl Yoselevitz the organiser and leader of the whole plan, and several Jews with a military background, who were not from Novogrodek.

People began to get organised. They were divided into groups with various missions, breaking through the different gates, cutting the barbed wire, and so on. The preparations went on for a full week. Some people opposed the whole plan and wanted to find another idea. Their attitude was, if we can live another day, why commit suicide today? Others argued, what's the use of living another day? In the end we will be killed, just like all the others.

One of those who spoke against the escape was the doctor's wife, Mrs Yaakobovitz. She wanted us to wait until a solution was found for her injured husband. These people organised a second committee, and came up with the idea of digging a tunnel. They had it all drawn up. Many people in the camp did not believe in this plan, but having no choice, they agreed to try. They had young people, and could get equipment from the workshops: drills for digging, logs for support, and everything else that was needed for the job.

The plan was to dig a hole in the living quarters, in the last stable building which was about 40 metres from the fence, and tunnel towards it. On the other side of the fence there were wheat fields. In the summertime, the wheat was one and a half metres tall. On a dark night we could pass through the wheat undetected. The forest was one and a half kilometres away.

The tunnel had to be completed by August, before the harvest.

One of the problems was the searchlight. An electrician named Rakovski took it upon himself to solve this problem by short-circuiting the camp's electrical supply. He suggested doing this several times beforehand, so that it wouldn't seem suspicious on the night of the escape. Another problem was how to dispose of the earth dug out of the tunnel. It was decided to fill up the attic of the living quarters with soil. Most houses in eastern Europe had an attic between the ceiling and the inclined roof.

The electrician Rakovski installed a device at the entrance of the tunnel which would warn the diggers of any sudden inspection. On several occasions the guards actually stood just a few metres from the tunnel's entrance while the digging went on inside. The warning signal prevented its detection.

Tools were manufactured in the metal workshop: shovels, drills, funnels and so on. Shaul's digging partner was Hone Kushner. They took turns, digging three to five hours every day. The tunnel ran about one and a half metres under the surface, and it was tall enough for a man to crawl through.

A further problem was keeping the tunnel from caving in. Every few metres the diggers would pierce the top with a stick, to measure the depth. This also allowed them to check if they were still digging in the right direction. The soil was heaped up in a corner of the stable. The tailors made sacks for its removal. When one attic was full, they moved on to the next. In order to get to the next attic, they made a hole in the wall separating the two attics, and passed the soil through there. Gradually all the attics of this building were filled up.

As the work progressed there wasn't enough air and light in the tunnel. For light, a cord soaked with oil was kindled, but when it wouldn't burn for lack of air, the diggers were forced to broaden the tunnel.

When they had dug about 20 metres, removing the sacks became difficult. They devised a cart pulled by two thick ropes, which the tailors made from cloth. Gradually the technique improved. A carpenter named Dvoretski suggested laying a wooden track with a wagon attached to a rope. Later on electricity was installed in the tunnel. Work went on energetically. People made great efforts and maintained secrecy, even though everybody knew about the tunnel. When the attics were full, double walls were built in the rooms, but even this wasn't enough. Then someone came up with a new idea. Sunday was maintenance day, when all the toilets, rooms and courtyards were cleaned. The toilets in the camp were holes in the ground. When they were full, new holes were dug and the soil removed in wheelbarrows. In the same manner, the soil from the tunnel was disposed of.

Gradually they approached the fence. At some point they ran up against some rocks in the tunnel. Another technical problem came up when the cart kept running off its wooden rails. But all such problems were solved. They started disconnecting the searchlight once in a while, so that the guards would grow accustomed to such power failures. Sometimes the searchlight would break down just before dark, and they would bring someone at night to fix it. The inmates would time how long it took to get it working again. But sometimes the Germans only repaired it the next morning. All this was repeated every two weeks or so.

The date of the escape was set for August. The order of escape was also set: who would leave first, who last, and so on. Those leaving first would carry guns, in case they ran into guards outside, and those at the end would also be armed, to cover the rear. They held practice drills. They also solved the problem of the people from the first building; there were too many of them and they couldn't get to the other buildings during the night. It was arranged for them to sleep in a building next to the tailors' workshop, then get out through openings in the attics. This was practised as well.

About a month before the set date the tunnel reached the wheat fields. Now, once the searchlight was disconnected, they could get out unnoticed. They waited for a stormy night and even prepared tin cans which would rattle in the wind and conceal the escape, giving our people time to get to the partisans or hide in the woods. It was estimated that escapees would have to cover a distance of about 20 kilometres.

Just when everything was ready, they heard that the Germans had blockaded the area with a whole division, and the partisans had been forced to retreat to the great woods at Naliboki, where they were also under siege. This siege lasted a whole month.

The escape was postponed. Once again the old argument broke out between those who wanted to escape and those who were against it. In the meantime, the wheat fields were harvested, leaving a vast area of open ground between the camp and the forest. The rainy season came, and the tunnel began to cave in at some points. People began to say that if they didn't leave right away, the tunnel would collapse completely. At this time 11 craftsmen were transferred from the camp to the concentration camp of Koldichevo. Shaul's father was one of them (and so was my uncle Yankel). More guards were brought in.

It was decided to dig further, beyond the hill at the edge of the wheat field. One 70-year-old carpenter from Karelitz, named Shkolnik, built wooden supports for the tunnel, and the work progressed. Shaul, too, worked every day. Early in September they reached the other side of the hill.

The early autumn weather was setting in, bringing wind and rain. The escapees heard that the partisans had returned to the outskirts of the town, and made final preparations. Several more practice drills were held, but the date was put off once again, because the weather was too sunny. A few people didn't want to leave, and found themselves hiding places in the camp. Operational and discipline commands were prepared, and a letter written to the German supervisor saying that they were liberating themselves, and would take revenge.

September 26 1943 was a cloudy, wet Sunday. The escapees got ready to leave. Each received a number for his place in the line. Shaul's was 82. As far as I know, there were no lots drawn. As it turned out, some of those who went first were killed, while others who were at the end of the line survived. But at the time it seemed better to be at the front. They had some weapons: pistols, rifles and hand grenades. In addition, there were some wooden guns, just to frighten the enemy. The operation began. The first 120 people entered the tunnel. Everyone stood in line, in total silence. As Shaul approached the exit, he could feel the cool air, the air of freedom. In all, about 250 to 280 people escaped that night. Shaul's sister Sonia and her husband Aaron Oshman were right behind him, and behind them came Aaron's brother, Yankel Oshman. Hearing gunshots they scattered in all directions. Shaul remained with Kushner, and said to him: 'I grew up here, I know the area. We'd better get as far away from the camp as possible.' But Kushner said he knew better. They started wandering about.

The night was very dark. Suddenly they realised they were approaching the camp gate. There was shouting and shots were fired. He turned around. Kushner had either disappeared or been killed. He was all alone and started walking through the fields. From a distance, he saw a Jew from central Poland named Feifer and another named Pakidel from Lomzha. They asked if he knew the area. Together they continued to wander through the night.

Later on I heard what happened. Some of the people who got out, wandered about in the dark and ran into some guards. Eighty of them were killed. About 170 reached the partisans safely.

They walked all night, found the railway tracks and reached the woods. At daybreak they saw that they were only about three kilometres from the town. At eight or nine o'clock, gunfire was heard from all directions. Jews were being caught and killed by the Germans. Shaul and his companions sat in the forest, among some nut bushes that hid them from view. At night they got out quietly. They went to one house and were turned away, because the Germans were nearby. They tried another house, and were given milk and bread, and then wandered through the forest all night without knowing where they were going. They wanted to get to a place called Larda, where Victor's partisans were supposed to be. They were told by the Gentiles that if they crossed the road, they would be in partisan-controlled territory.

The territory was divided into sections, and each part was ruled by a different partisan group. At dawn, after the second night, they reached a big forest. In the distance they saw a group of Jews, and among them they recognised Dr and Mrs Yaakobovitz, Daniel Ostashinski, Pinchuk, Feibelevitz and another man from Iveniec named Motke, who had a radio. They were told that the Germans had apprehended many Jews, and that they must get to the nearest group of partisans. That night, some peasants gave them food. The doctor's wife, Mrs Yaakobovitz, entered every place and got information about what was going on in the area. They were told how to get to the place where Victor's partisans were based. This was the area between the roads of Svitez and Novogrodek.

Once again, they walked all night. It was raining. Dr Yaakobovitz had an injured leg, and they carried him on their backs. The next morning they heard gunshots and saw men in German uniforms, but luckily, these were partisans from Victor's unit.

They promised to take Shaul and his companions to their head-quarters, gave them food and dry clothes, and showed them the way to Bielski's partisans. On the way they found different partisan groups, and were given food and directions by all of them. And so they carried on, until they reached the area of Otonoman where they found the Bielskis. They stayed there for about two weeks. Then they finally reached the Bielski partisan regiment, and Shaul's life as a partisan began.

Digging the tunnel and escaping was a supremely heroic act on the part of the Jews of Novogrodek, the last remnant of an illustrious, ancient community of about 6,000. The work was carried out day and night, for months on end, by starved, desperate people, who had lost their loved ones, in conditions of fear and dread, in a closed camp, fenced in and closely guarded, with watchtowers, searchlights and machine-guns all around, and the Germans holding inspections and searches without warning at any time, day or night.

The diggers themselves did not really believe that the tunnel would be completed. They expected the Germans to find it, knowing full well that this would bring about the immediate extermination of all the Jews in the ghetto. But digging the tunnel was an act of rebellion.

Under these conditions, the tunnel itself was a great engineering achievement. It was over 250 metres long and 60 centimetres high (about 2 feet), and it ran about one and a half metres beneath the surface. It is almost unbelievable that the Germans never found it, that the diggers were able to hide huge amounts of soil and solve all the problems as they arose: direction, cave-ins, water seeping into the tunnel, lack of air and other obstacles. The history of the Holocaust knows no similar deed. Eighty of the runaways were killed. Some were caught and tortured to death. But between 170 and 190 reached the partisans safely (among them Notke Sucharski and Idel Kagan) and most of these survived the Holocaust.

8 Reunion and the End of the War

THE REUNION with my dear cousin Idel was very moving. We laughed and cried. Idel was only 14, but had experienced many troubles, dangers and hardships. He had felt pain, torture and fear, and had lost both his parents. When he came to me, he was in very bad shape. He could hardly move. His feet were in a terrible state. The amputation wounds, which had partially healed, opened up again on the long journey from the ghetto to the partisans. They were bleeding and badly infected.

I was then with the Ordzhonikidze partisan fighting unit, which never stayed in any one place for very long. It was very clear that if I took Idel along, we wouldn't be able to keep up with the unit. In addition, the area we were in had become dangerous. Large police and army forces often raided the woods, searching for partisans.

We decided that Idel and I would travel separately, at our own pace. Whenever the company moved, the commanders told us where it was headed, and we travelled there in a cart. We made our way through the woods in the dark, hiding in the daytime. We got food from peasants in the villages. With God's help, we survived. Several times, on arrival at the company's new base, we found that while we were away, the company had encountered the Germans and lost some men. Idel and I were very lucky. I took care of Idel as much as I could. His young, strong body got over the injuries and good, nutritious food also helped. In a relatively short time he could walk again, and his feet were much better.

We realised that we couldn't go on with the Ordzhonikidze fighting unit and decided to join the Bielski camp in the Naliboki woods, which had been set up in the summer of 1943. The whole Naliboki region was partisan country, a Soviet-ruled enclave behind enemy lines. Only during the great manhunts, when the Germans brought whole divisions together, did they dare penetrate the Naliboki woods. When this happened, the partisans usually managed to get away. The German operations did not have satisfactory results, from their point of view.

The partisans' higher command and various headquarters were located in the Naliboki woods. Orders and instructions about military operations, guidance and organisation all came from there. There was even an airfield, where Soviet planes would land, bringing guns and ammunition, as well as Red Army officers, some experts in partisan warfare and politruks. The partisans kept in touch with the Russian army's front lines and carried out operations that damaged the Nazi enemy considerably and contributed a great deal to the Soviet Union's war effort. The planes would also take away our wounded men and bring us supplies and medication.

In the summer of 1943, the German advance on the Russian front was halted, the 'invincible army' suffered defeat in some battles and even began to retreat in several spots. The wheel of fortune had turned.

The partisans, operating behind the lines, considerably damaged the Germans' transportation and communication lines. The Germans knew that they had to get rid of the partisans and, at the end of July 1943, they held a most extensive manhunt in the Naliboki woods, searching for the partisans and their bases. Armoured units, planes, artillery and specially trained forces all participated in this operation.

The Bielski partisans, with their large civilian camp of women, children and old people, were in great danger when the Germans launched this operation. The leaders decided to abandon the base and find a hiding place for the group in the swamp area. An excellent guide, who knew the Naliboki woods very well, led us all into the swamps by a winding route known to him alone. We moved in the dark and kept very quiet to avoid detection. The terrain was very difficult, and progress was slow. The strong helped the weak. On the second day at dawn we reached our destination, a wooded area surrounded by water and swamps. We lay down in this grove, and artillery shells shrieked overhead as though they were aimed directly at us. The armed warriors and commanders of the Bielski partisans stayed with the family camp disregarding the regional command's orders to leave the area altogether.

For six days the people lay in the swamps without food. The filthy swamp waters we drank caused severe diarrhoea and poisoning, and people grew weak. But the people, who had known much suffering, overcame these troubles. No one complained and discipline was maintained. When the shelling stopped and our patrol informed us that the Germans had gone, the Bielski regiment returned to its base in the Naliboki woods. I myself, together with a company of warriors, left the Naliboki woods and returned to the Ordzhonikidze partisan unit.

The Bielski partisans' base in the Naliboki woods was in many ways a miniature copy of a Jewish town with its population of over 1,200 Jews, all refugees from various ghettos in the area, mostly the ghettos of Novogrodek and Lida. There were 'streets' in the camp, with huts constructed on either side, their wooden roofs camouflaged with vegetation – an expert job. Some of the huts were quite large, housing 30–50 people. Smaller huts belonged to important people, the commanders or their families. In addition, there were public buildings in the camp: the headquarters with its various divisions, a common kitchen, sickroom, surgery and a bath-house. But most important of all were the workshops for shoemakers, tailors, watchmakers, tinsmiths, saddlers, armourers, metalworkers, carpenters and builders, and butchers who made sausages and preserved meat. Craftsmen, including women, worked in these workshops. These Jews, unable to take up arms, were proud of their work and contribution to the war effort. They felt useful and needed. The workshops at the Bielski camp served partisans from all over the area, who came when they needed professional craftsmen or medical assistance for their sick and wounded. The partisans would barter these services for guns, ammunition and food. These transactions gave the camp both material and moral support. The craftsmen did their job joyfully, with a deep sense of responsibility, knowing that they were needed and useful to the fighting men.

The camp was run as a military base. Each person knew his job and his place. The fighting men were organised in companies and trained in the use of guns, defensive combat, sabotage, hit-and-run attacks, partisan warfare and so on. The commanders were experienced ex-servicemen. The craftsmen worked in the various workshops from morning to nightfall, and manufactured exceptionally fine products, considering the working conditions and the materials at their disposal.

The names of the guards on duty, special orders and work schedules were posted every day on the billboard next to the camp headquarters. On special occasions we would muster in military fashion and listen to reports on the political situation and news from the front. The district headquarters published a daily newspaper. We conducted various cultural activities and held classes for the children. Everyone was kept busy.

The Bielski camp proved itself productive. It had the vitality and endurance needed to survive. It was a miracle that this assemblage of ghetto Jews, near to breaking point both physically and mentally, bereaved of their loved ones, could still be useful, contributing to the war effort, taking up arms, inflicting damage upon the enemy and taking revenge.

Most of the Jews who had escaped from the ghetto at Novogrodek through the tunnel came to the Bielski camp in the Naliboki woods, my uncle Notke among them. When I arrived with my cousin Idel, we built a cabin with my uncle Notke and some friends, 12 people altogether. It was comfortable, having been built under the professional supervision of our friend the carpenter, Moshe Nignivitski. Cudek, the camp chef, also lived in our cabin, so we got the best food. Several women, the wives of some of the men, also lived with us, and kept the place tidy and clean.

As a fighting partisan, I was usually away from the camp, participating in missions or obtaining provisions for the camp. In order to provide for a camp of 1,200, our supply units had to travel long distances and operate very close to the cities. It took days and sometimes weeks before the units returned with supplies, meat, flour and other basic provisions. The roads were bad, and there were ambushes and traps. Many men died on these missions, but they were vital to the camp, and we did them out of a sense of responsibility. Whenever I returned from such a mission, I would always bring supplies to our cabin, especially for my cousin Idel – mostly meat and fat – and clothes as well. Idel's health improved considerably. At the base, Idel looked after me. He got me hot water to bathe in when I got back all covered in filth, and also washed my dirty clothes.

In February 1944, several dozen Jews arrived at the Bielski camp. They had escaped from the Koldichevo labour camp, where my dear uncle Yankel, Idel's father, had also been imprisoned. They had made a hole in the fence and escaped. They told us that my uncle Yankel had escaped with them, and we hoped that he too would arrive. We were excited and tense with anticipation. Days went by, and my uncle did not arrive. We got increasingly anxious. I decided to go out to the area and make inquiries in other partisan groups. But I discovered nothing. My uncle Yankel must have been killed during the escape. It is also possible that he committed suicide, using the cyanide pills he kept in his possession. The men from Koldichevo told us that my uncle Yankel was very depressed, having lost all his loved ones. He mourned for them ceaselessly. He often spoke of his son Idel who had been left alone, ill and wounded in the ghetto of Novogrodek, and said frequently that he didn't want to live anymore and would rather die.

One day, in the winter of 1943, six of us left the base at Naliboki, to get supplies. My friend Yudel Slutzki (who now lives in Israel), Zvi Leibovitz (nicknamed Yorke) and Eli Ostashinski (commander of the squad) were in that company. Our destination was the village of Revniki, near Novogrodek. We intended to take some cows and sheep from the peasants there. A few days later, on a Saturday, we reached an isolated farm near the village of Horodechno, also near Novogrodek. The farmer told us that two young Belorussian policemen from Novogrodek were visiting their parents in the village. They were a wild, brutal pair, who terrorised the whole region, raping and robbing at will. They bragged of having taken part in massacres and killing many Jews, and brought home a lot of goods taken from Jews. The farmer gave us their names and told us exactly where their parents lived, and we decided to go out at night and try to catch the two villains. It was quite dangerous. There were only six of us, and we were quite sure the scoundrels were armed. But we just couldn't pass up this opportunity. And we were successful. We surprised the two policemen, took away their guns, dragged them out of their parents' homes, tied them up and threw them into the sleigh, and left hurriedly with them. That night we reached Revniki, got the supplies we needed and set out on our way back to the camp, a distance of about 50 kilometres. We spent the daylight hours in an isolated farm.

Our prisoners were a real pain in the neck. We had to guard them, and doubted that we could take them all the way to the camp. When we interrogated them, they confessed to having participated in the massacres in the ghetto of Novogrodek. They said they had only been obeying German orders, that they and their parents actually loved Jews, and that they were willing to join the partisans and fight against the Germans.

We held a trial and sentenced them to death. They were executed by the partisan Zvi Leibovitz (Yorke), who killed them with an axe, saying it was a shame to waste bullets on such scum. Yorke also made them dig their own graves in a wood before he killed them. We got safely back to camp, reported the incident and earned an honourable mention in a special ceremony.

The spring of 1944 brought significant Red Army victories all along the front. The might of the German army began to crumble, and the Germans were retreating.

Towards the Labour Day holiday of 1 May 1944, the regional partisan command issued orders to the units, instructing them to cut off the important railway line between Vilnius and Minsk, through which the Germans sent supplies to their front lines. A Bielski unit, of which I was a member, was instructed to blow up a bridge near the town of Vilika. We were given explosives supplied by the Red Army. Our destination was far from our base, and well-guarded. It took us several days to get there. The stormy weather on the night of the operation was in our favour. We rejoiced when a loud explosion destroyed the bridge. Partisan attacks on the enemy's transportation lines were now very frequent. At night the partisans, in well-planned and co-ordinated operations, would simultaneously sabotage the railroads in different places, blow up trains, and cut off the enemy's lines of transportation for long periods of time.

In June 1944 the Soviets broke through enemy lines near Vitebsk and advanced rapidly towards Minsk. The Germans fled, retreating from large portions of Belorussia. Many German divisions were encircled in the battle of Minsk. At night we could hear long, faraway rattling sounds, like distant thunder in the eastern skies. These sounds were like music to our ears. We would sit up half the night, listening for these signs of the approaching storm which would soon bring us freedom. Our excitement and anticipation grew from day to day. The thunder of the front lines grew louder and clearer. Scattered groups of German soldiers appeared in the area, trying to escape the Soviet siege. The central command passed down instructions: be alert and watchful. The great hour we had been waiting for was near. Bielski's armed troops attacked Germans wandering in the forest. The partisans ambushed and wiped out many German units on the roads crossing the Naliboki woods. Our armed troops also encountered groups of German soldiers.

The partisans and Germans had switched roles: now the partisans were hunting down Germans. Our spirits were high. We were enthusiastic and vengeful, glad to batter the enemy. Every evening, when we returned to the base, we spoke excitedly and joyfully of the day's events. The Germans, at this point, were like hunted, frightened animals, trying to escape, hiding in the bush, hungry and exhausted. Their resistance grew weaker. These were the wretched remnants of the German army that had wanted to conquer the world. Four German prisoners were brought to our base headquarters, and executed for all to see. We were all overtaken by feelings of rage and vengeance. The central command constantly warned us to stay on the alert: the front line might pass through our area and then large German forces might penetrate the woods with great force, trying to eliminate the partisans and secure their own retreat. Our base prepared itself for sudden evacuation. We held practice drills, teaching people how to abandon the base.

One morning a large German unit surprised us, entering our camp. The armed troops were away fighting at the time, and the camp was virtually unguarded. The Germans fired in all directions and threw grenades into the huts. Fortunately, they only passed through and went on. We lost nine people in this surprise raid. My friends and comrades-at-arms, Eli Ostashinski and Zvi Leibovitz (Yorke), were among the dead. Later on the German unit encountered a partisan force and were wiped out.

The next day, the first Red Army troops passed by our camp. Everyone went out to meet them. We surrounded the dust-covered, sweaty soldiers, embraced and kissed them, and shook their hands. The soldiers were in a hurry to get on, and couldn't stay long.

The central partisan command sent word that the whole region had been liberated by the Red Army, including my native town, Novogrodek. We were free.

9 *Building a New Life*

THE PARTISAN chapter of my life was over. It had been a unique period, especially for anyone who had survived the massacres, horrors and terror. It had been very hard, but full of excitement. As partisans we never dreamed that we would one day be liberated. We did not expect to survive. There were so many dangers and hardships and terrible incidents, that it often seemed as though the inevitable end had come. We never planned for the future, and the liberation came to many of us as a complete surprise. Suddenly we were faced with all sorts of questions and problems: what were we going to do from now on?

For many of us, our first thought was to go back to Novogrodek. But on reflection we thought, what for? We will only find the graves of our loved ones there. The community no longer exists. The town is in ruins. But in the end we had no choice. We had to go back. At this stage it was better not to think too much. We didn't know what the future had in store for us. The war wasn't over yet. It was a strange feeling, leaving the base, coming out of the forest in which we felt concealed and secure. Over the years we had grown accustomed to the partisan way of life. All of a sudden, everything had changed.

Early in the morning we got ready to leave the camp. We were ordered to demolish the huts, so that the 'white', Polish partisans, who might now be taking our place, wouldn't be able to use them. We set out on our way to Novogrodek. Along the paths that crossed the forest we saw bodies of dead German soldiers, and the burnt-out remnants of military vehicles. We passed by the Kermin lake, and went on, through the dense woods.

The summer heat made us tired and sweaty. It was a hard journey, especially for the women, the elderly and the weak. My cousin Idel kept up with us and never complained, despite his crippled feet. He walked beside me, and never requested a ride in the carts which carried the ill and the weak.

93

Gradually a blue mist descended upon the forest, growing thicker as we progressed. We could smell smoke. The woods were on fire. The battles raging in the forests ignited fires that spread rapidly over vast areas. The smoke made it difficult to breathe, and our eyes watered. Flames were spreading all around and the heat became unbearable. We reached the Niemen River, which blocked the fire, and camped out in the open. And so, after a march of several days, we approached the outer edge of the woods.

We emerged from the forest and took the heavily travelled road. We passed through a large village, and the villagers all came out and watched in disbelief: such a large party of Jews. We entered the town of Lubcz, where the formerly large Jewish community had been completely wiped out in the Holocaust. The Christians all came out, and stared in amazement – so many Jews! They didn't even try to conceal their hostility. Some even refused to give us food and drink, and there were several clashes. We left the town, disgusted. The hostility we encountered there was indicative of the prevailing attitude towards the Jews.

At the outset, we travelled in military order, with armed troops leading the way and bringing up the rear. But later on we scattered, forming groups that proceeded at their own pace. Somehow, there was no joy in our hearts. As we passed through places where Jewish communities once flourished, we became aware of the extent of our tragedy. These places had changed. The people were different. Jewish town-life had ceased to exist. There were simply no more Jews there. They were all dead. We went on, becoming more and more depressed. The houses of Novogrodek could be seen in the distance. But we could feel no joy. We didn't really want to go into the town. Many of us couldn't hold back our tears. We reached the outskirts at night, entered through May 1st Street, and camped in a large farm at the edge of the city.

Neither my cousin Idel nor I could sleep that night, despite our exhaustion. We felt grief and sorrow. We talked about the loss of our loved ones, our unique warm home, our parents, our murdered brothers and sisters, and the large family that was completely wiped out.

The next day we all gathered in the farmyard for one last muster. Tuvia made a moving speech, and announced that he was disbanding the regiment, and each of us was free to go wherever he wished and do as he pleased. The partisan period was over. In doing this, Tuvia disobeyed the explicit orders of the central partisan command, namely, to place the complete partisan units, as they were, at the disposal of the Soviet authorities. Tuvia Bielski disobeyed this order courageously, of his own accord, because he predicted that the Soviets would immediately recruit the troops and send them to the front, where the war was still raging. And this is exactly what happened to those partisan troops that weren't disbanded. The Soviets, of course, did not approve of what Tuvia Bielski had done, and wanted to interrogate him. He was forced to leave Novogrodek and move to Lida.

The people of the Bielski camp scattered throughout the neighbouring towns and cities. Many of them got themselves jobs which exempted them from further military service. Others, of suitable age, were drafted into the Red Army, and continued to fight bravely against the Nazis. Many of them were killed in battle.

We must mention here the illustrious partisan commander Asael Bielski who fought the enemy bravely as a soldier of the Red Army, and was killed near Königsberg. Asael set an example of courage and bravery. He was a hero whose exploits contributed an exemplary chapter to the history of the Holocaust.

We walked through the streets of our native town, which we had once liked so much. We felt like strangers. Great portions of the town lay in ruins. Over the ruins and vast empty spaces, stood the gate to the Jewish cemetery, as a monument commemorating the illustrious community annihilated in the Holocaust. We walked through the streets, and the Christians of the town watched us with amazement, wondering how we had survived. They showed us no sympathy and seemed indifferent to our bitter fate. In fact, many were sorry that the Germans hadn't finished the job. They never bothered to conceal their hatred for the Jews, and had been easily convinced by Nazi propaganda. Some of the town's Christians now lived in Jewish houses and had taken part in the plunder of Jewish property. Now they were afraid that they would be forced to give it back.

We did not feel triumphant at all. Quite the contrary. We were defeated and depressed. We stood in silence beside the common graves at Skridlevo, Litovka and Horodzhilovka, where over 10,000 Jews lay buried, whole communities that were brutally butchered, among whom were our loved ones, our families, parents, brothers and sisters. The graves of our martyrs were covered with vegetation. In some places we found exposed bones and human remains where the local villagers had desecrated the graves, digging for jewellery and other valuables. We stood there, appalled, remembering the martyrs. We prayed *Yizkor* and said *kaddish* and some of us wept inconsolably. It was very moving, and many collapsed.

A strange emptiness now took over. Our lives were no longer organised and ordered by the partisan group, and we had to face a new reality in the town, to find our way somehow, plan the future, go on living. This meant finding food and other daily necessities, getting a job, the compulsory enlistment at the recruitment office for anyone of draftable age with military training. The war raged on, taking a heavy toll. Great numbers of young men died in the battlefields.

My cousin Idel, my uncle Notke and I found a room in a house on the castle hill, near Zamkovi Street in Novogrodek. Twenty Jews now lived in this deserted house.

I was recruited by the police force, and appointed superintendent of one of the town districts. My cousin Idel was only 15, and my uncle Notke was past draft age. Therefore we all stayed in Novogrodek. My uncle started working as a tinsmith and my cousin enrolled at a Russian secondary school.

The meagre salary I got from the police was insufficient, and my cousin began to trade illegally, which was quite dangerous. Idel was gifted and resourceful, and his business went very well. He would travel by train to various Russian cities, dressed in uniform, posing as a crippled war veteran. There he would buy and sell clothes and footwear which were in great demand, smuggle food and cigarettes and deal illegally in gold and foreign currency. While he did this, our financial situation was quite good.

A few months went by, and then my uncle Notke became ill with severe poisoning and complications in the digestive system. He died during surgery at the town hospital, and was buried at the Jewish cemetery of Novogrodek. Then I moved with my cousin Idel to the Delatitski house on Brazilanski Street, near the Provoslavian Church. There were about 15 Jews living in that house.

Several hundred Jews gathered in the town of Novogrodek – all that remained of the surrounding communities. Our conversations revolved around the great tragedy, the Holocaust, the partisans and the future. We drank a lot of alcohol, mostly vodka, trying to drown our grief and misery.

About 100 Jews took part in the Kol Nidrei service on Yom Kippur, 1944, which took place in the home of Wolfovitz on Zamkovi Street, in a large room which had once been a restaurant. Several Jewish soldiers from the Red Army, whose units were passing through Novogrodek, also attended. I shall never forget this moving occasion. The cantor was an elderly Jew from Novogrodek who had lost his whole family in the Holocaust. He had found a prayer book somewhere and read the prayers, while the whole congregation, men and women, stood and wept uncontrollably. There was a sense of holiness in the air.

Non-Jewish policemen and Red Army officers who happened to be there, stood still and watched, even though they did not understand what was happening. The unusual scene touched them and they did not disrupt the service or disperse the 'unlawful gathering', but let it go on.

On 9 May 1945 Germany surrendered. The brutal war that had raged for over six years and killed many millions of people, including six million Jews, came to an end. Never in the history of our long-suffering nation which has known many killings, exiles, inquisitions and pogroms has there been anything like this Holocaust. The very existence of the nation was threatened. The victory over the Nazi beast brought about joyful outbursts in all the occupied lands, national pride and admiration for the Soviet people, the Red Army and its commanders, and praise for the leaders of the Soviet Union. But we, the surviving Jews, remained indifferent to the Gentiles' jubilation, which was quite justified, for our hearts were full of grief and sorrow.

Once the war was over, we were faced with a very uncertain future. We felt like strangers in our native town. Clearly, we couldn't stay in this place, so full of tragic, dreadful memories, where every corner and every street was a monument to the illustrious past of the Jewish community and the horrors of the Holocaust.

In the summer of 1945 the government of the Soviet Union and the temporary government of the Polish National Democracy signed an agreement, whereby anyone who had been a citizen of Poland before the Second World War living in western Belorussia and the western Ukraine, which had previously belonged to Poland and were now annexed to the Soviet Union, was permitted to choose between the states. They could either stay in the Soviet Union or emigrate to the Polish National Democracy within its newly defined borders.

Most of the Jews remaining in Novogrodek chose to go to Poland, and registered at special emigration offices set up for this purpose. The Soviet authorities couldn't understand our motives. They tried to convince us to stay, with strong arguments: Poland was a land where antisemitism was very widespread and deeply rooted, where the worst, most deadly concentration camps had operated, where the population was indifferent to the Jewish genocide, where pogroms had taken place and Jews murdered in some major cities (Kletzk, Radum, Cracow and others) even after the Nazi defeat.

But our final destination was not Poland. We wanted to get away from the places where the horrors had occurred, to leave the Soviet Union whose borders were hermetically sealed, hoping that perhaps from Poland we would be able to go on somewhere else, though we didn't know where.

I continued to serve in the police force. One day I was summoned to headquarters and questioned as to whether I had any relatives or connections in Palestine. I said no, and they told me that a letter had arrived, addressed to Berl Kagan in Novogrodek. The letter came from a person named Meiri Gershon, in Tel Aviv, Palestine. I said I didn't know a person by that name, and had never had any contact with him. I was then asked to read the letter and translate it into Russian. The letter said that its author was a native of Novogrodek, and his former name was Gershon Eicher. I remembered Gershon Eicher, who had been a member of the Hashomer Hatzair youth movement in Novogrodek, and had emigrated to Palestine in the 1930s. I recalled that his family had a fish shop. Somehow, I don't know how, Gershon heard that I had survived, and in his letter he asked me to write him about what had befallen the Novogrodek community in the Holocaust, in particular his own large family, and about those who had survived. In his letter, Gershon emphasised that all natives of

Novogrodek who were now living in Palestine were most willing to extend all assistance possible to the survivors from our town. In their name, he expressed sympathy for our grief and concern for our well-being, saying they all felt it was their duty to help us in every way.

Gershon's letter was like a ray of light in the darkness. Suddenly we realised that somebody cared. And more important, we had found ourselves a destination, a goal: we must reach Eretz Yisrael, where we could find comfort for our grief, and a new life. Gershon's letter served as a driving force, impelling us to set out on our way towards the unknown, despite all difficulties.

My cousin Idel and I both decided to go to Poland, but I had a problem. I was serving in the police force, and was just about to be sent to a special NKVD (KGB) school in Minsk. I was desperate, but we had no choice. We decided that Idel would go to Poland on his own, and I would stay behind. Luckily, the authorities decided to expel all Jewish students from the school in the spring of 1945. There were three of us. And so I was back in Novogrodek. With my cousin Idel's assistance, I was admitted to the pedagogy department of Minsk University. Then he also helped me get the forms I needed in order to get a release from the police force. Illegally and unofficially, for a certain sum of money, I got the papers and immigration certificate, and we were ready to go, hoping I wouldn't get caught.

At about this time we received a letter from my cousin Leizer Sanderovski, from the town of Samarkand in the Uzbek Republic, in the distant south of the Soviet Union. We were very happy and excited. Another member of the family had survived, an elder brother. Leizer was already married, and we looked forward to meeting him and his wife. We did all that was needed, submitting the required requests, recommendations and other papers, to speed up the reunion. And sure enough, Leizer, his wife Michle and another family, Michle's relations, Yisrael and Miriam Ganz, arrived in Novogrodek. Mr Moshe Steinberg, who had been the headmaster of the Tarbut Hebrew School in Novogrodek also came at about the same time, from Uzbekistan. We were very happy, but our joy was mixed with sorrow, because so few had survived from our large family. The newcomers, discovering the terrible truth of what the Holocaust had done to our nation in general and the Novogrodek community in particular, were shocked and devastated.

Several weeks later, in the autumn of 1945, we left Novogrodek en route for Poland. We had very few possessions, only some clothes and a few personal belongings. Taking out any valuables was strictly forbidden, and we expected to be searched on the way. Anyone caught trying to smuggle anything out would be punished with long prison terms. My cousin Idel had a few gold coins, including a large 20-dollar American coin, and we decided to take the chance, and bring the coins with us. We hid the American gold coin, which was worth a great deal in those days, in the heel of my cousin Leizer's boot.

We travelled by freight train, 20 people in each compartment. It took weeks. We had long stops in all sorts of out-of-the-way stations. One night, in one of these stations, thieves came into the compartment and stole Leizer's boots, where we had hidden the gold coin. There was nothing we could do, but accept our bad luck. Officers frequently conducted searches and inspections, and the way to Poland was paved with excitement and anxiety. A young man from Novogrodek by the name of Moskovitz travelled with us on the train. His whole family had been murdered and he, the sole survivor, had been in the Bielski partisan regiment. He was travelling alone, and carried nothing but a violin that had belonged to his dead father, and which had been kept by the Gentile neighbours who settled in his family's house. The young man was depressed. He kept to himself and didn't talk much, but just sat in a corner, absorbed in his own thoughts. The violin was most precious to him. It was the only thing left of his father and family. Once in a while he would take out the violin and play a little, caressing and polishing it, then wrapping it up in a soft cloth.

In general, the atmosphere on the train was heavy. We were all sad and anxious about the future. On one particular occasion, the train had been standing for several days in a small, remote, deserted station. It was very cold, we were tired and our spirits were very low. Suddenly Moskovitz took out the violin and began to play. He played well-known Russian tunes, partisan songs and then Hassidic and Jewish tunes. We listened, enjoying the music, when all of a sudden Moskovitz stopped playing and threw down the violin, shattering it to bits. Then he burst into tears, and crying bitterly he shouted that he didn't want to live, that he'd rather die and join his family. He cried for a long time, inconsolably. This incident deeply affected everyone in the car. The scene touched our own pain and misery and we were deeply shocked. To this day, this memory stands out clearly in my mind. The train journey covered about 500 kilometres. It took roughly five weeks. Then, finally, we crossed the border into Poland. My cousin Idel and I, together with some friends from Novogrodek, found a place to live in the Polish city of Lodz.

Quite a few Jews, survivors of the Holocaust, came to Lodz at this time from all over Poland and Russia. Various clubs, offices and organisations assisted the new arrivals. There were several active Zionist organisations in Lodz. Young people found a place in the kibbutzim which had been established there. Emissaries from Eretz Yisrael came and gave us information about the Jews in Palestine, the struggle to open the gates and let the Holocaust survivors in, and the desire to welcome and absorb the surviving victims of the great horror.

Having settled in Lodz, my cousin Idel once again started doing business, travelling to various Polish cities, buying and selling products that were hard to come by in those days, clothes, footwear, food and cigarettes. He also dealt in foreign currency and smuggled forbidden goods. On one of his trips, to the port of Stettin, he noticed that he was being followed. With considerable difficulty and luck he managed to get away from a police raid, but was forced to flee across the border to Germany. In Germany, he travelled dangerous roads across the area occupied by the Russians. He stayed in Berlin for a while, then reached American territory, Bavaria and the refugee camp in the town of Landsberg am Lech.

I was no good at business on my own, so after Idel left I joined the Bein Gvulot kibbutz on Tsegelrdna Street in Lodz, which belonged to the Hashomer Hatzair youth movement. The young men and women who congregated in this kibbutz were mostly survivors of the Holocaust who had been partisans or who, returning from Russia after the war, had found their homes burned down and their families murdered, and no place in the world to go to. The pioneer kibbutz movement founded in the cities of Poland provided a home and refuge for those who had lost everything.

Berl Kagan, May 1947

The goal of the kibbutz movement was to bring these young people to Eretz Yisrael, the homeland. The instructors gave the members information about Palestine, Zionism and the efforts to establish a national home for the Jewish people in the Land of Israel.

The history of the survivors who remained in Europe is a tale of woe and grief. Only remnants of the great communities of Europe were finally liberated from the camps, and they enjoyed little freedom. These survivors longed for a home of their own, the warmth of a family and a safe haven, but the gates of Eretz Yisrael were closed against them.

10 *Journey to the Homeland*

Aᴛ ᴛʜᴇ Bein Gvulot Kibbutz, I met my future wife, Ita Rabin, who was 17 years old. Ita and her mother Sarah were the only survivors of a large family. Her father, David, had been murdered by the Germans in the town of Hoshze, near Rovno in the western Ukraine. This happened in the summer of 1941, shortly after the German conquest of the Ukraine. Together with her mother and brother Asher, Ita, who was 13 at the time, escaped from the ghetto. Throughout the War, they hid and wandered in the region, permanently in danger. They endured hunger, the winter cold and the constant fear of being captured by the Germans or their local collaborators or, worst of all, by the Ukrainian hoodlums, who tortured and murdered Jews who fell into their hands. Ita had personally witnessed such atrocities. Her own relatives had been murdered in front of her eyes. Ita's brother Asher, an 18-year-old youth, couldn't bear it any longer and in the spring of 1944, shortly before the arrival of the Red Army, had came out of hiding and turned himself in to the Germans. He was shot and killed right away.

In their wanderings, Ita and her mother met some Jews from their native town who were hiding out in various farms. Ita and Sarah tried to help them: they brought them food, kept in touch and moved them to safer places in times of danger. In doing this, they risked their own lives. Holocaust survivors from the town of Hoshze tell amazing stories about the help they received from Ita and her mother in those terrible times. Ita's memories from those dark times are dreadful.

At the kibbutz in Lodz, Ita and I met and became friends. I liked her for her honesty, her manner and simplicity, her kindness and also, undeniably, for her good looks. Ita did not remain indifferent to my attentions, and we came to love and admire one another, as we do to this day.

The central leadership of Hashomer Hatzair in Poland decided that in the fall of 1946, kibbutz Bein Gvulot should move to the town of Reichenbach in Upper Silesia, a German district which was annexed to Poland at the end of the Second World War. When the members of our kibbutz arrived in Reichenbach, we began to renovate our building, and the kibbutz started to grow. Soon it became a centre which attracted survivors of the Holocaust who were living in the area.

Our kibbutz at Reichenbach went into business. We opened a barber's shop, a bakery and a sawmill. Kibbutz members worked in these places and made a decent profit, which helped in purchasing food, shoes, clothing and other necessities. I was treasurer of the kibbutz, a very responsible job, which I tried to perform to the best of my ability and to the benefit of our collective. Our kibbutz flourished financially. We managed to save a good deal of money which was essential for our future.

The gates of the Land of Israel were shut tight at the time and Holocaust survivors were not permitted to enter. The British Mandate fought illegal immigration. But soon it became clear that long-suffering survivors of the ghettos and concentration camps could not be stopped. Relentlessly, they made their way to the homeland, where they hoped to rebuild their lives.

Against this background, a wondrous, heroic phenomenon emerged: the Escape and the 'Ha'apala', namely, the illegal immigration to Palestine.

Long columns of Jewish refugees would set out under the dark cover of night, men, women and children, old and young. They would cross international borders, rivers and snow-covered mountains on their way to Palestine. Not just a handful of Jews, but great masses, longing for their homeland. Nothing could stop them. Their will and their yearning became the power which overcame all barriers and hardships. The power of life and the will to live that throbbed in the hearts of the survivors created this movement.

Our kibbutz remained at Reichenbach for a relatively short time, about six months. We were in transit, and our final destination was the safe shores of the Land of Israel. Our kibbutz also took the route of the Escape and Ha'apala. We experienced the same hardships and dangers as all other Holocaust survivors, who feared nothing on the long and arduous journey to the borders of the homeland.

In the autumn of 1946 we crossed the border between Poland and Czechoslovakia illegally and travelled through the Carpathian Mountains, sometimes sinking waist-deep in snow, crossing rivers and obstacles, overcoming hardship, fear and danger. We pressed on relentlessly, making our escape. It was a difficult test, which required strength and resourcefulness. The persistent, relentless striving and yearning for the final goal, the Land of Israel, drove us on, kept us from falling and failing, and enabled us to succeed. The strong helped the weak, and the column kept on going.

We reached Bratislava in Czechoslovakia. The 'Bricha' (Escape) organisation worked very efficiently. They provided camps, food, certificates and rail travel for our journey. From Bratislava we went on by train to Vienna. We were given the papers of Greek refugees and were instructed to say nothing but 'Greek' at the border check-point, and not to enter into any conversations or arguments.

An amusing incident occurred while we were waiting at the checkpoint on the Czech–Austrian border. Some Greeks who were working nearby heard that there was a train carrying Greek refugees at the station. They came to greet us and spoke to us in Greek, which of course we didn't understand. We replied in Hebrew and conducted something like a conversation between the deaf and the dumb, until the disappointed Greeks gave up and left the place. To the border guards who had witnessed the scene, we explained in Russian that we were natives of a remote region in Greece, and spoke a special dialect, which other Greeks could barely understand.

We stayed in Vienna for several weeks and went on to West Germany. We reached the resort town of Bad Reichenhall, located in the Bavarian Alps, not far from Munich. We found a place in one of the buildings of the refugee camp – a former German Army camp. The mountain views were breathtaking. Bad Reichenhall is situated near the town of Berchtesgaden, located under the mountain where Hitler had his 'Eagle's Nest' villa, headquarters and bunker.

Jewish refugees soon filled the transit camp at Bad Reichenhall, as they filled other refugee camps established on German soil. These were all Holocaust survivors from eastern Europe. All they wanted was to carry on and reach the safe shores of Palestine despite the relative comfort of life in the camps and the generous assistance of the American military authorities and various philanthropic organisations like the Joint (Joint Distribution Committee).

Our kibbutz had already gained considerable experience at getting organised quickly, and soon we occupied a central position in the camp. Our members took an active part in the administration and on various cultural and financial committees. The kibbutz members worked, trained and studied, in preparation for the future.

We wanted to get to Palestine and continue with the kibbutz way of life, establish our own independent kibbutz or join one of the existing kibbutzim of the Hashomer Hatzair movement, 'Hakibbutz Ha'arzi'. With this future in mind, we managed to purchase various agricultural and industrial machines in Germany, and sent them to Palestine, as a basis for our subsistence and economic development once we got there. We also bought shoes and clothing for the members, most of whom had nothing at all. We got each member a backpack in which to carry his or her few belongings, and made preparations for departure.

Ita Rabin photographed in Bad Reichenhall, 1947

We remained at Bad Reichenhall for about eight months. I was the kibbutz treasurer and also worked at cutting down trees in the woods. Ita worked in the kibbutz kitchen and clothes store-room. During our stay, we toured the whole area, but we spent most of our time learning about the Land of Israel and Zionism, and studying Hebrew.

In Germany I met up with my cousin Idel, who was living at the refugee camp in the town of Landsberg. Idel had contacted our cousin in London, Rachel Konigsberg, née Gurevitz. After a long series of medical treatments, Idel left for England where he made his life. He has since raised a wonderful family, done well in business, and is a productive, energetic and generous man. Barbara and Jack Kagan have three children: Michael (named after Barbara's late father), Jeffrey (Yankel, named after Jack's late father, Yankel Kagan) and Debby (Dvore, named after Jack's late mother, Dvore Kagan). As for myself, I was determined to go to Israel.

The Hagana vessel *Exodus 1947* was approved for 'Ha'apala' to the Land of Israel in the spring of 1947. In its better days, it had been a riverboat in America. It had been purchased from its owner by the Hagana, altered and fitted for sea travel.

We set out from the refugee camp in canvas-covered trucks. On the way we joined a long column of many dozens of trucks, headed for the German–French border. Everything was extremely well-organised, including stops and concentration points. Silence and discipline were maintained.

We travelled through the night, and every once in a while, as the truck came around a bend, we could see the entire column – a wonderful sight. The headlights flashed in the distance, and the whole column was twisting and turning along the winding road, like a giant serpent. We reached the border at dawn. By now we had become quite accustomed to crossing borders, and the guards of foreign countries generally caused us no excitement. But, at this point, our hearts were beating fast. This wasn't just any border. This was the last border between us and the sea, between us and the ship which would take us to our homeland. At last they waved us through and the border post lay behind us. We were on French soil.

We were taken to a camp of tents and huts near the city of Marseilles, where we waited for several weeks, until the ship was ready to sail. Finally, the moment we had waited for so impatiently arrived: the night of the Aliyah. At midnight we got on the trucks, and the convoy left the camp. Our hearts were full.

At dawn, we arrived at the small French port of Sète, where the ship was waiting. The local people watched the column of trucks with bewildered eyes. We got to the docks, where there was considerable commotion. Hundreds stood in lines, ready to board the ship. Trucks arrived at regular intervals, unloading their human cargo. Our kibbutz stood in line like everyone else and waited to board the ship. The boarding proceeded fairly quickly, since there were several embarkation points. We settled in the place assigned to us on the ship. It was terribly crowded, with 4,500 passengers on board.

Evening came, and brought bad news. The British had found out about our ship, and were trying to convince the port authorities that they should prevent our departure. Our captain asked for a navigator to lead us out to the open sea, and was refused. At midnight we suddenly heard the anchor being raised, and the ship began to move off slowly. The ship manoeuvred for a long time, and finally managed to leave the harbour. It appears that the captain and crew decided to take the ship out to sea without the help of a navigator at great risk, and against all the rules.

The courageous act was successful. The ship reached the open sea and picked up speed, heading for Palestine. Conditions on board were dreadful: it was hot, stuffy and disorderly, with limited sanitary facilities and supplies of food and water. Most of the passengers got seasick, and there were some cases of dysentery, bad stomach pains and food-poisoning.

From the very first day, we were followed by a British destroyer. Several days later, it was joined by several other British battleships. We sailed on, well protected by His Majesty's navy.

Ita and her mother were quite sick. They lay on their bunks, unable to get up or eat anything. They vomited frequently and grew weak, but they did not complain. The voyage took about a week. We even had a bad storm, during which the ship creaked, water leaked in and we thought it wouldn't make it. But it fought bravely, like an old battle-horse, and didn't fail us. It continued along its planned route, and the captain and crew proved to be responsible, brave and skilled.

On the ship itself, things got worse every day. The stench of garbage and vomit, the filth produced by thousands of people was everywhere. The washing facilities were clogged. The water ration was reduced to half a litre per person per day. And yet, nobody complained.

The ship approached the shores of Palestine. We knew we would have to fight our British escorts, who would do everything they could to keep us from entering the gates of our homeland. The battle against the British destroyers began as we approached territorial waters. In the dark, two destroyers came up to our ship and pressed against it. The ship groaned, as though it were about to break. Our fighters of all ages stood on deck and hurled cans at the British soldiers. We turned on pumps and sprayed them with water and boiling oil, and threw overboard every British sailor who managed to board our ship. But we knew it was a losing battle. The British soldiers took over our ship and led it, captive, to the port of Haifa. We had a few dead and wounded, and our spirits were very low.

We approached the shore. We all stood on deck, at the doors and windows, to see the shores we had yearned for. We reached Haifa at dusk. Our ship docked in the harbour and British ships and guards were placed around it, to make sure no one escaped. We had reached our land, but were prevented from entering it. We saw Mount Carmel and the town of Haifa so close and yet so far away. The 'Hatikva' burst out of every throat. We stood there all night, unable to take our eyes off the town of Haifa and its breathtaking beauty.

The next day we were taken off our ship, the *Exodus 1947*, and put on three British prison ships for deportation. Thus began the journey back. We expected to be taken to the illegal immigrants' prison camps in Cyprus, but this was not to be. The British had decided to teach us a lesson, in an attempt to put an end to the illegal immigration once and for all. We were taken back to France. After weeks of travelling in dreadful conditions we reached the French port of Port-de-Bouc. The British and the French authorities pleaded with us to get off the ships, they made promises but to no avail. We were promised French citizenship if we got off, but that was no use either. We were determined to go to Palestine and nowhere else. This was our sole and final destination. The British decided to take us back to Germany. We began a long and very difficult journey, back to that vile land, Germany.

We remained on the deportation ships for two months, in the oppressive summer heat, under prison conditions, surrounded by barbed wire. The food was very poor, and water was scarce. But our spirits never fell. We kept on singing and dancing the 'hora', and the British soldiers were quite bewildered by this strange phenomenon. The British had hoped to break our spirit, but they failed. We prevailed, in spite of everything. The hardships only made us stronger and more determined not to give up, to continue our struggle.

We were taken to the German port of Hamburg and, despite passive resistance, were taken off the ships. The British soldiers had to carry many of us ashore. Some were carried off on stretchers. Those were the stubborn ones, the ones who held on to their bunks and wouldn't leave the ship. The soldiers' task was far from easy.

The *Exodus 1947*, in which I sailed with Ita and her mother, wrote a heroic chapter in the history of the 'Ha'apala'. The whole world watched with admiration, wondering at the courage of the Holocaust survivors, and their determination to reach the Land of Israel.

We were quite exhausted after two months aboard His Majesty's prison ships. Many of us were ill and weak. Now we were taken from the ships to the camp of Papendorf, near the town of Lübeck. This was a camp of tin huts, and 50 of us – men, women, old people, youths and children – were housed in each hut, sharing the three tiers of wooden bunks. It was terribly crowded. The huts were unbearably hot in the daytime and cold at night. And the people had nothing. Their clothes were quite inadequate. The sanitary facilities at the camp were terrible and the food was poor. Disease began to spread among the 'ma'apilim': bad colds and various infections.

The British army was in charge of this camp. They tried to prepare correct, up-to-date lists of the people of the *Exodus* who were at the camp with each individual's personal data, country of origin and the last country he or she had resided in before boarding the ship. But they failed. We all gave false names and said we were Palestinians, residents of the Land of Israel, who had been arrested and kidnapped from our homeland by British soldiers and taken to Germany by force, to be imprisoned in a concentration camp, just like it was under the Nazis.

After a month at Papendorf, the British realised they would never break the spirit of the 'ma'apilim'. So they moved us to two other camps, near Emden, a German port on the North Sea, near the Netherlands, which had served the Nazi navy. At Emden we lived in a former military camp. It was overcrowded, and conditions were very difficult.

At Papendorf, Ita and I, like many other members, had left the kibbutz. Now Ita, her mother and myself lived in one of the barracks with nine other people. Two of us slept in each of the narrow beds. We received our food in weekly rations. The food in this camp was somewhat better, due to the assistance of Jewish and philanthropic organisations all over the world – especially the Joint and from the United States.

My cousin Jack Kagan, who was already in England, found out that I was at Emden. He sent me food packages, and his help came just in time, and was very important. I also received food packages from the Organisation of Novogrodek Jews in the US, and from the late Mrs Wagner, who had known our family in Novogrodek. I was deeply moved by her warm letters, her suggestion that we should immigrate to the US and her willingness to assist us in every way.

My cousin Jack urged me to come to England. He promised that he and our other relatives would do everything they could to obtain a permit for me. Jack used arguments which were hard to refute: that he and I were our family's only survivors, and that he wanted us to be together and run a business in full partnership, just like our late parents had done.

I considered this for quite some time, and finally decided that Palestine was the only place for me, the land in which I wished to make my home and raise a family. I realised that I would face many hardships in Israel. I was penniless and had no profession. The situation in Palestine was also difficult and uncertain at the time. The country was at war, making incredible efforts to maintain the Jewish population and open the borders for the many thousands of Holocaust survivors who were knocking at its gates.

On 29 November 1947, the United Nations made its historic decision: the Land of Israel would be divided, and a Jewish state would be established. Jews around the world rejoiced, especially the refugees and survivors of the Holocaust, who were still living in camps in Germany, Austria, Italy, Cyprus and elsewhere. It was a ray of light in the dark. We knew that full independence and a state of our own were still a long way off, and that difficult struggles lay ahead, against hostile forces and the armies of all the Arab states, who had vast resources of money and weapons.

The Jews in Palestine and around the world knew that we would have to stand alone against our enemies, and that no one would help us. But our faith was strong. We believed that we would prevail and defeat our persecutors. Jews in Palestine and abroad knew that this was a struggle for the life of the nation, for its very existence. All of us, the young people at Emden, got very excited. The young men all volunteered to set out for Palestine at once, join the army and take part in the holy war.

We remained at Emden for about a year. I used the time to learn a trade, and became a dental technician, hoping that this would enable me to make a living in Palestine. I finished my studies and apprenticeship, and got a diploma. I was quite good at my work and received favourable evaluations. My girlfriend Ita studied and worked as a nurse in the camp hospital. She did well, advanced in her profession and was appreciated and praised.

On 3 April 1948, Ita and I were married. The wedding took place at Emden camp, in the room where we lived. Everyone rejoiced though there wasn't much food, and the ceremony adhered to all the rules and traditions of the Jewish faith. Ita's mother would have it no other way.

Before the wedding, Ita had to go to the refugee camp at Bergen-Belsen, several hundred kilometres from Emden to bathe in a mikvah (a bath for ritual purification) which, for some reason, could only be found there. I went with her, and we had to travel all night in a truck. Ita bathed in the mikvah in the presence of a strict *rabbanit* (rabbi's wife), who made sure every detail was observed. Finally Ita was found worthy and received the marriage permit, and the wedding date was set. At that time, Ita's mother was very ill and was being treated at the Bergen-Belsen hospital. She gave us her blessing, and we hoped she would soon

Our wedding picture with Sarah Rabin, Ita's mother

recover. We had enough problems, but a happy end makes up for everything.

We were married and everyone rejoiced. I was blessed with a wife after my own heart, a woman of many virtues: pleasant, quiet, gentle, almost too honest, dedicated, loving and a good housekeeper. We spent our wedding night and honeymoon in the same place, the room at Emden camp which we shared with ten other people. The only change was that Ita left the bed of her friend, Rachel Reznik, and came to sleep with me. But even this wasn't simple. I had a hard time talking her into it. Ita was shy and reluctant, and kept finding excuses and putting it off. She finally agreed only because she was afraid our friends and the other people in the room would make fun of her. Our wedding night was not very enjoyable. Our room-mates didn't sleep that night, and in this situation, as a young couple, we were quite nervous and tense. Later on we got used to this state of affairs, and it seemed quite natural, especially as there were a few other couples who slept together in our room.

On 14 May 1948, Israel was declared an independent state, and at Emden camp we celebrated. Our joy was indescribable. We were witnessing a historic moment and we were elated. The spontaneous singing and dancing went on all day and all through the night.

The date of our final Aliyah to the homeland we had longed for drew near. Right after the declaration of independence, the Arab armies invaded Israel, intending to destroy the newborn state, throw the Jews into the sea and establish an Arab state named Palestine. These weren't just unorganised gangs. They were trained armies, operating under the command of their governments. The defence forces in Israel were poorly equipped, but they had courage and resourcefulness, and were willing to sacrifice themselves and fight to the death. They knew they had to win. They had no choice. The War of Independence is a glorious page in the history of Jewish courage. A handful of Jewish warriors, equipped with courage and determination, defeated the armies of the Arab states just as David overcame Goliath.

In August 1948, our time came. We left Emden camp, and sailed from the French port of Marseilles in a ship called *Pan York*. This time we were not afraid, and His Majesty's battleships did not escort us. Our dream of going to our own homeland, the State of Israel, was finally coming true. We had very few possessions and were penniless, but our hearts were full of joy. We were finally going home. The journey was hard. Ita was pregnant, and she felt sick and vomited endlessly but at last the *Pan York* docked at Haifa. This time we went ashore and walked on the soil of our homeland as free people.

11   *Life in Israel*

W<small>E ARRIVED</small> in Israel towards the end of the War of Independence. The young, recently established state was fighting for its life against the armies of the Arab states, which invaded it with the aim of destroying it. The threat to the existence of Israel's Jewish population was very real indeed. Great resources of strength, money and manpower were required to drive back the invaders.

From the ship *Pan York* we were taken to a temporary tent camp (ma'araba) at Agrobank, near Hadera. Over 1,000 new immigrants were living there at the time.

The absorption process was exhausting, and conditions almost unbearable. We lived in one tent with two other families, ten people altogether. The month of August was extremely hot, the sanitary facilities were insufficient, water was rationed, food was scarce. Infectious diseases and allergies spread throughout the camp. Ita, who was four months' pregnant, felt sick, and her mother was chronically ill. I was very worried about the future. We had arrived penniless, and our anxiety was very real.

After two weeks in the camp we were sent to the Abandoned Property Custodian's office in Jaffa and given a small two-room apartment with a tiny kitchen in an Arab house in Jabaliah, near Jaffa. Many Arabs from Jaffa and other towns had abandoned their property and fled to Jordan when the War of Independence broke out. New immigrants arriving in Israel settled in their houses. The Arab house in which we had our apartment was shared by six families, including ourselves. It was very crowded; only one lavatory for all the tenants, no bath or shower and certainly no hot water. Despite these discomforts, we were happy. At last we had a place of our own. We got some furniture, two iron beds and straw mattresses, a wooden box for a table. I fixed up a closet and some shelves, and we were happy. Our apartment was always spotlessly clean.

The small loan we had received from the Jewish Agency upon arrival ran out, and there were few jobs available at the time, especially since the country was at war. Every day I'd go to the employment office, which sent me to various odd jobs: digging cesspools, clearing work and construction. I was happy to get anything I could. Ita's mother found employment as a cook in a restaurant and Ita, despite her advanced pregnancy, cleaned people's homes and did their laundry. At night, Ita and I cleaned cloth for a textile factory and did various other odd jobs.

After a while, some acquaintances got me a job at a noodle factory in Tel Aviv. I was overjoyed: a regular job! The owner was well satisfied with my work and even gave me a raise. I also got packs of noodles to take home every once in a while, which was very helpful. We ate lots of noodles at every meal. I worked at the noodle factory for about a month, until I was drafted by the Israel Defence Forces in October 1948.

The IDF was in desperate need of all the human resources it could recruit in order to drive back the attacking Arab armies. It therefore drafted all ex-soldiers from among the newly arrived immigrants, trained them briefly and sent them to the front. Many friends of mine, all new immigrants, were killed on the battlefield.

On 13 January 1949 our daughter was born. We named her Shoshana, after my mother who had been murdered in the Holocaust.

Our financial situation became much worse. As a soldier I only got a meagre allowance, and Ita couldn't work. Sometimes we didn't even have enough money to buy the basic necessities or pay the electricity bill. To make matters worse, Shoshana suffered from a respiratory allergy as a child. All in all, our spirits were rather low.

When she could work again, Ita made a little money, and I also worked during every leave. When I think back, it seems unbelievable that we actually managed to make a living, and even save a little. Our home was always clean, Shoshana was tidy and prettily dressed. My dear cousin Jack sent us food and clothing, especially for Shoshana, which was a great help. Ita never complained. She accepted things as they were, adjusted and did everything she could to manage our home and provide for the family. When I completed my mandatory military service at the end of 1950, the army asked me to stay on, on a regular salary, and I agreed. Our financial situation improved considerably. In 1954 we moved to the Regular Army Housing Project near Ramat Gan. We were very happy in our new home, which seemed like a palace to us. Three rooms, a bathroom, a kitchen, a shed, a porch, and even a small garden, in which we planted fruit trees and grew various vegetables. I built a small hen-house, and all this contributed a great deal to our standard of living.

On 25 June 1954 our son David (Dudu) was born. He was named after Ita's father who died in the Holocaust.

In 1960 Ita opened a nursery school in our home, which was attended by children from the neighbourhood. 'Ita's Gan', as it was called, had a good reputation and the teacher herself was well-liked and appreciated.

We liked our neighbourhood very much. We were on warm, friendly terms with our neighbours, and our children also made many friends there. There was only one problem: the faulty construction of our apartment. Many cracks formed in the walls, the floor subsided repeatedly and all repair work was to no avail. My cousin Jack convinced us to sell the apartment, and in 1967 we moved to a comfortable, spacious house in Ramat Hasharon, where we live to this day.

I served in Israel's regular army for 25 years, and held senior positions in the fields of intelligence and investigations. I studied law, sociology and criminology. I retired from service as a lieutenant colonel, and continued to work in the Defence Ministry for 15 more years before retiring in 1995. Throughout the years, my family and Jack's have maintained a close, warm relationship. We are proud of them, and Jack and his wife Barbara are devoted to us. We are very grateful for their substantial assistance in times of need.

Our concern, thoughts and ambitions focused mostly on our children. We went without comforts and luxury so that they could have everything they needed. Some say that Holocaust survivors are over-protective as parents, worrying too much, driving their children to superior achievement in their studies and professional lives. Our daughter Shoshana completed her studies at Tel Aviv University, and is today a successful lawyer. In 1972 she married Gidon Sacher, a senior metal engineer. They have three sons. The eldest, Danny, is today an officer in an armoured unit in the IDF. He plans to study computer engineering after completing his military service. The second son, Nadav, joined the army in 1995. The youngest, Gur, celebrated his Bar Mitzvah in 1996.

Our son, Dr David (Dudu), is a dentist, with an excellent professional reputation. His wife Orly is a family doctor, employed by Kupat Holim, the national health insurance scheme. Dudu and Orly have four children, three boys and a girl, all talented and beautiful. Shoshana and Dudu live in roomy houses in Ramat Hasharon, and we visit each other daily. We are proud of our children and grandchildren. The family is close and warm and gives us great pleasure and satisfaction.

Most of the survivors of the Holocaust from the Jewish community of Novogrodek (only a few hundred from a population of over 6,000), came to Israel, rebuilt their lives and raised families here. The Holocaust has considerably influenced their lives. The horrors and fear we experienced in that earthly hell cannot be erased from our memories.

As survivors, as the last embers remaining from that great fire, we have a sacred duty to our loved ones who died, to do everything within our power to preserve their memory for all generations to come. In Israel there is an organisation of Jews from Novogrodek and its surrounding district. Its main purpose is the commemoration of the sacred martyrs massacred and otherwise horribly murdered by the Nazis and their helpers. This organisation is working to remind our children, the next generation, to take part in this sacred mission, so that the annihilated community may never be forgotten.

One of the most important projects was putting up monuments on the common graves of the martyrs of Novogrodek. This was done three years ago by Jack. He was the main driving force behind this initiative, which he himself financed. Every year, groups of natives of our home-town come from Israel, the US and other countries to visit Novogrodek and remember the martyrs.

The Novogrodek Jews of Israel thank and congratulate Jack for erecting the monuments on the graves of our martyrs, for his many activities relating to the commemoration of the Holocaust and the fate of the Jewish community of Novogrodek, and for generously assisting the Organisation of Novogrodek Jews in Israel.

118

Part Two

HOW I SURVIVED

by

Jack (Idel) Kagan

12   *About Novogrodek*

O<small>N</small> 13 M<small>ARCH</small> 1881 Tsar Alexander II was murdered by revolutionaries. His advisors felt it necessary to avenge their ruler's death so turned their anger against the Jews, which resulted in a wave of pogroms across Russia. Jews started to emigrate, mainly to America, 'the Golden Land' – 2,378,000 emigrated between 1880 and 1924 and from Novogrodek 4,500.

I found an old article in an American Jewish newspaper asking the Jews of Novogrodek to go to the States and they would be sent money.

A census took place in Novogrodek in the year 1897. Out of a total of 13,656 inhabitants, 8,137 were Jews.

During the First World War the Jews in the area of Novogrodek suffered badly, first from the German occupation, then from the Bolsheviks and various antisemitic Polish bands. Finally the war ended in 1921 after the Riga Agreement, and Novogrodek became part of Poland. Another census was taken in 1921 and of a total of 9,230 inhabitants, there were 4,500 Jews. At the same time a count took place in the Novogrodker Synagogue at 101 Hester Street, New York in which it was discovered that 4,500 Jews from Novogrodek alone lived in New York.

In New York they formed six Committees to help the people they left behind: Navaredker Congregation; Navaredker Lodge No 536 IOBA; Navaredker Women's Verein; Navaredker Branch 146 W.C.; Women's Club of Navaredker BR. 146 W.C.; and the Navaredker Brothers Society. Every Novogrodker was registered.

One of the principal leaders of one of the committees was Alexander Harcavi. Alexander was born in 1863. He left Novogrodek in 1878, went to Vilnius and later arrived in New York. He educated himself to the highest degree, becoming in the process a linguist and writer. In 1888–90 he edited the first English–Yiddish, Yiddish–English dictionary. He was teaching Jewish immigrants English by means of newspapers. He translated many books from

English into Yiddish. He never forgot his birthplace. He united all the Novogrodek committees into one Alexander Harcavi United Novogrudker Relief Committee. The Committee worked hard to collect money for the impoverished Jews of Novogrodek. Harcavi issued a book about the town and its life, sold it and the profit went to the committee. Concerts were given and they collected the grand sum of $40,000, which was sent to a bank in Vilnius.

In 1921, Harcavi and an assistant left for Novogrodek. The Polish government had just settled into power. Harcavi arrived in Vilnius, notified the Governor that a large sum of money he had sent from the USA had arrived at the bank, upon which the Governor arranged an escort, Harcavi picked up the money and then arrived in Novogrodek to a great welcome by the whole population. He was like a ray of light and hope.

He spent five weeks there planning for the future needs of the community, and also helped to write and advise on a constitution for the Novogrodek Jewish citizens. Democratic elections were held. All men and women over the age of 20 could vote and propose candidates to the Main Committee and 15 subcommittees, eight for social help, six for cultural matters and one for justice (*Bet Din*). The social committees comprised: a committee for the orphanage (in 1921 there were 60 orphans to support); a committee for the

Alexander Harcavi

122

Main Committee, Novogrodek

Hospital Committee, including Notke Sucharski (with arms folded on right)

Committee for the Old Folks Home

home for the elderly (*Moshav Skanim*). At the time there were 30 residents; a committee to support the Jewish hospital (*Hecdesh*) of 25 beds, a chemist and an ambulance; a committee for the Red Magen David (distributing medicine and food to the needy); a committee to support the soup kitchen making 600 to 660 meals a day, with the subcommittee funding 60 per cent of the money, the rest to be met by the main committee fund; a committee to support the soup kitchen for adults where 300 meals daily were given; a committee to support the ORT school (*Shokdei Mlacha*) for children to learn a trade: girls to be seamstresses and boys, joiners; and a committee for the Interest-free Loan Society (*Gmilat Chesed*)

The cultural committees included: a committee for the Tarbut (Hebrew school) called Chaim Nachman Bialik, where 800 children studied (the curriculum was the same as in Eretz Yisrael); committees to support the kindergartens; a committee for support of Gan Trumpeldor (Cirey Zion) for 100 infants; a committee to support adult education for 80 students; a committee to support Talmud Torah classes; and a committee to support the school of agriculture.

My favourite picture – the children's choir

The Soup Kitchen

Showing the richness of footwear

The Hebrew School Tarbut

Maccabi Novogrodek (the Sports Youth Movement)

Rabbi Abovitz giving a lecture in the Religious Academy

The cultural committee was responsible for the library, which contained 7,000 books in Russian, German, Yiddish and Hebrew. And there was the justice (*Bet Din*) committee.

The main language for the Jews was Yiddish and in many houses modern Hebrew was spoken, school classes were taught in Yiddish or Hebrew, the local population spoke Belorussian and the official government language was Polish.

The committees were set in motion and with the help of the money sent from America progress was made. In 1931 Harcavi returned to Novogrodek with more money. He was pleased with the improved Jewish way of life in Novogrodek. He took lots of photographs and made a film of life in the town, as he wanted to show the Novogredker Jews in New York the improvements which had been made over the past ten years. (This film was found in New York in the early 1960s. I made many copies of this film which were sent to numerous universities and museums. The Diaspora museum in Tel Aviv added sound to it.) Whenever I give

Pupils of the Yeshiva (Religious Academy)

a talk about the destruction of the community I use this film. After Harcavi's death, Jacob Maslow took over the Chairmanship and Abe Meyerson became Secretary.

I found many letters in the Yivo Institute in New York and below is one from the Joint Distribution Committee to Mr Maslow, the Chairman of the Novogrodker Committee. It is one of the last letters written before the outbreak of war.

```
Mr. Jacob Maslow,                           April 5, 1939
100 Van Cortlandt Park,
Bronx, N.Y.


Dear Mr. Maslow:                         Re: Novogrodek

It is indeed with great delight that we have learned
that your Committee has started the campaign to raise
funds for the unfortunate, impoverished, persecuted and
oppressed Jews in Novogrodek. It is still more
gratifying, since your Committee has agreed that all
moneys collected by them would be turned over to the
Joint Distribution Committee, and hence every penny
collected will without question reach the unfortunate
people.

'We do not have to emphasise again how dreadful the
conditions of the Jews in Novogrodek are at present,
and how imperative it is for American landsleute to
extend their utmost assistance. We understand that you
have assigned committees to visit your landsleute and
hope, therefore, that your campaign will be most
successful.

On behalf of your unfortunate brethren overseas, we
wish to take this opportunity to thank you personally,
as well as the other members of your Committee, for your
great interest and noble efforts.

Wishing you again success in your important work, we
remain.

                              Sincerely yours.
                    LANDSMANSCHAFTEN DEPARTMENT
                    Joint Distribution Committee
                          Norman V. Gilmovski
                                    Secretary
```

131

13 *My Family and the War*

I WAS BORN in 1929 into a unique family. Two brothers married two sisters and harmony reigned in the house! Even though we had two houses, we lived in one. Everything was togetherness. The most important thing in life was family.

My father Yankel was a businessman. My uncle Moshe was a hard worker who loved his work and looked after the small sandal factory and saddle-making workshop which my grandfather Leizer had founded. Leizer was known all over the district as an honest man. Until the end, the farmers in the area always said they were going to Leizer to buy.

My mother Dvore was a businesswoman who looked after our two shops where we sold the saddles and sandals produced in our workshops; my aunt Shoshke was in the house cooking and cleaning. I had a sister, Nachama, two years older than myself. My uncle and aunt had two children. The older one, Berl, was named after my mother's father, and the younger one, Leizer, was two years older than me, a lively and likeable friend, named after my grandfather.

We were a middle-class family; not short of anything. The boys followed the normal routine of *shtetl* life by going to Menaker's *cheder* to learn how to pray and about the meaning of the Torah, and from there they went to the Tarbut school to learn Hebrew. The Tarbut was considered a very good school; it had 800 pupils and all subjects were taught in Hebrew, with the exception of Polish which was taught as the national language. We had excellent teachers like Leikin, Mr and Mrs Levin and others. The headmaster was Mr Moshe Steinberg, a most dedicated man. When the German–Russian war broke out, Steinberg retreated with the Russian army, and became a teacher in Russia. He returned to Novogrodek after the war to find that his wife and twin daughters had been killed by the Germans. We left for Poland together. Years later I heard that Mr Steinberg had gone to Israel,

My parents, Dvore and Yankel Kagan

where he changed his name to Sharig. He was sent by the Jewish
Agency to be a director of a Hebrew school in Buenos Aires, where
he stayed for seven years. He finally returned to Israel with his
second wife and died in Tel Aviv in 1990.

Berl went to the Polish elementary and secondary school.

Novogrodek was a district town and, in my eyes, a completely
Jewish one. On the Sabbath everything was quiet, no farmer came
to town, nearly all the Jews were in the synagogue. We were
traditionalists – Mitnaggedim as opposed to Hasidim – and, looking
back, I do not think we were a particularly religious community.

The Jewish population of between 6,000 and 6,500, made up
half of the town's inhabitants. The remainder were Belorussian,
Polish and a small community of Tatars. There were really no
problems between the Jews and the poor local population. But
from 1935, after Marshal Pilsudski's death, the situation began to
change. Poles from western Poland started to settle in our town.
They brought strong feelings of antisemitism with them. The
Endeks (Free Poles Party) shouted their slogans: 'Jews to
Palestine'! 'Don't buy from Jews!'

The synagogue where our family prayed

The Jews lived in the centre of town and most of the shops belonged to them. They formed the majority of the professional people. Jewish community life was organised through the synagogues and unions. Each trade had its own synagogue and each businessman had to contribute to charity. The emphasis was on helping the poor and encouraging scholarship. There were many political parties among the Jews: Zionists, Revisionists, Communists, Bund members. There were religious parties and anti-religious parties but there were no Jewish criminals, and no Jewish illiterates.

There were all sorts of Jewish institutions: hospitals, *cheders*, Hebrew schools like the Tarbut, religious schools like Toshia, orphanages, ORT schools for orphans to learn a trade, carpentry for boys and dressmaking for girls.

There was a Jewish theatre, a library, a bank for lending money free of interest (*gmilat chesed*), Jewish newspapers, and all sorts of unions, linked to each trade and to the synagogues. In addition there was the Maccabi sports club, Rabbi Yozel's famous Beit-Yosef Yeshiva, and a burial society.

All this changed on 17 September 1939. War had broken out on the first day of September. We were very worried about a probable

The ORT School, Novogrodek, 1931

German occupation but on the afternoon of the 17th we heard the roar of the Soviet tanks coming from Karelitzer Street. Some Jews cried with joy. They ran towards the tanks with flowers in their hands, blocking the way and waiting to kiss the soldiers of the Red Army. The poor farmers gathered in the middle of the market square and there they noticed a tall man with a new long overcoat walking towards Mickiewicz Street. It took only one person to shout out, 'There goes the judge who used to send us for years to terrible jails', for hundreds of people to start running towards him and then to rain him with blows. Red Army soldiers, seeing a riot, ran to the scene and saved the poor man. They asked him who he was, to which he replied that he was Refoel the poor cobbler who had gone home to put on his Sabbath overcoat. He was no judge but had come to welcome the Red Army.

We were pleased, as the alternative to the Red Army was occupation by the Germans. On the first night, some Poles opened fire on the Russian troops, and all night long there was shooting. My uncle was on guard at the fire brigade. He was arrested but soon released. A militia was formed. Most of its members were

135

The Interest-free Loan Society

Jews who belonged to the secret Communist Party.

Our life changed. We had to run down our shop, as private enterprise was not allowed. We were allowed to sell the goods we had but we could not hide anything. The Russian soldiers bought everything: goods that had been in our loft from the First World War were cleared out. We had to close our shops and workshops, and stop going to the synagogue. No more Tarbut, because Hebrew was not allowed.

Everything Jewish connected with religion or Palestine had to stop. Every institution that was Jewish had to change, like the Jewish hospital and theatre. The famous Navaredker Yeshiva was moved to Vilnius, as Vilnius became part of Lithuania. (Most of the students were saved as they went from there to Japan.) Many Jewish refugees flooded into our region from western Poland, which had been occupied by the Germans; later many of these same people requested to go back there.

It became a different life. The rich business people were arrested during the night and sent to Siberia together with the leaders of the community. Informers fared best of all. If you didn't like somebody, you informed on them. They were arrested and had to wait years for their cases to be heard.

My father and uncle worked as saddlers in a co-operative. As for me, I started to go to Yiddish school. All subjects were taught in Yiddish. We also learned Russian and Belorussian. I was very upset that I could not join the Pioneers, as I was a member of the former 'capitalist class', and to be a Pioneer you had to be from a working-class family. Our home was measured, and according to the municipality it was too big for our two families so we had to take in tenants. Soldiers from the NKVD searched our home, looking for leather and any unsold goods they thought that we might have concealed. On 7 April 1941 I had a very nice 12th birthday party that I remembered for many years to come, as it was the last party that we celebrated as a family.

Thinking back on it now, the Russians wanted to destroy our rich Jewish culture by closing the synagogues and all Jewish institutions, and by prohibiting the use of Hebrew. The leaders were sent to Siberia. In the long run, we would have been Russians with the word 'Jew' only stamped in our passports.

Arrests of ordinary people went on up to the day of the Russian retreat. The war between Germany and Russia broke out on 22 June 1941. Already the following day, the whole Russian army was in retreat. Everyone holding a Communist Party card was allowed to move east. At the old frontier, papers were checked and people sent back. (My cousin Leizer Sanderovski from Zdzienciol was at that time on holiday near Minsk, so he managed to retreat with the Red Army. He survived the war in Samarkand.)

We knew that we would suffer under the Germans. We expected labour camps and imprisonment, but could not imagine that they would try to liquidate us all. I remember the discussion between my father and my uncle. 'There is no point in running. We are used to work, they won't kill us!' Some of the refugees even wanted to return to their home areas now under German occupation. Because of the Molotov–Ribbentrop agreement the Russians were not broadcasting anything negative about Germany at that time. We knew nothing about what was happening to the Jews in occupied Poland.

And so we stayed. On 24 June 1941 the town was bombed. Four days later, on the 28th, planes flew overhead and dropped fire

137

Leizer Sanderovski

bombs. Most of the town was burnt down. All the centre, including Racelo Street where we lived, was destroyed: not a single house was left. Large numbers of people lost their lives.

We, the Kagan family, lost everything. I was left with a pair of short trousers and a shirt. I started to make journeys by foot to my grandmother in Karelitz, 21 kilometres away. So as not to wear out my shoes, I walked barefoot. It was difficult at the beginning, but I got used to it. 1 used to bring back items like blankets and other necessities. We found an empty house and moved in with about eight families. As there was not enough room on the floor, our friend Zamkovi gave us a small room and my mother, sister and I had to sleep there. (Zamkovi's son Michael survived the war in the Ordzhonikidze detachment. He then went to work for the tax office in Lida. On his way to work one morning, he was killed by Polish murderers.)

The Germans entered Novogrodek on 4 July 1941, and immediately started enforcing anti-Jewish laws. Yellow stars had to be worn on the front and back, Jews were not allowed to walk on the pavement, everyone from the age of 12 to 60 had to report

Novogrodek: part of the market place, December 1941

for work. *Jews lost their rights of citizenship*, which meant that if someone wanted to rob you and many did, you could not complain to the authorities, for you had no protection. Lots of Poles became *Volksdeutsche* (ethnic Germans). They started taking revenge on the Jewish population for greeting the Red Army. As in other places a Judenrat was formed from the community leaders, but they were immediately arrested and disappeared.

They arrested a young man by the name of Abram Ivenecki for the single reason that he had a Polish girlfriend. They kept him for three years in prison as their informer. As soon as a Jew was brought to prison he was sent to Ivenecki's cell, so that the latter could obtain information from him, but this ploy was discovered, and the arrested Jews made certain not to disclose anything. The Germans killed him a few days before their retreat.

My father and uncle were working as saddle-makers. Farmers brought bread to pay for the repairs done to their saddles. Food was not a problem. I remember my aunt Shoshke and my mother fasting on Mondays and Thursdays. My mother, aunt and others, including myself, were working on clearing up the bombed streets and recovering bricks, wherever possible. For that we were issued food cards for 300 grams of bread and potatoes.

On Saturday 26 July 1941, some Jewish men were rounded up by the local police and brought to the centre of the market-place, where a group of SS men were waiting. I was in the market-place, so I saw the SS and ran to Racelo Street and hid behind the ruins of a burned out house. I heard shots being fired and an orchestra playing music. I waited there quite a while and when I reached home I heard the awful news that the SS had selected 52 men and shot them. Jewish women were ordered to wash the blood off the cobble stones. The bodies were put on carts and taken to the old cemetery for burial. (At the time nobody mentioned the music and so I thought I had imagined it until recently, when I received a document from the Vatican which stated that in July 1941 the Germans had killed 50 Jews and a military band had played music – Strauss waltzes – all the while.)

From time to time after that, groups of Jews were caught in the street and told that they were being sent to work. But later we would find out that they had been shot a short distance from town. An order was issued that the Jews must bring all the gold they possessed to the *Komendatura*, the Nazi headquarters. If hidden gold were found, the penalty was death. On Friday, 5 December 1941, the SS and the Lithuanian police arrived and town posters appeared, stating that as from 6 o'clock that evening no Jew could leave town and that the next morning all Jews must assemble at the court-house. They could only take with them whatever they could carry. Many tried to escape; we estimate that about 300 were killed that night by the *Wehrmacht*, including my friend Feivel Feivelevich with his mother. They guarded every little road and shot on sight everything that moved.

Saturday was a bitterly cold day, −20 degrees Centigrade. The court-house was a kilometre from town. The 6,500 Jews assembled in the yard. We waited all day in the cold. Late in the afternoon, they opened the doors to the four buildings (one building had four floors, another had two, and the other two were sheds). There was just about room to stand. There was no sleep that night. We were locked up there Saturday and Sunday.

On Sunday, the *Wehrmacht* arrived, some on horseback, and took a party of about 100 men to build a fence around 28 houses in

Peresika (a suburb of Novogrodek) to create a Ghetto. They took them to the market-place on Minskaya Street and ordered them to break the fence up into large segments, then to lift and carry these to Peresika. The wood was wet and heavy, their journey took them round the outskirts of town, they had to walk through deep snow, and very soon the first casualties occurred – anybody that could not manage to lift or carry the weight was shot.

How many were killed that day by the *Wehrmacht* was not known. Artmann's verdict (see below) states that he took 70 people with him because that was all that came back. The rest were buried in Britianka.

Early on Monday morning, 8 December 1941, lorries arrived with the SS and local police. The chief of the SS (his name is unknown to me) came in and we had to form a line, families together. The head of the family had to approach the SS man, and two questions were asked: 'Profession?' and 'How many children?' There were no further questions. From the SS man, there was just a sign with the glove, right or left: life or death. My uncle with his family went first: 'Profession?', 'Saddle-maker', 'How many children?', 'Two children'. Sign from the SS man to the left. My father followed: Saddle-maker; two children, sign to the right.

As my uncle with his family were walking to the yard, a German officer shouted that he needed an auto-mechanic. My cousin Berl answered and this saved his life. Five thousand, one hundred were selected to the left, taken off to the village of Skridlevo, beaten up on entering the forest and ordered in parties of 50 to lie face down on the ground. If anyone lifted their heads up they were severely beaten; from there again in parties of 50 they had to give up all their valuables, undress in the bitterly cold weather and be driven by these terrible people to the pits where they were shot by the *Einsatzgruppe*. That day, we lost my uncle Moshe, aunt Shoshke, Leizerke, and a cousin staying with us, Berele Kapushevski from Karelitz. It was an appalling blow to us all.

I found out later that the man in charge of the *Wehrmacht* was Johann Artmann. He was accused of mass murder and brought to court in Traunstein in 1965 but the case was dismissed. The killing of so many Jews did not count.

Here is the first page of the 10-page court verdict. An English translation of the entire transcript follows.

Ausfertigung [202 AK-2-372/59]

AK 3/65 LG Traunstein

914 *bereitet*

verfahrensabschließend
ausgewertet 21. NOV. 1983

B e s c h l u ß

der 2. Strafkammer des Landgerichts Traunstein vom
11. Januar 1966 in der Strafsache

gegen   A r t m a n n   Johann
wegen   Mordes.

P
DO

I. Der Angeschuldigte Johann Artmann wird
außer Verfolgung gesetzt.

II. Die Staatskasse trägt die Kosten des
Verfahrens.

G r ü n d e :

Am 8.12.1941 erschossen SS-Einheiten vor dem Ort
Nowogrodek (Weißruthenien) eine große Zahl von Juden.
Der Angeschuldigte, damals Oberleutnant und Chef der
7. Komp. des Inf. Rgt. 727, lag zu dieser Zeit mit
dieser Einheit in Nowogrodek. Er war auch Orts-
kommandant; weil damals bereits Zivilverwaltung einge-
richtet war, beschränkten sich seine Befugnisse auf
militärische Aufgaben. Angehörige der 7. Komp. waren
an dem Erschießen der Juden am 8.12.1941 insoweit
beteiligt, als sie das Gelände absperrten und dadurch
eine Flucht der Juden verhindern sollten.

in ZK bereits
erledigt.
21.11.83 Sell

Source: Zentrale Stelle Ludwigsburg 202 AR-Z 94e/59 Bd V pp. 914–23

A-K/3/65 Traunstein

Verdict

of the second Court of the District Court at Traunstein on 11
January 1966 in the Trial of ARTMANN, JOHANN accused of MURDER.

1. The case against JOHANN ARTMANN dismissed.

2. The legal costs of this Trial will be borne by the State.

Reasons

On 8.12.1941 Units of the SS shot a great number of Jews at a
place called Nowogrodek in White Russia. The accused, then a
First Lieutenant in command of 7. Company, 727. Infantry
Regiment, was at that time stationed with his unit in
Nowogrodek. He was also Town Major. As at that time a Civil
Administration was already in place, he concerned himself only
with military matters. Members of 7. Comp. were only involved
with the shooting of Jews, in that they surrounded and isolated
the area to prevent the escape of the Jews.

The accused is supposed to have committed the criminal act of
aiding and abetting in the crime of Mass Murder, in that he
ordered the men of his company to surround the area for the
purpose of preventing the escape of the Jews who were to be
shot. An additional charge to this criminal accusation could be
that he knowingly tolerated members of his unit to take part in
the measures taken to prevent these escapes.

Investigations and pre-trial interrogations have shown, that
it can not be proven that the accused took part in the criminal
act of the murder of the Jews on 8.12.1941.

1. The measures taken against the Jewish population began on
5.12.1941 with a public wall poster announcement by the area
administration in Polish and in German. It ordered all Jews, in
possession of an authorisation issued by the local Labour
Office, to assemble with their families, in the building of the
Law Court, early in the morning of 7.12.1941. Old people and the
sick were to remain at home (evidence of witness S. G.). To
ensure that on the 7.12.1941, all Jews fit to work, had been
caught, members of 7. Comp., the only unit of the German
Wehrmacht stationed in Nowogrodek, surrounded the area of the
town with double sentries. Their duty, to prevent the escape of
Jews to the surrounding areas and if necessary to use their
firearms. As shown, by the evidence of many witnesses, the exit
roads and a railway bridge were guarded by soldiers of 7. Comp.
for one or two days, but certainly for one night. That escaping
Jews were actually shot, is according to those statements,
not clear. It was not possible to establish who gave the order

to block all the escape roads. According to the evidence it must be assumed, that the accused, in his capacity of Company Commander and Town Major, must have at least been aware of the Order.

On 7.12.1941 the whole Jewish Population were packed together into the building of the Law Courts. Approximately 70 Jewish workers had to tear down wooden fences at the Town Square and other places and carry them on their shoulders to a part of the town, known as Pieresiki, where a Ghetto was established. Jews, mainly old people who had remained in their houses, were transported to the school of the Sisters of Nazarene. That German Soldiers took part in these events, is not possible to ascertain for certain, according to the evidence of the Jewish witnesses (G. among others).

The reason why those events were taking place, was given by the Office of the District Commander. Namely, that the occupation authorities wanted to concentrate all the Jews in one place for their own safety. There was most probably, the intention right from the start to allow those to stay alive who were fit to work, but on the whole to exterminate all the Jews. Yet, this was not possible to establish with absolute certainty, when looking at what happened on 8.12.1941. Certainly, the intention to kill a part of the Jewish population, was not known to those not involved. The accused probably also belonged to those who were not involved, because his contacts with the District Commander and his office were only as required by official business. He maintained no personal contact with any member of that office.

The facts are that he made members of his Company available. In view of the size of the town it must have required the larger part of the 260—280 men comprising the Unit on 7.12.1941 and beforehand, for the purpose of sealing off all escape from the town, or else tolerated their use for this purpose. It does not follow from this that he wanted to assist and aid the murder of the great number of Jews which occurred on 8.12.1941. The same applies also to the members of the Company who were used to guard the building of the Law Courts.

2. On 8.12.1941, the Jews who had been brought to the building of the Law Court, were haphazardly and arbitrarily separated into two groups, by members of the district administration (wearing brown uniforms with swastika armbands). One part had been brought to the Ghetto, which had been prepared the day before and remained there, unharmed until 7.12.1941. The other group was brought (partly on foot, partly by lorry) to an area, several kilometres outside the town, where a mass grave had already been dug, and where they were shot by persons who can not be traced, but who belonged to the SD, SS, Free Lithuania and Civilian Police. The same fate befell those who had been brought to the school of the Sisters of Nazarene and the old people, women and children taken away from private homes.

144

Whilst the shooting was in progress, the Execution area was surrounded and blocked off by No. 1. Platoon of the 7. Company, the purpose of which was obviously, to prevent persons that had been selected to be shot, from escaping and so save themselves. According to statements from witnesses, members of the other platoons were in the building, and were obviously there by chance or came out of curiosity. This was brought out by a statement made by the witness J., who at that time was a Sergeant and deputy leader of Platoon No. 1. So far as several witnesses declared that the whole company was deployed, this error is most likely to have been made, because stretcher bearers (statement: O., H.), kitchen personnel, clerks (Statement: S., R.), were ordered to join No 1 Platoon, in order to strengthen it. According to the statement by witness J. the order to surround and isolate the area was given by Lt. M.

It is therefore obvious to assume that Lt. M. received the order from his immediate superior, the company commander, the accused Artmann. Because Lt. M. fell later in the war, this can not be proven.

The accused himself denies ever having given such an order, nor was he aware what duties his No 1 Platoon was performing. According to his statement he became aware that a large part of the Jews were to be exterminated. He only ordered the closure of the approaches to and from the town with double sentries, to prevent the Jews from escaping, and to protect the company (against partisans). He maintains he also inspected the sentry line which isolated the town, on horseback together with Lt. M. Those steps were taken on the day the shooting was carried out. Apart from that, he had ordered his men to secure their quarters because he expected that there could be a revolt by the Jews or an attack by the Partisans.

This last statement by the accused was confirmed by several witnesses: S. (3. Platoon) who stood guard near the billets, together with B. (3. Platoon). S. (2. Platoon) did guard duty at the Ghetto. According to the witness B. (platoon leader, 3. Platoon) Artmann gave an order not to leave the billets.

The accused also declared that, at that time, he had not received any order from higher quarters to take any of those measures. Although Major S., in his opinion a Jew hater, once, at a discussion with Company Commanders had made it known, that there was an order from a higher level, that Jews were Partisans and as Partisans had to be finished off. On the other hand he knew of a later divisional order forbidding members of the Wehrmacht to take part in any action against Jews. The existence of this Divisional Order was confirmed by the witnesses: J., N. (Battalion Adjutant), S. (Sergeant), N. (Sergeant Major), P. (Colonel and Reg. Commander) and Freiherr von M.-B. (Major general and Divisional Commander).

The company commanders, amongst them the accused, were of the opinion that they were to make their own decisions, as the

localities where they were stationed were some distance from
the Battalion Commander and his staff (Baranovichi). It is
unthinkable that the accused would have given orders to men
from his unit to shoot Jews, if that would have meant acting
against a direct order, besides, when asked to do so, by the
civilian authorities, he could then refer to this order. In
view of his personality it is difficult to assume that the
accused acted on his own initiative. He was already 48 years
old, and in the unanimous opinion of all those members of the
company who were interrogated he was correct, definitely not a
Jew-hater, good-humoured, yes, genial, and no martinet who
would make his men jump through the hoop. He was aware that
civilians, regardless of the fact that they were Jews or not,
had to be treated decently. Until the time that the Civilian
administration was established, the relationship of the company
towards the population was very good. The leader of the 2.
platoon, Lt. H. was entrusted with all the matters concerning
the local administration. He also gave a free hand to his deputy
Lt. M. in dealing with matters outside the Company.

The only accusation against the defendant, which was
unsubstantiated, was the statement made to the police by the
witness W., according to which Artmann at a parade, is supposed
to have said, something like: 'We were supposed to carry out a
barbaric order. As you know, the Jews are all being caught and
taken to Germany. We were supposed to take all the Jews in
Nowogrodek and drive them out into the forest. There we were
supposed to shoot them. I have been able to manage it up to now,
that we only have to surround the town, so that no one can
escape. You don't have to take your task so seriously; if a few
Jews get out, it is also not so terrible. The shooting will be
done by Lithuanians.' This supposed talk by the accused, with
the meaning implied, could not be confirmed by a single witness.
The witness himself, in front of the examining judge has
explained the meaning of his statement to the police, namely,
that Artmann implied that he had an order to use his Company to
murder the Jews, but that he refused to do so, because he was a
soldier and did not want anything to do with it. Without doubt,
his statement regarding the encircling duty relates to the area
of the town and not to the execution area. Besides there are
grave doubts about the witness's truthfulness, because he admitted that he had made false accusation against the co-
defendants S. and K.

In view of the results of these proceedings and the pre-trial
investigation there exists no reasonable suspicion, that the
defendant took part in the murder of Jews in Nowogrodek on
8.12.1941, or that by the use of the 1. Platoon and a number of
other members of the company he then encircled the execution
area, or that he knowingly tolerated the encirclement by men
under his command.

A statement as regards the involvement of the 1. Platoon in
the shooting of the Jews by sealing the execution area without
the knowledge of the Company Commander, finds that Lt. M., who

gave the order to his platoon, acted on his own initiative. The fact that he also ordered the men of the service unit to join in, can be explained by the manner in which he behaved as deputy to the Company Commander. His arrogant behaviour expressed his character, his appearance, and his attitude towards Jews. Sergeant N. described him as nosy compared to Artmann. He liked to make the decisions in the Company, he was ambitious, and wanted to be promoted to Company Commander. The witness O. describes M. as overbearing. The witness M. as a most independent person who did not want to be told anything, and for whom nothing went fast enough. According to B., the 1. Platoon which M. led, was the Elite Platoon, which was the one most frequently used when anything happened. In the statement made by the witness K., Lt. M. was more fanatical than Artmann, (whom he described as a pleasant chap). He (M.) did not like the Jews. In contrast to Artmann he maintained personal connections with the area commissariat, the plumed peacocks. As a man of the forest he was invited to hunt with them and was friendly with one of the secretaries in their office. In view of this attitude towards the Jews and those personal connections, it is not impossible to assume that Lt. M. acted on his own accord and exceeded the standing divisional order. He did not have to worry about a reprimand for his action under the National Socialist Regime.

   After all this, a verdict of guilty against the defendant Artmann, because of the publicly charged crime against him, is for reasons of the evidence based on actual facts, not to be expected. The defendant therefore is found not guilty. The decision is according to the application of the State Prosecutor.

Decision on cost: 464/1, 467/1, STPO.
Signed:Ehrnsperger
Superior District Judge
Uschold
District Judge
Ruecker
District Judge

And just in case no Jew should have remained alive, Rabbi Rogatinski, with two others, made a statement and gave it to Mr Roznov, a non-Jew, for safekeeping, to hand over to the authorities after the War. In 1942 the Rabbi knew that the Nazi policy was to exterminate every Jew in the German Reich.

   The document overleaf was given to me by my friend Tamara Vershitskaya in 1994. She is curator of the museum at Novogrodek. Rabbi Rogatinski wanted it as a testimony of what happened in Novogrodek.

Source: Museum Novogrodek

148

НАВАГРУДСКІ
ГІСТОРЫКА-КРАЯЗНАЎЧЫ МУЗЕЙ

231400 Рэспубліка Беларусь, Гродзенская вобл.
г. Навагрудак, вул. Гродзенская, 2. Тэл. (297) 2-14-70, 2-23-95

Дн. 14. March, 1993
Mr. T. Kagan
Leor Plastics Ltd. (off Oxgate Lane) London NW2 ???
Horseshoe Close

Statement   N 66
                 113

March 20, 1942
Drawn up by the commission with Rabbi
of the Novogrudok community Rogatynski M.R.
at the head and its members Shelyubski L.I.
and Roznov X.E. on the fact, that on December 8,
1941 mass manslaughter of Jews from Novogrudok by German fiends and their brothers-in-arms
took place, 4500 people were killed. The killing
was done in the following way:
   On December 5, 1941 all Jews from Novogrudok
and surrounding places were driven to the
District Court in Minskaya str. where they
were kept in the open air at the temperature
of 20° below zero. guarded by belarussian police
till the morning of December 6, 1941. On December 8 the Gestapo having arrived made a
selection and took them by cars to the place
beyond the Novogrudok barracks, shot them
down and buried alive in 2 pits at 40m x 3m
in size.
   That is certified
Commission:
Head of the Commission
Rabbi of Novogrudok   Rogatynski
                                   Raznov
Members: Shelyubski

149

```
                            Statement
                                            N66  113
20 March 1942
```

Drawn up by the Commission with Rabbi of Novogrodek
community Rogatinski M.R. and members Shelyubski L.I. and
Roznov X.E. on the fact, that on 8 December 1941 a mass
slaughter of Jews from Novogrodek by German fiends and their
brothers in arms took place, in which 4,500 people were
killed. The killing was done in the following way:
  On 5 December 1941 all the Jews from Novogrodek and
surrounding places were driven to the District Court in
Minskaya Street where they were kept in the open air at a
temperature of 20 C below zero, guarded by Belorussian
police till the morning of 6 December 1941. On 8 December
the Gestapo having arrived made a selection and took them by
lorries to a spot behind the Novogrodek barracks, shot them
down and buried some alive in two pits 40mtr x 3mtr in size.

That is certified.
Commission:
Head of Commission Roznov
Rabbi of Novogrodek Rogatinski.
Members Shelyubski

Roznov and Shelyubski were members of the NKVD.

The remaining 1,500 of us were taken to Peresika, where the
ghetto was formed. It was small. Bunks were built: 60 cm (approx.
2 feet) space per person was allowed; if you had to turn over in the
night, you would wake up the nine people who slept in your row.

It was an open ghetto. This meant that there was no work inside
and we had to go out to work. Two main workplaces were formed,
one for skilled people, in the workshops in one of the court-house
buildings. There were shoemakers, tailors, furriers, saddlers,
joiners and various others. Approximately 450 men and women
worked there. The other place was the Russian barracks, where
about 250 worked, mostly men. The remainder worked in the
town.

My father worked as a saddler, and my mother worked stitching
fur gloves for the German army. I worked in the barracks in
Skridlevo. The work was difficult. In the early days I worked with
joiners from Zdzienciol (a neighbouring town). The day started

The infamous Court House

early. I had a four-kilometre walk to work. I was barely 13 years old and found the going hard. I believe that I was the youngest worker in the barracks and after a short while I was transferred to a better job: to wheelbarrowing stones. This work was also hard and I received plenty of beatings. A wheelbarrow loaded with stones is very heavy and it was difficult to find the right technique for lifting it up and then controlling it on a narrow path of wooden planks.

Even on the hottest day I wore a padded jacket: it gave me some protection in case I should get a hiding. There was a Nazi, whom we called 'Hazza' (after a dog which used to come into our yard before the War) and when he was around fear was in everybody's heart. Three times as much work was done. You loaded more stones than you could lift, and after a crack from his whip you fell down and stopped the line. He had lead fitted to the end of the whip. That was his pleasure: riding up and down on his horse, whipping everybody.

We received 200 grams of heavy black bread and some soup each day and an extra portion of soup for working in the barracks.

The Gebiets Commissar of Novogrodek was responsible for the Jews of Karelitz, Lubcz, Delatits, Iveniec, Derevna, Vsielub and other small towns.

At the beginning of May a decision was made by the SS to liquidate the Jews from the small towns around Novogrodek. The Jews of Karelitz were consequently marched to Novogrodek ghetto and the Germans then turned their attention to other small communities with Jewish populations. The SS together with the Lithuanian and Belorussian police set off in four lorries and rounded up all the Jews still living in Rovizshevitz and Iveniec. They asked them to hand over their gold and other valuables, beat them up and marched them outside Rovizshevitz where they were all killed. After finishing their work, they started drinking and continued their way to Lubcz to kill the remainder of the Jewish community. The only way to Lubcz was through Naliboki.

When that came to the knowledge of the leader of the Partisan group Stalintsi the leader decided to ambush the four lorries on the way out of Naliboki. They lay in wait at the edge of the forest. Late in the afternoon they heard the noise of the engines and when all four lorries were in range they opened fire, killing some and wounding others.

The lorries stopped and the survivors came out with their hands up. They fell on the ground and begged us to spare their lives for they were only carrying out orders to round up and kill the Jews from small towns.

The partisans looked in one of the lorries and found three Jewish girls whom the Germans had taken with them. The leader of the Partisans asked if the girls wanted to join them, which they did. They searched the lorries and found the gold and other valuables. They took the ammunition, asked the Germans and Belorussian Police to undress and killed them on the spot, burned the four lorries and retreated back to the forest. Following is the German version of the event.

TRANSLATION FROM GERMAN   450/93

Copy

The Commander of the
Security Police and the Security Service   Riga, 16.6.1942
  — Ostland —
Dept. 1 P Diary No. 1919/42

To the
Reich Commissioner for Ostland
Riga

Subject: Partisan attack in Baranowitsche

The Baranowitsche Unit of the Commander of the Security
Police and the Security Service, White Ruthenia, with a
strength of 8 German SS-Unterführer and Unterfüher, 2
members of the District Commissioner's Office, Novogorodek,
1 Lieutenant and 1 Sergeant in the Gendarmerie and 15
Lithuanians and Russians, had gone out on an operation
against Jews and at about 5.00 p.m. on 9.6.1942 reached
Walibokie north of Stolpce. The village is in a fairly large
wooded area; in front of the village however there is a
fairly large, completely open and flat area.

When the Unit's cars and lorries had left the wood and
wanted to drive into the village, they were fired on from two
sides by heavy machine-guns. The Unit left the vehicles and
tried to storm the village. In the open ground it was,
however, exposed to strong fire. Besides the fact that the
terrain was unfavourable, in that it offered no possibility
of cover, the Unit was also at a disadvantage because the
weapons they had brought with them had too limited a range
compared with those of the partisans. In the unequal battle
all the members of the Unit fell one by one, only an SS-
Oberscharführer and an SS man along with 4 interpreters and
drivers could withdraw and fight their way out alive. In the
course of this one interpreter was wounded.

On 10.6.1942 the Commander of the Security Police and the
Security Service, White Ruthenia, set out for Baranowitsche
with almost all the forces at his command. He received
reinforcements from the motorised gendarmerie and the local
police. He found 15 dead bodies in Walibokie, just as they
had fallen in battle. All those who had fallen had had their
boots taken off, the SS men had also been undressed down to
their underpants and all their identity documents and
identifying marks had been stolen. One SS-Obersturmführer
had had a swastika and a Soviet star burnt into his chest.
From an interrogation of villages it was established that

4 Germans, namely probably two SS-Unterführer and the two gendarmerie officers, had been captured and taken through Walibokie on a lorry stolen by the partisans. They had placed red flags in their bound hands. In addition the partisans had scornfully shouted: "Look, these are your masters!" The bands of partisans conisted of 90—100 Russians, including parachutists wearing Russian uniform. They were armed with heavy weapons and had radio equipment.

From further questioning of villagers it has been established that the four captured officers were shot on 9.6.1942 in a wood near Walibokie. A search operation for the bodies has been set in motion.

Measures necessary to combat the partisan group have been taken without delay, but because of the weakness of our forces these have so far not been successful.

On instructions
sgd. Stuber
ss-Sturmbannführer

Source: Bundesarchiv (BA) R6/354 p19. Commander of Security Police Ostland to Reichskommissar 16.6.1942

The Germans had tried to liquidate the partisans, but were unable to. And below is a German document to this effect.

Report of   0076   Wilejka, 18 June 1942
SS Unterscharführer Lipps
Wilejka Group
to
SS Untersturmführer Burgdorf

My last report covered the period to 24 May 1942.

The time between 24 May 1942 and 18 June 1942 has been filled with more or less unsuccessful operations against partisans who have been disagreeably active in this area in recent weeks.

On 30 May 1942 we brought in two parachutists who surrendered to us voluntarily. Between 1 June and 3 June we concentrated our operations in the region of Dolhinow where, according to reports, a large band (of partisans), which had a fortified encampment in the forest, was carrying out acts of terror. We located the camp on the third day, but the partisans had left it the previous day.

On 4 June the entire *Waffen SS* group was ordered to Minsk, where a major operation was to be launched against the partisans in the area. On 5 June we drove to Stolpce, 75 km SW of Minsk. On 6 June we came back to Minsk, only to return to Stolpce again on 7 June. The operation began on 8 June. Substantial forces were committed. The preparations had taken several days. After all that, the operation was a total failure! We found one camp, but it was deserted. All our efforts against the partisans, in conjunction with the *Wehrmacht*, came to nothing because the machinery operates too slowly. On the evening of 9 June we returned to Minsk and on 10 June continued on to Wilejka. On the evening of 10 June we received orders to return to Minsk. We set out early on the morning of 11 June. Our route took us through Wilna-Lida-Nowogrodek to Mir, where we met up the next day with the Minsk group. We had been summoned because a detachment from the Baranowitschi group had been ambushed by partisans the previous day. It was an unfortunate encounter in which fifteen of our men, mostly Lithuanians, were killed. Six others, including four Germans, were taken prisoner by the partisans. The dead were buried in Baranowitschi on 13 June. We then returned to Minsk. On 14 June we came back to Wilejka and on the same evening received orders to return once again to Minsk. *SS Obersturmführer* Burkhardt had unfortunately been killed in action against the partisans. The group set out for Minsk once more on 15 June, took part in the funeral ceremony for the dead *Obersturmführer* and returned to Wilejka on 17 June.

This concludes my report of the major events between 24 May and 18 June.

There have been no incidents within the group which would give any cause for complaint.

[Signature]
Lipps
SS Unterscharführer

Source: Military History Archive Prague. Group Wilejka to Burgdorf 18.6.1942

Various regulations were coming out daily against the Jewish population; I found one while I was in Novogrodek. Following are copies of the original, in Belorussian and German, followed by my own English translation.

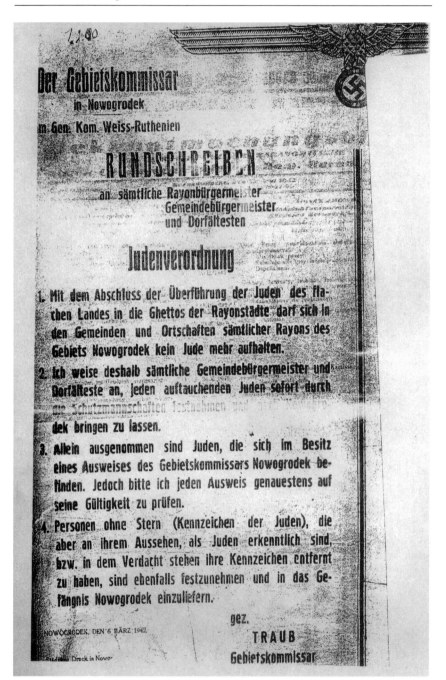

Source: Museum Novogrodek

АКРУЖНЫ КАМІСАР
у Наваградку
Ген. Ком. Беларусі

АБЕЖНІК
да усіх Раённых Бурмістрау
Гмінных Бурмістрау
і Соцкіх.

Загад адносна жыдоў.

1. З заканьчэньнем пераводу жыдоў з усяго абшару у гэтта раённых гарадоў, ані адзін жыд ня можа знаходзіцца у вёсках і гмінах паасобных раёнаў Наваградскай Акругі.

2. Дзеля гэтага загадываю усім гмінным Бурмістрам і Соцкім кожнага натрапленага жыда зараз жа затрымаць паліцыяй і загадаць адправіць да Наваградка.

3. Свабодна адпушчанымі могуць быць жыды, якія маюць пасьведчаньне Акружнага Камісара Наваградка. Аднак прашу кожнае пасьведчаньне дакладна прааналізаваць адносна яго важнасьці.

4. Асобы бяз зорак (разпазнальныя азнакі жыдоў), якія аднак па свайму воннаваму выгляду могуць быць прызнаныя жыдамі, або падазронныя, што скінулі азнакі, павінны таксама быць затрыманымі і дастаўленымі у Наваградскую цямніцу.

падпісана
ТРАУБ
Акружны Камісар

НАВАГРАДАК ...н. 6. САГАВІНА 1942 г.

Source: Museum Novogrodek

```
The District Commissar
in Novogrudok
in the Gen. Kom. White Ruthenia
```

Announcement

to all District Mayors
and Village Elders

REGULATION CONCERNING JEWS

I. With the conclusion of the Transportation of the Jews of
the Flaten (plains) to the Ghettos of the Towns of the
District no Jew is allowed to be in the Communes and
Localities in the District of Novogrudok.

2. I therefore order all Community Mayors and Village
Elders that if any Jew appears, he be arrested by the Police
and brought to Novogrudok.

3. The only exception are Jews who are in Possession of an
Identity Document issued by the District Commissar of
Novogrudok. Nevertheless, I request that every one of the
Documents be thoroughly scrutinised to check if it is
genuine.

4. Persons without Stars (Recognition Badge of the Jews)
but who by their appearance are recognisable as Jews, in
other words, can be suspected of having removed their Jewish
Recognition Badge are also to be arrested and delivered into
the Prison of Novogrudok.

```
Novogrudok, 6 March 1942
Signed TRAUB
DISTRICT COMMISSAR
```

The Gebiets commissar decided to bring the Jews from the little surrounding towns and villages to Novogrodek. At the beginning of May, the first lot of families started to arrive in the ghetto – from Karelitz 530 individuals, Lubcz 1500, Vsielub 1500, Derevna 280, Iveniec 1200 and other small places. Among them were my uncle Yosef Gurevitz, my aunt Breine Feigel and their children, Nachama and Hassia, my other aunt Malke Kapushevski, her son Nochim (her husband, Haim, was sent to Dvoretz to build an airport and was killed there and the other son, Berele, was killed on

8 December 1941) as well as my old grandmother Hannah Gitel. We moved to the loft to give our places to our family from Karelitz. Altogether the ghetto now held about 6,500 people. Every centimetre of space was utilised.

It is difficult to describe the misery of that time. People were walking around aimlessly knowing that they were sentenced to death, but not knowing when the execution would take place. Yet there was nowhere to run to.

One day, at the beginning of July, we arrived at work as usual. At lunch time, I drifted away from the workplace as I had done every day, to search for cigarette ends or pieces of bread, which German soldiers would throw out (whether for us or for the birds, I will never know, but for me it was a great thing). My uncle Yosef Gurevitz was a smoker and I was his cigarette provider. Suddenly, out of nowhere, a German soldier jumped at me shouting, 'Raus, raus du verfluchter Jude!' I felt a crack from the butt of his rifle, and he pushed me into the middle of the barracks square, together with about 50 other people. The troops surrounding our group were all from the SS. They shouted insults at us and made us line up in a single row. I was in the middle. Within a few minutes a machine-gun was assembled and I thought they were going to shoot us. My legs became like jelly. I turned up my collar and looked away from the machine-gun, but immediately received a slap in the face with a white glove to make me turn back. They kept us there for a long time. Eventually Reuter arrived. Reuter was a high-ranking SS officer in charge of Jewish affairs for the whole area of Novogrodek. He did not say anything but just released us and we went back to work.

Before the German occupation a Jewish farmer lived next to the barracks. The Jewish farmer handed over his farm to a non-Jewish 'friend'. Now the farmer's two sons worked in the barracks and, from time to time, during the lunch break, they used to sneak out under the barbed wire and the 'friend' gave them food. But on this particular day the 'friend' notified the Germans that Jews would be calling on him, and two soldiers were waiting inside the house. When the brothers noticed the Germans, they ran off after hitting one of them and stealing his rifle. And the only reason why the Germans did not shoot us was that it was very near to the second action and they did not want to create panic.

That was my last day of work in the barracks. The next day I went to work with my father at the court-house to learn saddle-making. My father was friendly with the foreman and he had given permission for this. On the first day of work I went over to a large empty building and started searching the basement, scavenging through it to see if I could find anything useful, and did indeed find something really valuable – a fireman's hose. It took me a week to cut it up into pieces, take out the wires from the corrugation and bring it to the ghetto for sale for rubber soles. I also found some municipality plans and by accident I wet them and found there was linen under the paper. The linen was of poor quality but a saleable commodity nevertheless.

We all knew that an action would soon take place, and escape was easy. But where do you go to when nobody will let you in? The winter is severe, temperatures can go down to minus 25°C and that is cold.

We arrived at work as usual on 7 August 1942. Immediately we were surrounded by the police and the SS. There were about 500 of us, men and women. They guarded the main entrances but left one side unguarded. At the same time they surrounded the ghetto and the barracks, but many children with parents in the work-shops managed somehow to smuggle themselves in. Among them was my sister. The Germans took everybody from the ghetto to Litovka, two kilometres away, to prepared mass graves. They killed everybody from the ghetto: all my relatives from Karelitz, including my old grandmother. By that time, 750 Jews were working in the barracks. The Germans sorted out 500 men and women. The remainder were also brought to Litovka to be shot.

On that day 5,500 men, women and children were killed in Litovka. My cousin Srolik Sucharski tried to escape and was shot at the gates of the barracks. The 500 that remained were kept for three days and nights without food or water and given no toilet facilities. That same evening, everybody in the workshops had to line up and be inspected. I stood next to my father, dressed in my father's jacket and long trousers to look older. The Nazi Chief passed and did not say anything but all the children who were hidden in the loft, and some in the basement, were found and thrown out of the windows and then taken by lorry to Litovka where they were killed. From that day the ghetto in Peresika contained 500 Jews and the court-house 500 skilled tradesmen. I was one of the youngest among them. From our family, mother, father, sister, cousin Berl and myself, had survived so far, and from the Sucharski family, Notke, Haike and Sheindel had survived. We were kept locked up for a number of days without food or water. Then a van was driven in to where we were assembled and loaves of bread were thrown at us. The Germans took pleasure in seeing us struggle to get hold of a piece. Then the camp commandant Reuter told us we were the lucky ones, we would remain alive because the Reich needed us but we would have to work hard. Numbers were issued. We had to stitch one on the back of our clothes. Mine was 334. Now it was no longer a ghetto but an *Arbeitslager*. The skilled joiners (from Zdzienciol) were brought from the barracks. However, before the place could be fenced in, most of them escaped to join the partisans.

We were enclosed by two encirclements of barbed wire with a wooden fence on the outside. Towers with searchlights and machine-guns were installed. Because of the wooden fence, we could not see the guards, and therefore never knew how many were watching us. The camp had no water facilities. Every day a number of workers had to fetch drinking water. This was our contact with the outside world. The Belorussian guards (we called them 'black crows') were bribed with gold to buy pistols, ammunition and food and, from time to time, to let somebody disappear.

14   *Escape and Life with the Partisans*

AFTER THE second massacre, young people began to escape. There would be a lot of whispering, then they would disappear at night. Contact with the Bielski partisans in the woods had been established, and the ghetto youth prepared their escape. The Bielski brothers gave me hope, a place to run to. I must admire the inmates of our camp. They were not afraid to let the young people escape, even though Reuter had issued a warning that mass shooting would take place if he found out that Jews had escaped from the camp.

I knew the youngest brother, Archik Bielski, very well. We went to the same school, were in the same class and for certain lessons we shared the same bench. The Bielski family consisted of father David, mother Beila, nine brothers and two sisters. They lived in a village called Stankiewicz, and were the only Jewish family amongst the ten families there. Their income came from the water mill and several acres of land.

Life was hard, in Stankiewicz. As a stranger, you had to defend yourself continuously and be tough-minded and unafraid. The Bielski brothers were all strong lads, tall and broad-shouldered. One had to think twice before starting an argument with them.

Tuvia was born in 1906. At the age of 21, he was mobilised by the Polish army. In 1928, after six months of service, he became an instructor and taught new recruits.

Tuvia was very clever, very shrewd and knew the local population extremely well. He was a judge of character, knew whom to trust, kept cool – in fact, a born leader for a partisan movement. The biggest test of his qualities came in July 1943, when the great blockade (Operation Herman) was launched.

Tuvia died in New York on 12 June 1987. His remains were then moved to a special military leaders section of the Har Hamenuchot Cemetery in Jerusalem, and received full military honours.

Asael was born in 1908. Very good-humoured, he always had a

Tuvia Bielski, the leader of the Jewish Partisans (left) and his brother Asael

Yudel Slutzki by Tuvia Bielski's grave in Jerusalem

Zush Bielski   *Archik Bielski, 1991*

smile on his face, and managed to stay calm in the worst of situations. He looked like a farmer with all the local mannerisms, but turned out to be an excellent reconnaissance man. He was killed near Königsberg while serving in the Red Army in 1944.

Zush was born in 1912, got married before the war and lived in Novogrodek, where his wife and baby perished in the first slaughter. Zush served in the Red Army, was very strong, very tall and very brave. The farmers were afraid of him. He knew the countryside and the local farmers well. He died in New York on 18 August 1995.

The youngest brother, Archik, was born in 1928. He, too, knew the countryside and participated in giving advice. He now lives in New York.

The four brothers refused to submit to the German terror and went into hiding in the forest. Their parents, two brothers and sister were killed in Novogrodek in the large mass killing of 8 December 1941.

In the spring of 1942 the Bielskis were joined by the Dzienciolski and Boldo families, making a total of 20 people. In the summer,

YAD VASHEM יד ושם

Holocaust Martyrs' and Heroes' Remembrance Authority רשות הזיכרון לשואה ולגבורה

Jerusalem, 16 January 1994

Mr. Vladimir Kozlovsky
Str. Warshavskaja 23
Gorod - MOGILOV
BELORUS

Dear Mr. Kozlovsky,

   I have the pleasure to inform you that the Special
Commission of the Designation of the Righteous, at its session of
22.12.1993 decided to confer upon you, your late father Mr.
Kustyk Kozlovsky and your brother Genady its highest expression
of gratitude: the title of Righteous Among the Nations.

   This recognition entitles the previously-named to a medal
and certificate of honour and the privilege of having your names
inscribed on the Righteous Honor Wall, at Yad Vashem, Jerusalem.
A copy of this letter is being mailed to our embassy in Minsk
(Mr. Eliahu Valk, Hotel Belarus, Minsk, Tel: 00-7-0172-690-804).
They will be in touch with you for further information on the
distribution of the awards.

   Please accept our congratulations and best wishes.

Sincerely yours,

Dr. Mordecai Paldiel
Director
Dept. for the Righteous

decision/m.p./s.o./

5927#

cc: Mr. Eliahu Valk, Embassy of Israel - Minsk
   √Mr. Dov Cohen - Israel
    Mr. Y. Sloszki - Israel
    Mrs. Y. Abramowicz - Israel
    Mrs. Tova Nochimowski - Israel
    Mrs. L. Rodnicki - Israel

2

The letter from Yad Vashem to Vladimir Kozlovsky

with the help of Konstantin Kozlovsky (he died after the War and his son Vladimir received a medal from Yad Vashem as a Righteous among Nations, which is the greatest honour that can be bestowed by the Jewish people [see letter on previous page]), the first ten people arrived from the Ghetto in Novogrodek. The Bielski brigade was formed and they called themselves *Otriad* (detachment) Zhukov, with Tuvia Bielski elected as commander.

And once it became known in the Ghetto that there was a place to run to, people began to take the chance and run. To me the Bielskis are among the greatest of Jewish heroes. And it is a pity that not many people know about them.

By the end of October 1942 the group consisted of more than 300 people. In November Ishie Oppenheim, from the Bielski group of partisans, left the forest briefly to enter the camp, where he organised a group of young people for an escape. My cousin Berl Kagan was among them. I was put on look-out duty, and they managed to get out of the ghetto safely. I watched the older boys and envied them: they could escape to freedom, war and revenge.

Every so often somebody disappeared from behind the toilets and under the wire or from the water party, and went either to join the partisans or in search of a friendly farmer who might hide them. Very few farmers wanted to risk their lives and the lives of their families to save a Jew. The penalty for just having contact with a Jew was death. But there were some good farmers who risked their lives and hid children or entire families.

Opposite is a picture of Bella Dzienciolska, taken in 1993, examining the place where she had been hidden during the War. Her parents had entrusted her to a farmer to hide. She was blonde and she did not look like a Jewish child, but at two years old, she already spoke Yiddish. So the farmer made a hole under the floor and kept her there during the day for a year until she forgot to speak Yiddish. He then took her out and told the neighbours that a relative's child was staying with them.

The Bielski family became famous, and we knew that they were operating around Lida. The name Kozlovsky and that of the dogcatchers (Bobrovski) became known. The story was that if you were planning an escape, you should go 14 kilometres from Novo-grodek to Lida to Kozlovsky's farmstead. He would then direct you to the partisans and of course everybody knew where the

Bella Rubin née Dzienciolska, 1993, visiting the house where she had been hidden

dogcatchers lived. And they also had contacts with the partisans. Sometimes partisans managed to slip into the camp, to get their parents, wives or girlfriends out, and most of these escapes were successful.

I started to prepare myself for escape, too. Getting out was still quite easy. The danger was that in winter you could freeze to death. Then there was the problem of food, and the fact that the outside world was unfriendly, people were ready to sell you to the Germans or just give you away for the sake of it.

I got friendly with the warehouseman who was in charge of the store of felt boots. He had lost a son who had been my age and therefore wanted me to succeed in my escape. He risked his life and gave me a pair of the most beautiful, hard felt boots. I took one boot at a time and hid it in my bunk. I told my parents that I planned to escape and they gave me their blessing.

At about this time, Ruvke Oppenheim, Ishie's brother, slipped into the camp to get his mother out. I watched him as carefully as I

Ishie and Ruvke Oppenheim and their sister, 1944. Ruvke was killed in Latrun, Israel while serving in the Israeli Army.

could. On 22 December 1942, the gates were opened to let lorries in, to unload raw material. It was very cold. I saw Oppenheim in his warm coat and I went to the room to put on my special hard felt boots. Inside them it was like a hot oven. I loosened the yellow star and number and tore them off when I came nearer to the gates. There were no guards to be seen. I did not hesitate but walked through the gates without looking back. I crossed the highway, went on to the small forest where already a few people were waiting. By the afternoon there were 14 of us. We waited until dark, then started to walk around the town to reach the dog-catcher's home by midnight, because Oppenheim had a rendez-vous with the partisans at that time.

The going was very difficult, with waist-deep, soft snow. We had to cover approximately eight kilometres, in order to skirt around the town so as to keep away from the houses and barking dogs. We reached the little river Britanka. We felt the ice under the snow, but suddenly the ice gave way and most of us fell in. The water flows so fast in this river that even at this temperature, of about −20 °C, it had not frozen over. I was the worst off. I had felt boots and the fabric immediately absorbed the water and snow started sticking to my boots. Each step became more difficult; it seemed as if I was walking on stilts. My feet became heavy and I could not keep up, but I knew where the dogcatcher lived so I started to go at my own pace. I caught up with the group about half an hour later.

We all reached the place but too late! The partisans had not waited. They were due to come back three nights later. The dogcatcher refused to let us stay in his house or in the barn. He advised us to go to the small forest and wait there for the next three days. His wife gave me a plate of hot soup, but out in the yard. After a while, I just wanted to sleep. I started to dream and realised immediately that if I fell asleep now, it would be forever. I fought hard with myself and made a decision: I must return to the camp. Otherwise I would freeze to death.

I crawled to the road and put my life in the hands of fate. I was fortunate. A peasant passed by in his sleigh. He sat wrapped up in his coat, and didn't notice me when I climbed onto the back of the sleigh. Luckily, he took me through Peresika Street, right next to the ghetto. I saw the guards. The sleigh took me to the market place and down Karelitzer Street. When we got near the camp I just fell off and started walking towards the well. I knew that in a few hours' time the first party would come to fetch water. I waited in the bitter cold for the first party to arrive.

Eventually they came. The guards were so wrapped up that they could not see anything. I moved forwards and was noticed by one of the carriers. He must have immediately told the others, as I found myself in the middle of the group. Before I knew what was happening I found myself back in my room.

My father tried to take off the boots but it was impossible. A file and sharp knife had to be used. My toes were black with frostbite on both feet. There was a doctor by the name of Yaakobovitz but he could not help because a few weeks before he had lit a cigarette in the dark and a guard had shot him through the leg. So there was no doctor to help and no medicine, no bandages, nothing. A dentist was called and he suggested waiting a week or so and then having my toes cut off. After a few days the flesh started to rot and the smell was unbearable. I was examined again and the dentist decided to amputate the toes the following day.

Four people held me as the dentist performed the amputation. It was not painful when he cut the flesh but when he used tooth pliers for the bones, it was agony. Worst of all, I felt sure that, even if other people might survive, by luck or miracle, I had signed my own death certificate: that is by being in a camp and not being able to walk.

The strain on my parents and sister was unbearable. If I couldn't work, I couldn't bring in any food which meant a decrease in rations for them. Ruvke Shabakovski lived in our room. One day Ruvke was called into town to do a special job for the German commandant. When he came back he brought with him half a sack of flour and later he took out a radio from the bottom of the sack. A joiner was called, they went up into the loft, chiselled out a hole in the beam and hid the radio. And so we got to hear the world news. The news about Stalingrad made us feel especially good. And also hope arose that perhaps we would be left to stay alive. After all, we were helping their officers with fur coats and boots and gloves.

On 4 February 1943 we heard the bad news that the Ghetto had been liquidated in the early hours. And on the following day there was an additional Jew in our camp. He said that he had escaped from the massacre and managed to get into the camp. It had not snowed that night, the leaders looked for his footprints near the toilets, but could not find any. He had been planted by the Germans. A meeting was called by the escape organisers and it was decided to behead him. The execution was done the same day. The following day Burstein (the Judenrat representative) and Shabakovski were arrested. Two days later Shabakovski was brought back by the local police. He was carried. His back was so black from the beating he had received that he was too weak to speak but when he felt better he told us they wanted to know the route to the partisans and what had happened to the informer. Neither had given anything away but unfortunately Burstein did not survive the beatings. On the prison wall was written in blood in bold letters **TAKE REVENGE**.

Reuter appointed Daniel Ostashinski to be in charge of the Jews. I started feeling better, but a new enemy began to show up: bugs

(*Wanzen*) – millions of them. They made my life a misery. Because of the dirty conditions, lice and bugs reigned. They got under the so-called bandages and disturbed my wounds. I had to scratch and with the slightest scratch the wounds would bleed again.

One night I woke up with a terrible pain in my head. I was going crazy, then I soon realised that a bug had crept into my ear. The only way for me to get it out was to crawl to the edge of the bunk and urinate in my hand and flush the bug out. It worked, but I had to wait until the morning to be able to get a small amount of water to wash my hand and face.

Of course, there was no electricity in the camp. We cut up pieces of kindling and burned them. Depending on the angle at which they were held, the light was brighter or dimmer. I used them all night to burn the bugs off the wall. I was moved to the top bunk, so as not to disturb other people. I was so sorry for my parents, they had aged. In my room before the War there was a placard on the wall. On it was a Jewish boy with a sad face and under it was written 'Lo tov ba'olam' 'It is no good in the world'. It must have been printed in 1935 during the riots in Jaffa. I was lying on my bunk terribly hungry and thinking, what reason did he have to complain?

In early April, my aunt received a message that a farmer sent by the partisans would be waiting to take Sheindel Sucharski and her friend Michle Sosnovski to the partisans. They managed to slip away from the water-carrying party, waited for a while and reached the large market-place outside the town. There a Polish girl who had gone to school with them before the War recognised them and called the police. They were arrested, tortured and killed in prison.

In April 1943 the camp commandant, Reuter, announced that he was satisfied with the work of the inmates and that from now on, 250 of the specialists would get extra food rations, 100 grams of fat and another portion of bread every week. To get it, they would have to go to the assembly hall inside the workshops and not to the gates as before. My father fell into this category. Every week I watched the assembly, heard the calling out of the numbers and the beatings take place on the assembly area and saw how the specialists were marched away to get their extra food.

The morning of 7 May 1943 was nice and sunny. The window was open, and I watched the muster of the specialists as usual.

Suddenly I saw lots of local and foreign police running about, hitting out with their rifles at everybody. My mother came to the window, to reassure me, 'It is nothing', she said. I was sure she had come to say goodbye (during that period you had a feeling about things and when my mother came to me like that, it was as if she were saying goodbye). I could no longer stand hearing the shouting and seeing the beatings. I turned towards the wall where the so-called pillows were supposed to have been. I covered myself, put my fingers in my ears and lay quietly, crying my heart out. After a while I heard shooting.

What would I do if I was caught? They would beat me to death because I still could not walk. Suddenly I heard the guards coming into the room. They had killed everybody and now came to rob, but we did not have anything. With anger and curses they took some belongings and threw them on the top bunk and so covered me more. How long I lay there I don't know, but soon I heard people crying and realised that the specialists had been sent back. Among them was my father and uncle Notke Sucharski. All the others, including my mother, sister and aunt, had been taken just opposite the camp and killed.

After this, food was cut down to 125 grams of bread mixed with straw and a bowl of soup a day – a slow starvation diet. It was impossible for me to get used to the hunger. I was not occupied and the days passed by very slowly waiting 24 hours for the next slice of bread. In the early days I used to dream of the good food we had in the past, but I would wake up even more hungry.

An escape committee was formed because it was now certain that nobody would be left alive at the end. Regardless of whether German soldiers would be saved from freezing to death by the supply of winter clothing we were making, it seemed that the War against the Jews was even more important to the Nazis than the War against Russia.

The first plan was to wait for a dark night and to throw hand grenades into the guardroom and escape. Some would definitely reach the forest. But what about me? I could not run and I could not let myself be taken alive. So my father prepared two nooses. As soon as we heard the first explosion we would hang ourselves.

After a few nights this escape plan was dropped and a new plan was devised: to dig a tunnel 100 metres long to the other side of the barbed wire into a field of growing wheat. The work started sometime in June. The tunnel was to be 70 cm wide, and between 60 and 70 cm high. The electricians had to find a way to connect electricity in the tunnel with fuses so that they could play about with the electricity to the guardroom and searchlights. The tailors collected most of the torn blankets to make bags to carry the sand, and laces for pulling a trolley. The work went on around the clock. Wood had to be stolen from the workshops for rails and the trolley.

One morning Refoel, one of the joiners, was caught with a piece of wood under his coat. The following morning after the roll call, he was hanged by the wrists. After fainting he was revived by having water thrown over him. He was left hanging for half an hour. But that did not stop us from stealing tools and wood.

At the beginning of July 1943, my father came to me during the working day, took some belongings and said goodbye to me. He told me that they were sending him for a short while to a different camp. They took 11 skilled tradesmen, one from each trade and sent them to a Russian prisoner-of-war camp at Koldichevo. It was a very sad day for me, the parting was so quick, and to this day I see my poor father with the small packet in his hands putting on a brave face, saying he would see me soon, knowing very well that this was goodbye forever. Koldichevo was a training school for Belorussian hoodlums and therefore the worst camp in Belorussia. It is interesting to note that an order had been issued by the high authorities that this part of Belorussia was to be freed of Jews (*Judenrein*) as of 1 January 1944, but the camp commandant needed the 100 Jews in the camp. On that date while at the assembly place they were asked to remove the yellow stars, and from then on until the escape they were just called workers (*rabochie*). My father was killed, sometime in February 1944, when all the 96 Jews from Koldichevo escaped. About ten did not reach the partisans, my father among them. It was said that he committed suicide after leaving the camp. But they were not sure.

When I felt better I started to test my strength. After six months of lying still, I felt pins and needles and pain when I lowered my legs. I was very weak but tremendously determined. All the time, my wish was to know how it would all end: it did not seem possible that the free world would lose the war. If indeed that happened I would not care anymore. And I thought of the story by J. L. Perez, *Boncie Shwaig.*

First, I would arrive in heaven. There was no reason why I should go to hell as I was only 14 years old and had not done any harm to anybody. And when the question was asked: 'What would you like? You can have anything you want, anything you desire', my reply would be: *'Please can I have a fresh roll and butter.'*

As the Jewish population from the whole area had been killed, the Germans started atrocities against the Poles and Belorussians; many were arrested and sent to Germany as slave labour. It started a vicious circle, mobilisation was organised to take workers to Germany, young men ran away to the partisans, the Germans came and arrested and killed whole families to stop people running off to the forest. The more they killed, the greater the flight. On 31 July 1943 the Gestapo arrived at the monastery, arrested 11 nuns, took them to a basement opposite the prison and then early in the morning drove them to Skridlevo where they were shot. To date there is no known reason for this action; two inquiry centres were set up, one in Warsaw and the other in the Vatican.

For me, life became hard. I could more or less get around on my crutches, but I could not lie anymore on the hard boards for I was just like a skeleton. I had to live completely on charity for a slice of bread and some soup water. Even the lice on me were completely white. I had lots of help at this time, particularly from Efroim Sielubski, a saddler who had worked for our family for many years. I believe our family had acted as matchmakers between Efroim and his wife. We were very friendly.

The digging of the tunnel progressed very well. We were nearly 100 metres forward and well past the barbed wire. But suddenly there was a panic: the Germans had brought in a tractor to cut down the wheat. Would the weight of the tractor cause the tunnel to collapse? Thank God, it held out. A decision was made to dig 250 metres in total to just behind a little hill.

As it turned out, we were very lucky not to have made our escape in early August as you will find out later on when I write about 'Operation Herman'.

Nobody can imagine how much earth accumulates from such a project. First the loft was filled, then double walls were built and filled. The people responsible were very careful not to make any

СЛУГИ БОЖИИ – МАРИЯ СТЭЛЛЯ И ДЕСЯТЬ ЕЁ ПОДРУГ
ИЗ ОРДЕНА СЕСТЕР СВЯТЕЙШЕЙ СЕМЬИ ИЗ НАЗАРЕТА
Убитых в Новогрудке 1 августа 1943г. гитлеровцами.

The 11 nuns that were murdered by the Nazis on 1 August 1943
Source: Jedanascie Klecznikow Rome

mistakes which might result in all the inmates paying with their lives. They were careful to dig in a straight line, and from time to time a white stick was pushed through and watched from the loft. At the same time measurements were taken of the depth of the tunnel. The dirty condition inside the camp helped us, the commandant Reuter believing that if he stepped inside the living quarters he would catch a disease. Even before hitting a Jew he used to put on white gloves.

At the end of August there were further problems: rain was seeping through and earth was falling from the roof of the tunnel. Wood had to be stolen and some bunks destroyed to make supports. In the middle of September a meeting was called and a vote taken. There were still some who said it was better to die in the camp than to run, but the majority preferred escape. A list was drawn up. The first to go would be the tunnel diggers, followed by five of the armed men (the other five armed men would be in the rear to supervise the escape), then the strong ones and, among the last ones, Pesach Abramovitz (who had also lost his toes on one foot) and me, as it was felt that if anything happened and we blocked the tunnel we would endanger other people. I had to make a trial run and it went perfectly well. I was already walking without sticks (I had a look at my legs: they were like match sticks and I wondered how on earth they would support me). I made arrangements with Pesach Abramovitz that we would walk together (everybody talked of running, we talked of walking). Our plan was to go the same route as last time and not to follow the crowd since we would never keep up.

The planning that went into the tunnel was fantastic. While it was being built, a hiding place was dug and another place was constructed in the loft in the workshops for those who would be too weak to escape. The idea was that they could hide and perhaps escape afterwards. Most importantly, everything to do with the tunnel was kept secret from the bookkeeper, an Austrian Jew, who lived separately, because we believed him to be an informer.

We did not work on Sundays, Sunday was the day when we cleaned the camp. The escape committee had keys for the work-shops. On 19 September 1943 a meeting was called in the main hall of the workshop. Everybody turned up, someone from the escape committee talked and notified us that the tunnel would be completed the following week and weather permitting, we would make our escape then. The construction of the tunnel was an amazing project (especially when you look back and think of the way it was built, the hardship, the risk and the lack of the right tools and instruments to start and complete a 250-metre tunnel with precision). There was to be no discussion for or against escape but it was proposed to put it to the vote. There were still about 20 per cent against the escape as they did not believe that anyone would survive. The meeting lasted for just a few minutes, as we had to disperse quickly.

The longest week in my life had started but I was not scared. People were saying goodbye to each other, exchanging tips about the route and the best way to go. Some people were complaining that nobody was organising a precise escape route. It was thought, however, that if we all went our separate ways, we would stand a better chance of survival.

During the week I visited the tailoring workshop, and told them that I had my father's coat, which was originally in fact my cousin Leizer's. He had left it when he went on holiday near Minsk before the outbreak of the War. It was a lovely coat made from his Polish army coat with a fur collar. My father continued to wear it until they took him to Koldichevo. It was too big for me and I badly needed a pair of trousers and even more than the trousers I needed an extra piece of bread. I was offered both. The trousers were equally good, new, no holes. I was pleased with the deal and picked them up on Friday.

Saturday was a day of silence. It was raining on Sunday and we had confirmation that the escape would take place that evening.

26 September 1943 – our chosen day of escape. I went to the saddler's workshop and stole a belt with a holster for a German pistol. I had asked the metalworkers to make me a metal stick to lean on. Friends came to wish me a successful escape, as if I was the only one escaping. I understood what they meant; they thought that I didn't stand a chance. I could sense that they were feeling sorry for me. All of them would go away with tears in their eyes. However, I was not afraid. At about 8pm we assembled in the loft. To understand this, I must explain that we lived in two long sheds and a stable. The sheds were divided into many rooms, each with a door and a window but no communicating doors from one room to another. The only way for us to communicate was through trap doors in the ceiling into the loft. And during the night we could visit one another in this way. When the earth was dug from the tunnel, it was put in the loft on either side, leaving the middle clear for movement, and the ceiling was reinforced where the earth was placed. We assembled in the loft and formed a queue.

It was a dark and stormy night, the searchlights were cut off and some of the nails were removed from the zinc roof, to allow the wind to shake it and make a lot of rattling sounds. We assembled in a long line, according to the instructions given; from what I remember we were given numbers, and I was told to stand behind Pesach and Pesach behind someone whose name he had been

177

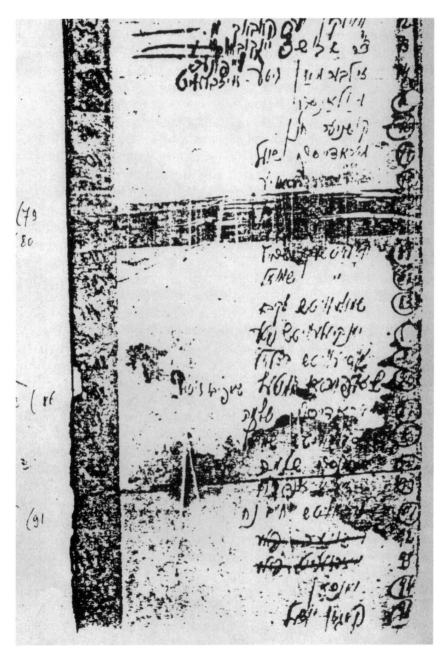

This is a list which was kept in the camp by an inmate. It was used to make up the escape list. My name (Kagan, Idel) appears at the bottom

given, and wait.... We waited about an hour. It was very quiet; and you could just make out the faces, in the semi-darkness. I sat quietly behind Pesach, and thought about my family and what had happened to us in such a short time. How strange that my mother envied her dear sister for being dead. I was hoping that my father was still alive and that maybe we would both survive this living nightmare. My only wish was not to be taken alive by the enemy.

Time passed quickly. At about 9pm a small hole was made to allow for ventilation and the line started to move forwards.

About 120 people went down into the tunnel. They sat in there for about 10 to 15 minutes until the final hole was punched through and the line started to move forward. We had not reckoned on the effect of the lighting in the tunnel. When people came out at the other end, the sudden darkness after the brightness in the tunnel disorientated them and they ran towards the camp, whereupon the guards opened fire. Although the searchlights were

A model of the labour camp. The front building houses the workshops and the sheds behind were the 'living' quarters

179

Model of the camp with the route of the tunnel

cut off, the guards still saw movement in the dark and probably thought partisans had come to liberate the camp.

When I came out of the tunnel I could see the whole field ablaze with flying bullets. I had great difficulty in following Pesach. On my later visit to Novogrodek I spoke to various people around the court-house and they all told me that the guards did not find out that we had escaped until about 4am. Reuter (the SS man in charge of Jewish affairs) turned up at 4.30am. The Belorussian guards were arrested.

The ten elderly people hidden in the loft heard the commotion early in the morning when the gate was opened and no Jews were to be found. The Germans took over. On the third day after the escape, lorries arrived and removed the machinery and raw materials and took away the German guards. On the fifth day the two groups of hidden Jews walked out through the unguarded gates and joined the partisans.

Pesach was in front of me. We stuck to our plan. We saw figures in the dark running towards the forest and we were certain that in the morning the Germans would make a search of the area. Since we would not manage to cover more than eight kilometres at most, we stood no chance of getting away. So our plan was to skirt around the town and wait on the other side. We stuck together. The fields were recently ploughed, so walking was difficult. I felt that my wounds had opened up again. The metal stick was useless because it sank into the ground when I leaned on it, so I threw it away. It was a heavy, soaking rain and I became totally drenched.

We took the same route I had taken on our first escape and crossed the same river. We saw the burned-out house of the dogcatchers. The Germans, sometime in February, found out that

*Pinie Boldo, Pesach Abramovitz and
Ishie Oppenheim after liberation*

the Bobrovskis (dogcatchers) were in contact with the partisans. The Gestapo set fire to their house and pushed the two adults into the flames and the 14-year-old girl and the 15-year-old boy were sent to Gross Rosen concentration camp in Germany. The boy died there and Maria came back, suffering from sugar diabetes, with the result that one leg had to be amputated. She now lives in Novogrodek. The Bobrovski family are among the Righteous Among Nations.

Morning started to break. We lay behind a bush and stayed there all day, about two kilometres from town. It was a sunny day but it took a long time for us to get nearly dry. We did not hear anything but saw shepherds grazing their sheep. As soon as darkness fell, we got up and went to the nearest house, knocked on the door and asked for food. I had the pistol holster on my belt that I had stolen before escaping. A man gave us a loaf of the most beautiful bread and milk. He told us that the Jews had escaped and the Germans were after them. We were very lucky! We were very hungry, but took only two bites of the bread and filled our pockets with the rest. That was the only place that we stopped for food. We drank from water puddles.

We walked for five nights in the same direction, not knowing the way. It rained a few nights and I was afraid to take off my torn shoes. Around the hole I could see hardened blood. During the day it was sunny and after a night's rain you could see steam coming off our clothes. On the morning of 1 October 1943, we started to rest after a night's walk when we saw a group of people with a cart and horses. We hid ourselves but then we heard them speaking Yiddish. I recognised Itzie Bernstein from Iveniec.

The partisans with Itzie were from the Ordzhonikidze brigade. These fighters were back from a mission and we were very lucky to have met them. How can one describe our joy? We had covered approximately 30–40 kilometres and were half way to Lida. It is impossible to calculate the odds of going into that forest, without really knowing the way, and reaching the group we were searching for. Had we fallen into the hands of the Polish partisans it would have meant death. Some Russian partisans might have shown us the direction, or even taken us to the Bielskis, but others would have just let us wander in the forest, where sooner or later somebody would have killed us.

Pesach was told that his brother had been killed in a battle with the Germans and local police. He had died bravely. I felt terribly sad for Pesach because he had been looking forward so much to meeting his brother again.

It all felt very strange to us as the night before we had finished the last grain of bread in our pockets. And now for the first time in more than two years there was no restriction on how much we could eat. I was given lots of milk but was cautioned to eat slowly, and very little at a time. They spoke from experience.

We heard about another Jewish family group headed by Zorin, which contained 800 Jews. Shimon Zorin was born in 1898 in Minsk, fought in the Communists cadres in 1918 and served as an officer in the Red Army from 1918 to 1924. He was a carpenter by trade before the War. When the Germans entered Minsk he, together with all the other Jews, was put in the Ghetto.

In 1942 he worked in a Russian prisoner-of-war camp. He befriended many former officers and Communists, and with their help and the help of Mr Smolar (a pre-war Jewish Communist in Poland, later in Russia), they helped 10,000 Jews to escape from the Minsk ghetto. Many were killed *en route* to the partisans. The children and elderly escapees found their way to Zorin and the remainder joined Russian detachments and fought the Germans. According to the Russian documents, in the Baranovichi district the Zhukov detachment had 673 partisans, among them 30 Jews; the Dzerzhinski detachment 617, among them 18 Jews; Ckapola 1,170, among them 239 Jews; Stalin 1,404, among them 140 Jews; Kirov 601, among them 150 Jews; Lenin 695, among them 202 Jews; Vperod 579, among them 106 Jews. There were very few detachments without any Jewish members. The Jews had to excel themselves in the fight against fascism and a lot of eastern Jews did not reveal their nationality; it was easier to serve as a Russian. This is just a list of the detachments in Baranovichi district – there were many others. (See documents at the end of chapter.)

The partisans took us to the base and there I was reunited with my cousin Berl. We laughed and cried at the same time. He never thought I would reach the partisans but as for myself, I was certain I would. Berl was one of the fighters in the group.

I reached the Ordzhonikidze detachment of the Kirov brigade.

Shimon Zorin, head of another Jewish family group

This was the name of the ex-Bielski fighting group of 180 men and women. It was two days before Yom Kippur. In charge of the detachment was a Russian commander, and Zush Bielski was in charge of reconnaissance. I remember that very early on the day of Yom Kippur, food was being prepared for about 30 fighters going on a mission to ambush a German convoy. After concealing themselves by the main road, they kept watch all day. But nothing happened; the road was empty, except for local movement. (By Autumn 1943, no German lorries could go singly on the highway around Novogrodek. They all had to travel in convoys as the roads

184

in that area were partisan territory and ready for ambush.)

Soon after Yom Kippur, Berl decided that we should leave the Ordzhonikidze and join the family group of the Kalinin detachment, better known as Bielski, so that we could stay together. He got permission for us to transfer, and we left the fighting group. We only had a short two-kilometre walk to reach the Kalinin group. The commander was Tuvia Bielski, and there was a Russian commissar who had been sent by General Platon, whose name was Shematovietz. Asael Bielski was second-in-command. The camp was a large temporary arrangement, with a big kitchen at its centre. I was by now well fed but I always carried a piece of bread in my pocket.

It was strange for me, seeing so many Jews in this place, quite unafraid, although it was so close to German police stations.

The reconnaissance arrived and told Bielski that the Germans and local police were on the move. That meant immediate evacuation of the camp. It could not have happened at a worse time for me. My wounds were just beginning to heal. Berl got a pair of shoes for me but I could not put them on. In the camp we had horses and carts and as I climbed onto one of the carts, I remember Tuvia Bielski riding a big horse and shouting. 'We haven't moved anywhere and the *malbush* (the name for a non-fighter) is already on the cart!' We moved out slowly in the middle of the day, a large convoy. The danger was great because we had to cross major roads. Berl decided that he and I should leave the convoy because if shooting should take place, I would not be able to run. He found out the route the convoy was taking and we left on our own, Berl, with a rifle in his hand and I with rags on my feet. Berl knew the way and we walked slowly.

We rested at my convenience but strangely enough, we covered a lot of ground. In the evening we went into a farmstead where there were other partisans. An old lady (a babushka) served us hot soup from a long metal container and everybody stood around dipping their spoons into the soup. I did not have a spoon so I had to wait until somebody had finished but by that time little was left. When I left the farmer's house I took a spoon with me. It was a similar story on the second evening: soup was served in a large container, very hot soup; I went up to this metal container, everybody had started on the soup but I could not drink it. They all

Detachment register Iveniec–Lida district

Наименование бригад, отрядов	Количество партизан	Чл. и канд. ВКП(б)	Членов ВЛКСМ	Национальность								
				Русских	Белорусов	Украинцев	Евреев	Поляков	Французов		Совхозный район	
Бриг. им. Жукова	673	55	158	131	448	73	30	9	11	4	64	40
Бриг. им. Дзержинского	617	64	142	208	322	38	18	7	24	2	9	24
Бриг. им. Чапаева	1140	139	257	472	306	79	229	5	39	11	32	90
Бриг. им. Сталина	1404	156	277	554	544	103	140	19	44	4	52	
Бриг. им. Фрунзе												
Бриг. им. Кирова	601	59	116	195	157	61	150	19	19	2	62	-
Бриг. им. Ленина	695	70	166	162	266	46	202	8	12	2	45	-
Бриг. 1го ...	1064	117	200	353	537	79	55	19	31	2	43	-
Отр. им. Кутузова	69	19	28	32	29	5	1	-	2	-	5	5
Отр. им. Дзержинского	124	1	12	10	153	1	8	1	-	-	1	2
Бриг. Ленинск. Комсомол	222	31	62	66	66	15	60	5	10	1	7	2
Бриг. "Вперед"	579	58	109	108	247	24	106	7	12	14	3	2
13 Барановск. кр. Парт.	350	22	102	45	256	14	27	4	4	1	14	3
Бриг. им. Щорса	392	37	84	72	272	24	5	5	9	1	44	
Слоним. МРЦ	295	12	49	61	212	7	11	2	2	-	14	1
Особ. Казачий	218	9	45	31	167	13	2	-	4	-	5	
											300	ор. ч/с
											Барановиче	

had wooden spoons but my spoon, being a metal one, got so hot that I had to wait for it to cool down and by that time there was very little left. I made sure from then on that I would always carry with me a deep wooden spoon tucked under my belt and later in my boots! In fact I brought one with me to Novogrodek after the liberation. My spoon was half my livelihood. We met the group on the following day and heard that shots had been exchanged with the local police. We had something to eat and moved on again to the next meeting place. I got used to sleeping in the forest without fear. We were in partisan territory which meant that we could walk during the day unless we ran into an ambush and so we carried on moving for the next few days. When it was safe enough, we rejoined the group.

Berl rejoined the Kalinin fighting group and received an order for 20 of the fighters to bring food to the Naliboki base. And so I reached the Naliboki forest. The forest was huge. We arrived at an old partisan base, met up with Pesach and found a flat piece of ground which was to be our home until a new base could be built about five kilometres away. We arrived late and I was very tired. With difficulty, I took the outer rags off my feet. 1 took off my sweater and wrapped it around my feet. We had a blanket, so we put it on the ground. I covered myself with an overcoat and fell asleep.

I woke up early in the morning. The pain from my feet was unbearable. There was frost on the ground and I felt so cold that I thought I would not survive. I took off my shirt and wrapped it around my feet but it did not help. Pesach went to the inner camp and from the kitchen there he brought me some hot water in a container. I put my feet against the container and immediately felt better.

I got up and went to the kitchen where soup was being prepared for the workers who were going to build the new base. I had a double helping of the piping hot soup and then Pesach and I had a walk round the camp.

I met a couple of friends and without telling anybody, we went to the new base. There, we found various teams at work building the huts – a task which had to be done fast before the ground froze. One team was digging large holes; they were one metre deep, five metres wide and about seven in length. The next team was preparing the wood to build roofs and another was making bunks for 50 people per hut. Some huts were already completed, and others were already occupied.

We went into an empty hut, brought in our belongings (I had only one pair of trousers and a torn towel and Pesach about the same) and made ourselves at home. The building work went on from morning to evening. For me the most important thing was the kitchen. I was constantly hungry and, luckily, getting soup was never a problem. I became friendly with Cudek, the cook. I found a large dish in which I put hot water to soften the rags from my feet. It was just like a miracle when the wounds started to heal.

When Berl arrived with the group, they brought with them lots of food, horses and cows, and gave me a sackful of food containing ham, butter, cheese and bread. On top of all that he had found me an overcoat. Berl and some friends decided to build their own hut in a drier place and within about ten days we settled in our new home. It was a nice crowd of friends, which included my uncle Notke Sucharski.

Berl was seldom at the base. His group was continuously on the move to find food. His journeys were long and dangerous. The Germans had burnt down the villages (sometimes with the inhabitants in them) around the forest and we could not take anything from the partisan region which meant that any food-taking was done in the villages near the towns, not far from German garrisons or police stations. There was no room for mercy, if we did not take some of the farmers' pigs or cows away, the Germans would. The young men risked their lives to provide food for the camp. The journey out to the operation carried a risk, but the return journey was even more hazardous. The carts were heavily loaded, the going was slow and some farmers would run to notify the police. Fortunately, the farmers never knew the strength of the groups, the figures were highly exaggerated and the police were afraid of the forest. But some unfortunate events did occur.

Sometime during the summer, a group of 11 men left the base on a mission to blow up telegraph posts and to bring back food on the return journey. They accomplished the first part. However, it took them longer than they had planned and as they were tired they decided to go and hide in a safe house, cleared by the partisan command. The house was about three kilometres from a German base. The farmer (by the name of Belaruss) greeted the partisans – after all, he was part of the organisation. He gave them food and vodka. The leader made a mistake. As they were all very tired, he did not put out a guard, but relied on the farmer. But the farmer was an antisemite and sent his son to the German commandant to tell him that Jewish 'bandits' were in his house. The Germans surrounded the house and with the farmer's help killed all of them.

When the boys did not come back, an investigation was held and it was discovered that Belaruss was responsible for their deaths. It was decided to take revenge. Asael Bielski was born on a farm, his speech and manner were those of the local farmers. Nor did he look Jewish. After an interval of three months, Asael collected men of similar background and one evening they paid a visit to the farmer.

The farmer greeted Bielski and his group. The farmer's wife prepared supper and drinking started. Asael said he did not like Jews. The farmer then told him the story of how his son went to the Germans and how he personally hit one of the Jews with an axe. At this point Bielski revealed who he was. The farmer's son tried to reach for a pistol but was stopped. Then the whole family was killed. All the farmer's relatives in the next village were also massacred. Leaflets were left in neighbouring villages that this was the punishment for betraying Jewish partisans.

Before the mission, Bielski had ordered that nothing was to be taken from the farmer, but on the way back, it was discovered that one of the men had disobeyed Bielski's order and taken the farmer's new jacket. Emptying the pockets he found a congratulatory certificate from Gebietskommissar Traub and a reward of 100 German Marks. (This letter was handed over to the partisan headquarters, and it should now be in the war museum at Minsk.)

Usually when Berl came back to the base he was so tired he could hardly move. He would take off his clothes, which I was surprised did not walk on their own, they were so full of lice. I used to put everything in boiling water and brush the bugs away afterwards. To keep warm he wore two pairs of trousers and did not undress for the duration of the mission, which usually lasted 10 to 14 days.

A partisan group (with the help of a young servant) assassinated the well-guarded General Kommissar Wilhelm Kube who was the

Group of Bielski partisans

big boss of Belorussia. He was killed on 21 September 1943, news of which reached us about a month later. We were very happy about it, but at the same time knew that the Germans would take revenge by murdering hundreds of innocent people.

The base developed into a little town, with a bakery, a salami-maker, shoe workshops, tailoring and engineering workshops and, later, a tannery. Partisans from all over the region used to come to Bielski, to repair their guns, shoes and uniforms, and exchange flour for bread, cows for salami. The Bielski group became a productive unit and helped the partisans in their fight against the Germans. I did all sorts of work in the camp. We had plenty of entertainment as the Russian partisans used to put on shows. By the middle of 1943, the partisans were a properly organised body ruled from Moscow. Major General Platon, with various high-ranking officers, visited our camp and were very satisfied with what they saw; it was a productive camp, helping in the war effort. We even had a partisan airport not far from us, where planes used to land to pick up wounded men and women. It was the task of Bielski's group to guard the airport. With the help of many kilos of sausages as barter, Bielski managed to get modern weapons from the pilots. At this point I too managed to get a rifle.

191

Bielski had to report everything to headquarters. And below is one of his reports, followed by its translation:

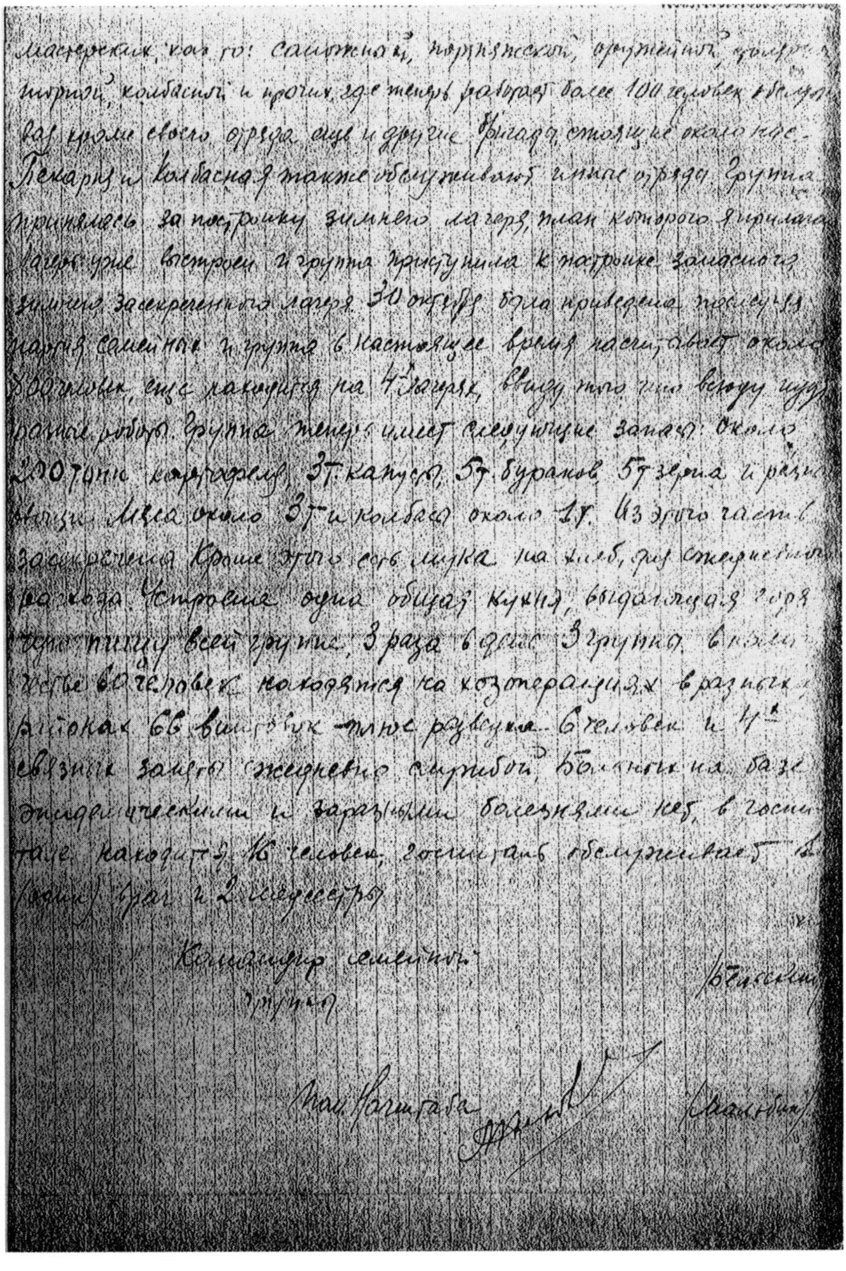

Abs.secret   94

Kirov Partisan Brigade

Detachment named after S.Ordzhonikidze

Family Group N-ki dense forest

   5-12-43

N 0020

Report to the Commander of the Kirov Partisan

Brigade Capt. Comr. Vasiljev

on work carried out

On September 17, 1943 on having gathered together the family group of 250 people and having left a fighting unit with the whole Staff in the area of our operation, according to the order of the brigade's staff and taking into account the impossibility of the coexistence of the detachment and families in the area of hostilities, I returned them to the old base in the Naliboki Dense Forest. Having arrived at the place I found out that the group of 36 people which I had left had grown to 63 people and was engaged in digging up potatoes for their own needs and building a summer camp. Having come to the representative of the CCCP/b/B in Ivenec Inter-district centre, in whose district the camp is situated, I started to build a base for 700-800 people. In addition, I received an order to gather together all the families, which were in the dense forest and in Stolpcy and Mir districts numbering about 100 people. We at once began a planned stocking-up of potatoes and building a winter camp. Taking into account our situation, we immediately started up a bakery and a mill of our own, seeing that part of the dense forest had been burnt down during the round-up. Moreover, we started to arrange different workshops: shoemakers, tailors, gunsmith, joiners, saddlers, sausage-making, and so on, where more than 100 people are working now serving other brigades located near us apart from our own detachment. The bakery and the sausage-making department serve the other detachments. The group began to build a winter camp, the plan of which is enclosed.

   The camp is already built and the group began to build a secret reserve, a winter one. On October 30 the last family group was brought in and now the group has about 800 people, it is still in 4 camps insofar as different kinds of work are carried out everywhere. Now the group has the following stockpiles: about 200 tons of potatoes, 3 tons of cabbages, 5 tons sugar beet, 5 tons of grain and different vegetables, about 3 tons of meat and 1 ton of sausages. Part of it is kept in a secret place. In addition, there is flour for bread for everyday use. There is one common kitchen, which provides hot food for the whole group 3 times a day. Three groups of 60 people are on economic operation in different districts. Sixty-six riflemen plus reconnaissance of 6 people and 4 messengers are on daily service. There are no epidemically or infectiously ill people on the base; there are 16 people in hospital, 1 doctor and 2 nurses work in the hospital.

Commander of the family group. Belski

Assistant to the Chief of Staff. Malbin

Source: Central National Archives (Partisan section) Minsk

This was the plan of our camp:

Map of the Bielski Otriad in Nalibocka Forest
During the Last Phase of Its Existence
(Fall 1943–Summer 1944)

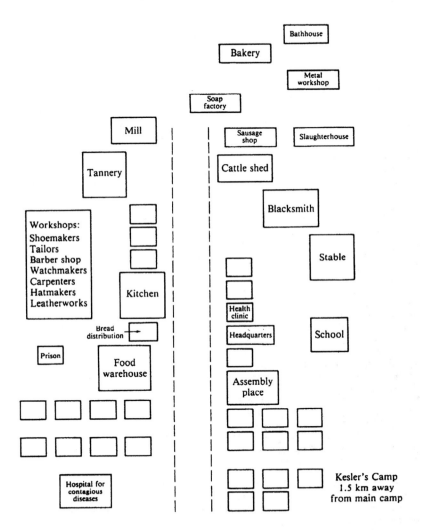

Unidentified structures are living quarters; all other structures are identified by the particular function each served.

This map is based on information provided by Chaja Bielski.

Plan of Bielski detachment

From the middle of 1943 there was a great influx of new partisans, many of whom were genuine young men ready to fight to liberate their territory from the German murderers who were killing, raping and destroying everything in their path and sending young men and women as slave labour to Germany. Among these genuine people, however, the Germans had posted a host of spies and below is a translation of a warning letter written by the Sidorok, the representative of the Belorussian Partisans.

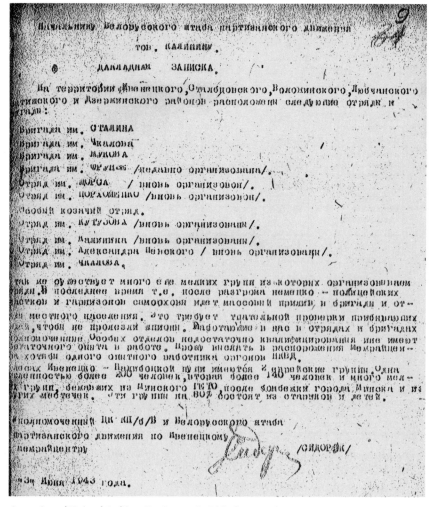

Source: Central National Archives (Partisan section) Minsk

To the Chief of Staff of the Belorussian Partisan Movement
Comr. Kalinin.

Report

The following detachments and brigades are stationed on the
territory of Ivenec, Stolpcy, Volozhin, Lubcha, Juradishki,
and Dzerzhinsk district:
Stalin Brigade
Chkalov Brigade
Zhukov Brigade
Frunze Brigade
Detachment Shchors (newly organised)
Detachment Porchomenko (newly organised)
Special Cossack detachment
Detachment Kutuzov (newly organised)
Detachment Kalinin
Detachment Alexander Nevski
Detachment Chkalov

There are also many small groups, which are in the process
of being organised into detachments. Last time, i.e. after
the crushing defeat of the German and police sectors and
self-protection garrison, there was a mass influx of the
local population to the brigades and detachments. The people
coming in must be thoroughly examined in order not to let
spies in.

Representatives of Special Departments working in our
detachments and brigades are not qualified or experienced
enough in the work, so I am asking you to send at least one
experienced worker of the NKVD to be at the disposition of
the Inter-district centre.

There are 2 Jewish groups in the forests of Ivenec-
Naliboki dense forest. One group contains more than 200
people, the other has more than 140 people and there are
many small groups, that escaped from the Minsk ghetto after
the bombing of Minsk and other towns. These groups consist
of 80 per cent old people and children.

Representative of the CCCP/b/B and Belorussian Partisan
Movement Headquarters on Ivenec Inter-district centre.

June 3, 1943   / Sidorok/

At the beginning of July 1943 German soldiers and the SS started
to arrive in the Novogrodek area, and the partisans from the
district moved to the Naliboki dense forest. The Germans kept on
bringing in troops to Molodechno-Lida, Dzerzhinsk and Stolpci,
Novogrodek and Baranovichi. According to the records of the
Partisan movement in Belorussia the Germans brought in 52,000
front-line soldiers, which included SS brigades and local police.

They started their offensive on 13 July and finished on 8 August. The code name of the operation was 'Herman'. Their aim was to wipe out the partisans from the area around Novogrodek, Lida, Iveniec and Naliboki.

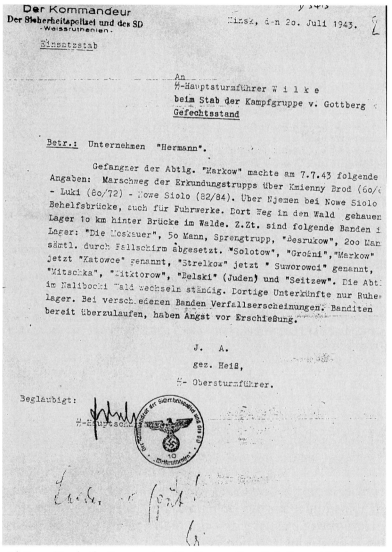

A letter written by the Commander of the German Security Police and SD during Operation 'Herman'

Source: Special Moscow Archive 500-1-769 p. 218. Commander of German Security Police to SS Hauptsturmführer Wilke

The translation follows.

```
The Commander                              D3413

of the Security Police and of the SD    Minsk, 20 July 1943.

White Russia.

Combatstaff

                    To

                    SS-Hauptsturmführer WILKE

                    with the Staff of Combat Group v. Gottberg

                    Incident Report

Re: Operation 'Herman'
```

Prisoner belonging to Section 'Markov' on 7.7.43 made the following statement: The route of march of the reconnaissance troops over Kmienny Brod (60/6)- Luki (80/72) — Nowe Siolo (82/84). Over the Njeman at Nove Siolo is an auxiliary bridge, usable also by vehicles. From there a path has been cleared into the forest. The camp is 10 km from the bridge, into the forest.

At the present time, the following Bands are in the camp: 'The Moscowers', 50 men, demolition troops, 'Besrukow', 200 men, all parachuted in. 'Solotow' now known as 'Suworowci', 'Mitschka', 'Witkorow', 'Belski' (Jews) and 'Seitzew'. The sections in the Nalibocki forest change constantly. The quarters there are only a rest camp. Some bands display a low morale. Bandits are prepared to surrender but are afraid of being shot.

```
                    J.A.

                    Signed: Heiss

                    SS. Obersturmführer
```

Confirmed: (Signature)

SS Hauptscharführer

(written by hand) 'Regret too late'

At the beginning the partisans worked together in blocking all the roads so as not to let the German lorries or tanks into the forest. When an order was given by the high command to fight a joint battle, Bielski sent 200 fighters to the united front. By the time they had assembled, it was revealed that a few battles had already taken place with partisan losses. When the leaders realised the strength of the German forces, they ordered the groups not to fight with the Germans. Each group was to act independently, to retreat and avoid contact with the enemy. It was the right decision. For the Russian detachment it was easy to retreat in an orderly fashion and by-pass the Germans with the help of the local population, but for the Bielski group there was a great problem in a fast retreat owing to the number of elderly people and children, so to follow the Russian detachment would spell disaster. The Bielski brothers kept calm and did not panic although the Germans were not far away and kept up a barrage of fire. Mr Milashevski from the Polish detachment and a neighbour of the Bielskis came to say goodbye to Tuvia whom he told to be brave. Retreating Polish and Russian partisans told Tuvia to move fast since the Germans were not far away and would be certain to reach that point the next morning, but Bielski knew that he must not follow them.

People started to panic. Tuvia begged them not to lose their heads and to keep together. 'You must listen to me', he said, 'I will bring you out of here alive.'

Two partisans, Michael Mechlis and Akiva Shimonovitz, approached Tuvia, and they suggested crossing the swamps to a small island called Krasnaya Gorka. They were certain that the Germans would not go into the swamps. Mechlis was a forest surveyor before the War and knew the forest well, and Shimonovitz was a peddler in the area of Naliboki and also knew the shortcuts in the forest.

Bielski immediately ordered the cows and horses to be let loose. He opened the food store so that everybody could take as much bread, flour, beans and grains as they could carry in their pockets or in little bags. He asked everyone to form a line and told them that they were going to march into the swamps. As soon as they reached them, the children would have to be carried on the shoulders of the adults, elderly people would have to be roped together with the young, and the rifles would have to be kept dry.

Mechlis and a few armed men went first, followed by the people with children. They walked into the swamp which became deeper by the minute. It took an hour to cover just one kilometre, so from time to time they rested. The island was about 10 to 12 kilometres away; they kept on moving in a slow, quiet procession as ordered. Bullets flew past their heads, they heard Germans shouting, but the group kept moving deeper into the mud and further away from the Germans. They had to rest often, to lean against the bushes and fall asleep. Tuvia asked them not to eat the food they had taken as it would have to last a long time. After a long trek through the swamps they reached the 'paradise' island of Krasnaya Gorka and dry land, with the sun shining and far from the enemy. A count took place when a few were found to be missing, but after a search in the area everybody was located. Shooting was heard in the far distance and artillery shells started falling over our heads. Bielski again begged us to be quiet: even if a shell should explode nearby we had to maintain order otherwise we would not survive.

After a few days food was running short. People were eating grass and drinking the swamp water which made them feel ill. After six days in the swamps it became quiet. Tuvia sent his brother Zush with 80 armed men to look for food and to find out about the situation in general.

Zush came back the following day with some wonderful news. He had seen the Germans packing up and leaving their base. The villages were in flames. He brought some food which was distributed, and the detachment was split up into small groups to leave the swamps and search the area for food and eventually to meet at the old base. In this big hunt after the partisans that lasted for 35 days (according to the encyclopaedia Belarus in the Great Patriotic War 1941–1945 published in Minsk, 1990), 130 partisans were killed and 50 wounded. The fascists killed 4,280 persons from the local population; 654 were arrested by the security and SD; 20,944 people, among them 4,173 children, were taken to Germany; and more than 150 villages were set on fire sometimes with their inhabitants, among them Delatichi and Kupisk from the Novogrodek area.

The Bielski detachment came out without any losses.

Zorin lost quite a few of his members, but the detachment survived. I believe the Russian figures were not accurate and that there were more casualties than the 130 quoted.

In the forest the Jewish partisans had another enemy – the White Poles. Their slogan was 'Poland without Jews and Communists', and many Jews who managed to escape from the ghettos were killed by them.

Following is Bielski's report on one of their battles.

Экз. №3

76

АКТ

Составлен 20 мая 1944г. в том, что группа конных разведчиков партизанского отряда им. Калинина в количестве 12 человек под командованием к-ра боевой группы Бельского Александра Давидовича и начальника штаба Мальбина Лазаря Абрамовича дня 18 мая 1944г. в 20 часов по распоряжению командира бригады им. Чапаева майора тов. Кузрина, отступив с селом из Айлиловских хуторов, залегла в засаду около дер. Кривичи. Группа встретила огнем приближающуюся колонну белополяков и после обстрела отступила.

По сведениям жителей дер. Кривичи убито 6 человек количество раненых не установлено.

Жертв со стороны нашей группы не было.

В засаде участвовали:

1. Бельский Александер Давидович - ком. боевой группы.
2. Мальбин Лазар Абрамович - нач. штаба.

Source: Central National Archives (Partisan section) Minsk

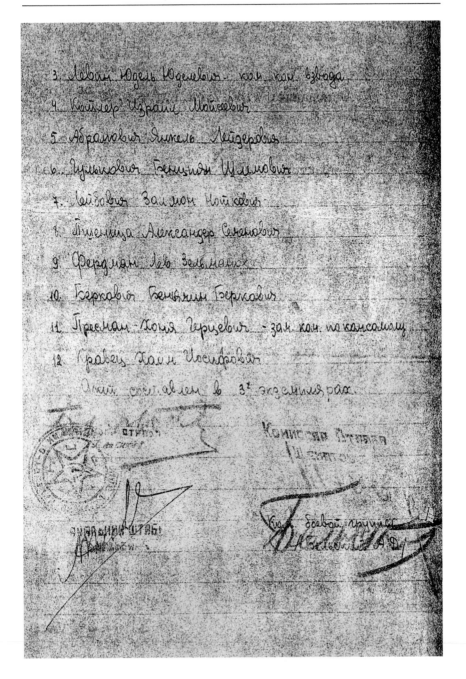

3. Левин Юдель Юделевич - ком. ком. взвода
4. Кайлер Израил. Мойсеевич
5. Абрамович Янкель Лейдеровиз
6. Цимкович Бенцион Шломович
7. Лейзович Залман Нойкович
8. Пшеница Александер Семенович
9. Фердман Лев Зельманич
10. Беркович Бенькиин Беркович
11. Пресман Хоня Геузевич - зак ком. по комсомлу
12. Гравец Хаи Иосифовна

Акт составлен в 3х экземплярах.

Transmitted on 26.5.44   Copy 3   76

Statement N 12

It is hereby reported that on May 20 1944, a group of mounted scouts from the Kalinin partisan detachment including 12 people under the command of the fighting group commander Bielski Alexander Davidovich and the Chief of staff Malbin Lazar Abramovich on 18 May 1944 at 20 hours having retreated from the fighting from the Atminovo farmsteads laid an ambush near the village of Krivichi by order of the commander of the Chapaev brigade, Major Comr. Kudrin. The group met the advancing column of the White Poles with fire and being fired on they retreated.

According to information from residents of the village of Krivichi 6 people were killed, the number of wounded has not been established.

There were no victims among our group.

The following took part:

1. Bielski Alexander Davidovich Chief of fighting Davidovich
2. Malbin Lazar Abramovich Chief of Staff
3. Levin Judel Judelevich Commander of the mounted platoon
4. Kotler Israel Leizerovich
5. Abramovich Yankiel Leizerovich
6. Gulkovich Benzion Shlemovich
7. Leibovich Zalman Notkovich
8. Pshenica Alexander Semionovich
9. Ferdman Lev Zelmanovich
10. Berkovich Benjamen Berkovich
11. Presmann Chonya Gerzevich
12. Kraviec Chaim Isifovich

The statement is drawn up in 3 copies

Commander of the detachment   Commissar of the detachment

   /Bielski/   /Shemyatovec/

Chief of Staff   Commander of Fighting Group

   / Malbin/   /Bielski A.D./

Yudel Levin, Commander of the Mounted Platoon, and Yankiel Abramovich
Source: Museum Novogrodek

Below is a German announcement in Novogrodek about their victory over the partisans printed 30 July 1943. Propaganda lies were rife. An English translation follows.

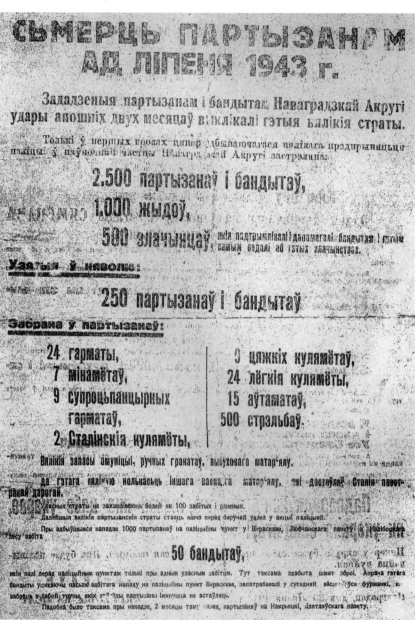

У гэтых баях расстрэляна шмат правадыроў бандытаў
і партызанаў.

Страйкоў быў забіты за свае злачынствы у Наваельні.

.....зны на .....романі.

Кузьмін быў забіты пад Верасковам.

Міцька, Польскі палкоўнік, забіты над Немнам.

Ключкоў правадыр брыгады Жукава, застрэляны.

Далей зьнішчаны нач. штабу брыгады **СЯМЁНАВА**
і правадыр кампаніі группы „Комсамольская".

Шмат іншых бандыцкіх правадыроў акружаны разам з іхнім штабамі і з іхнімі усімі бандытамі і будуць абавязкова зьнішчаны.

Восьма Сталінскім партызанам пэўна прыйдзецца .... як .... пасланы на вечную Чырвонай Арміі на фронце, якая ужо цэлыя вест-і зтрымлюе страты ....

Так ісьцяцца учыненыя над насельніцтвам злачынствы бальшавікоў!
Так .... терор бандытаў!

Так нясуць помсту нямецкія часьці за замардаваных партызанамі і бандытамі

мужоў, кабет і дзяцей-

За зрабаваную маёмасьць і добро, за спаленыя хаты, школы і гаспадаркі і за усе іншыя зробленыя злачынствы

За крыўду над соцкімі, настаўнікамі, духоўнымі і ся-
лянамі.

Бандытаў так праследавалі у апошніх тыднях што большыя іх группы у вычарпаным аусім стане пнайшлі у балота, ружжа і уцяклі да Нямецкіх часьцей ....

Я ранеі .... Кара наступіла

Я .... наступяць кары.
Усе бандыты ідуць насустрэч пэўнай сьмерці!

А таксама тыя, якія ўспамагаюць бандытаў і не слухаюць загадаў дзяржавы, яны будуць у будучыні тракта-
вацца як партызаны і бандыты.

Кожны сабе адумай, ці-ж хто захоча упарадкаваныя існаванне пад асланай дзяржавы прамяняць на праследаванне, прысу-........ на самоць духоўныя бандыты

Падпарадкуйся дзяржаве, іначай яна цябе укарае,
як укарала бандытаў!

Ципер у акрузе будзе стала працаваць нямецкая паліцыя. Яна будзе надзвы-
чайна чуйная.

падп **Т Р А У Б**

Наўградак, дня 30 ліпеня 1943 г.   АКРУГОВЫ КАМІСАР

German documents from Soviet archives. This is a reproduction of the poster put out by German Nazis in Novogrodek

Source: Central National Archives (Partisan section) Minsk

DEATH TO PARTISANS
OF JULY 1943

Strikes against partisans and bandits of the Novogrudok Akruga (region) during the last two months caused these great losses.

During the first steps only of the great action undertaken by the police in the northern part of the Novogrudok region were shot:

2500 –	partisans and bandits
1000 –	Jews
500 –	criminals who supported and helped the bandits and thus knew about these crimes

Arrested:

250 –	partisans and bandits

Taken away from the partisans:

24 cannons
7 mortars
9 antitank guns
2 Stalin machine guns
9 heavy machine guns
24 light machine guns
I5 sub-machine guns
500 rifles

Large stocks of ammunition, hand grenades, explosives and in addition a great amount of various other military materials provided by Stalin by air.

Our own losses do not exceed more than 100 killed and wounded.

Other great partisan losses were caused by the police, who took part in the action.

During the attack by 1000 partisans on the police post in Vereskovo, Lubcz district from the Naliboki forest were killed:

Fifty bandits fell before the police post with one person killed on our side only. A lot of weapons were taken here as well. Moreover, bandits running away after the repelled attack on the police post in Vereskovo took all the carts from the neighbouring village in order to take the bodies of the killed with them, which partisans always try not to leave behind.

The same happened during the partisans' attack on Nakryshki, Diatlovo povet two months ago.

During the fights many leaders of bandits and partisans were shot.

Stralkov –	killed for his crimes in Novojelnia
Grozny –	punished by death for his bloody crime on lake Kroman
Kuzmin –	near Vereskovo
Mit'ka –	Polish Lieutenant-Colonel, killed near the Niemen
Klynchko –	Commander of Zhukov's brigade

The Chief of Staff of Semyonov's brigade and the leader of the group 'Komsomolskaya' were also destroyed.

A lot of other bandit leaders together with their staff and all their bandits are surrounded and will surely be destroyed.

Stalin's partisans behind the front line do not feel any better for the fact that the Red Army in the front has been bearing losses for two months already without achieving any success in the offensive.

Thus the Bolsheviks' crimes over the civil population are avenged!

Thus the bandits' terror suffers!

Thus German units will take revenge for those killed by partisans and bandits:

men, women and children.

For the stolen property and goods, for burnt administrative buildings, schools and farms and all the other crimes committed.

For the offence given to the administration, teachers, clergy and peasants.

Bandits have been so hard-pressed during the last two weeks, that the largest of their groups totally exhausted, threw their weapons into the marshes and ran to the German units.

I have warned you beforehand, punishment has come, I am warning you further!

There will be more Punishment!

All the bandits are advancing towards certain death!

Also all those who help the bandits and do not listen to the orders of the state, will be considered partisans and bandits themselves in the future.

Be **obedient** to the state, otherwise it will punish you as those bandits.

Now the German police will be working constantly in the region. They will be extraordinarily attentive.

Lieutenant-Colonel Traub

Commissar

Novogrudok, July 30, 1943

That was the last large German offensive against the partisans in the Novogrodek–Lida area.

We heard the good news about the Second front. At the beginning of June 1944 all partisan brigades were ordered by Moscow to blow up German trains, to prevent the Germans bringing reinforcements to the front line.

While I was in Belorussia in July 1996 I found various documents about Bielski's activities, and is one of the documents of that time is shown here. Its translation follows.

Нач. Уполномоченного Центрального
Партизанского Движения и ЦК КП(б)Б по
Барановичской области.

тов. Соколову

Лидская Зона.

Боевое донесение.

22 июня

Доношу что группа партизан отряда им. М.И. Калинина
Лидской Зоны в количестве 7 человек ст. группы Кукелко Люба
минер Баран Беньямин участники Берман Яков Слуцкий ...
Слодер Эфроим Пальман Хил... Борецкий Иосель в ночь с 14 на
15 июня с.г. заминировала жел. дорожное полотно на линии
Лида - Молодечно возле станции Ча... 15 июня в 3 часа спущен
под откос вражеский эшелон следовавший из Молодечно в Лиду
повреждён паровоз и 14 вагона санитарных. Количество убитых
и раненых не установлено. Движение поездов приостановлено на
6 часов.

Той же группой, ту же ночь на том же месте заминиро-
вало жел. дорожное полотно и 15 июня в 7 часов спущен под
откос вражеский эшелон следовавший из Лиды в Молодечно, повреж-
ден паровоз и 5 вагонов с воен. техникою. Движение поездов
приостановлено на 8 часов.

Вышеуказанное подтверждено проводником Змитровичем Владис-
лавом, жителем хутора Застенок около дер. Русаки Ивьевского р-на.

Командир отряда
(Белоский)

Комиссар отряда
(Шентявец)

Ст. группы

To the Central Staff of the Partisan Movement and CCCP/6/B Representative of the Baranovichi region comr. Sokolov.

Lida Zone.

Fighting dispatch.

I report, from a group of partisans from the detachment M.I. Kalinin, Lida Zone, including 7 people, the man in charge of the group is

Kukelko Anton, Miner, Baran Benjamin.

Participants: Berman Jacov, Slucki Judel, Sinder Efraim, Golman Nina, Borecki Josel mined the railway on the Lida–Molodechno line near the station of Gavja on the night of 14-15 June. On the 15th at 3 o'clock an enemy echelon going from Molodechno to Lida was derailed, the locomotive and 4 sanitary carriages were derailed. The number of killed and wounded has not been established. The movement of trains was stopped for 6 hours.

The same group on the same night and in the same place mined the railway on June 15 at 7 o'clock and derailed an enemy echelon going from Lida-Molodechno; a locomotive and 5 carriages with military materiel were damaged. The movement of trains was stopped for 8 hours.

The above is confirmed by messenger Zmitrovich Vladislav, a resident of farmstead Zastenok near the village of Rusaki, Ivje district.

Commander of the detachment	Commissar of the detachment
/Bielski/	/ Shemyatovec /
Chief of Staff	Chief of the Group
/Malbin/	/Kukelko/

The Bielski group took an active part in fighting the enemy and in committing various acts of sabotage which included blowing up bridges and cutting down telegraph posts. Over a period of six months in 1944 the Bielski fighters stopped the German trains for 51 hours, which is a great achievement. While all partisan groups were known by the name of the group – for example, Stalintsy or Octyabr – the Bielski group was always referred to as Bielski and not Kalinin; as I am now in possession of headquarters documents I can verify that this is so.

At 4 o'clock on the morning of 22 June 1944, exactly three years after the Nazis started the terrible war against Russia, the Red Army began the great offensive on the Belorussian front. On

3 July, Minsk was liberated. When lying on the ground we could already hear the sound of artillery and so we prepared for a fight with the German army as we knew their retreat would be through the forest. Sure enough, one morning a large retreating group of Germans broke through our reinforcements. Unfortunately, ten of our members were killed.

On the following day, we heard that the Russian army was in Novogrodek. We were pleased that the nightmare was over but each one of us felt terribly sad. We were not returning to the unknown because we all knew what we would find in Novogrodek – a destroyed town without Jews and the people we had known before the War. Maybe they would be glad that we had survived and would say in Belorussian 'Aty jeshcio zywiosh?' '(You are still alive?').

It was decided that we should return to Novogrodek. Bielski requested that everybody should march out from the forest in an organised body and go through large villages and small towns in this way. And so it was. I walked without difficulty the 100–120 kilometres to Novogrodek and, thanks to Tuvia, Zush, Asael and Archik Bielski, 1,230 Jews arrived in the suburbs of the town on 16 July 1944.

Document dated 17 July 1944 stating that Idel Kagan was in the Kalinin Partisan Brigade
Source: Central National Archives (Partisan section) Minsk

213

A decision was made not to go into town until the next day. Although we were free, nobody talked or laughed or sang. We were all sad.

The following morning we received documents and were released from the group. Bielski went against his orders in doing this.

Some Reports from the Kalinin Partisan Detachment

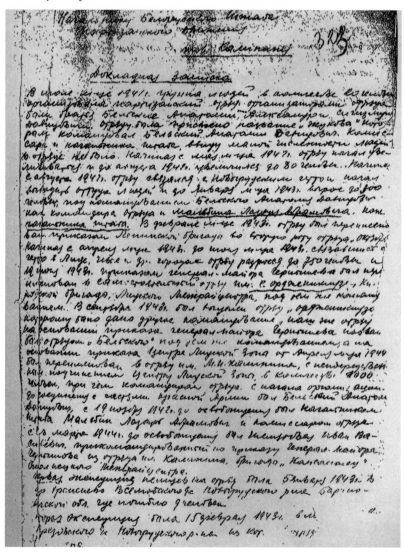

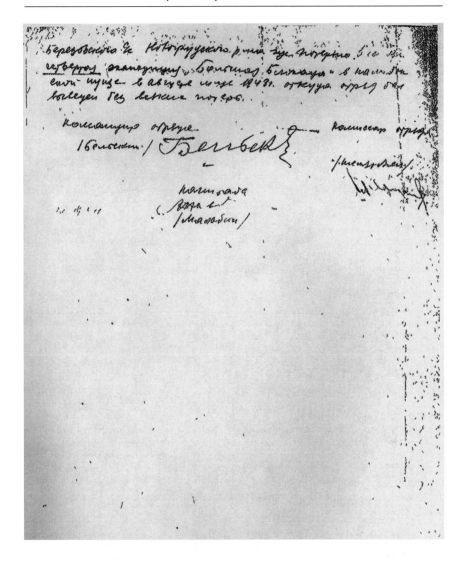

To the Chief of Belorussian Staff

of the Partisan Movement

Comrade Kalinin.

In July 1941 a group of 20 people organised a partisan
detachment. The organisers of the detachment were the
Bielski brothers, Anatoli, Alexander and Sigizmund
Davidovichi. The detachment was given the name of Zhukov,

with Anatoli Davidovich Bielski in charge. There was no
Commissar/ enlistment officer / and no chief of staff in the
detachment in view of the small number of people.

From May 1942 onwards the detachment began to grow and by
August 1942 the detachment put itself in touch with the
Novogrodek ghetto and began to take people out of it and by
January 1943 it grew to 300 people under the command of
Anatoli Davidovich as Commander and Malbin Lazar Abramovich
as Chief of Staff. In February 1943 the detachment was
renamed into the second company of the 'Octyabr' detachment
by order of the Lenin brigade. From April 1943 to June 1943
on having put itself in touch with the ghettos in Lida, Ivje
and other towns, the detachment grew to 750 people and on
1 June 1943 by the order of Major-General Chernyshev it
became an independent detachment renamed Ordzhonikidze,
Kirov brigade, Lida Inter-district centre under the same
command. In September 1943 the Ordzhonikidze detachment was
separated and given another command, and on Major-General
Chernyshev's order, our detachment was named the Bielski
detachment under the same command and by order of the Lida
Zone Centre of April 1944 it became the Kalinin with direct
subordination to the Lida Zone Centre with 1,000 people. The
commander of the detachment from its inception to joining
the Red army units was Bielski Anatoli Davidovich, and from
November 1942 to the Liberation the Chief of Staff was
Malbin Lazar Abramovich and Commissar of the detachment from
18 March 1944 to the liberation was Shemyatovec Ivan
Vasiljevich attached by Major-General Chernyshev's order
from the Kalinin detachment, brigade of Komsomolec Stolpcy
Inter-district centre.

The first German expedition against the detachment took
place on 5 January 1943 in the village of Chrepenovo and
Vsielub village, Soviet Novogrudok district, Baranovichi
region where 9 people were killed.

The second expedition was on 15 February 1943 in the
forest village of Berezovka, Soviet Novogrudok where 5
people were lost.

The fourth expedition was 'The big Blockade' in the
Naliboki dense forest in August 1943, from which the
detachment was withdrawn with no losses.

Commander of the detachment   Commissar of the detachment
        /Bielski/   /Shemyatovec/

It is strange that Bielski does not mention the third German
expedition – probably as it was not directed against the Lida zone
the detachment suffered no losses in it. It must be taken into
account that in the Ordzhonikidze detachment over 230 Jewish

fighters survived who had originated from the Bielski Detachment, where Zush Bielski had been in charge of reconnaissance.

It is only thanks to the fantastic heroic leadership of the Bielski brothers and the leaders that the losses were so few.

This is a list of the people in charge of the detachment that I found in Yivo document centre in New York.

Source: Central National Archives (Partisan section) Minsk

Commander of the detachment: Tuvia Bielski
Second in command: Asael Bielski
Chief of Staff: Malbin Lazar
Secretaries to the Chief of Staff: Kaplinska Raya, Bedzovski
Israel, Veiner Abraham
Quartermaster: Friedberg Pesach
Commissar: Shematovietz Ivan Vasilievich
Chief of Sabotage: Feldman Leibush
Chief of Special Operations: Wolkoviski Solomon
Section Head and Instructors: Bielski Yehuda, Shlosberg,
Ostashinski Eliyahu
Commander of the Camp: Potashnik Max
Head of Reconnaissance: Levin Yehuda
Reconnaissance 1st Section Leader: Reznik Moshe
Reconnaissance 2nd Section Leader: Abramovich Yakov
Section Leaders: Abramovich Chaim, Navicki
In Charge of the Medical Section: Dr Isler Hehrik
His Assistant: Dr Hirsh
Workshop Manager: Kaback Maciek
Responsible for Food Supply: Gershovski Mordechai
Kitchen Manager: Rosenhous Itzhak
Building Manager: Engineer Ribinski
and there were managers for each trade in the workshops.

A fascinating report from Feigelman, the Commissar of Zorin's detachment, to headquarters is reproduced, along with its translation. All this took place under the very noses of the German occupiers, their forces were not far away, their spy organisation was excellent. They knew that groups of Jews were quite close, yet they could do very little about it. Life in the forest went on in a normal way. Their air force, tanks and artillery were of no use to them.

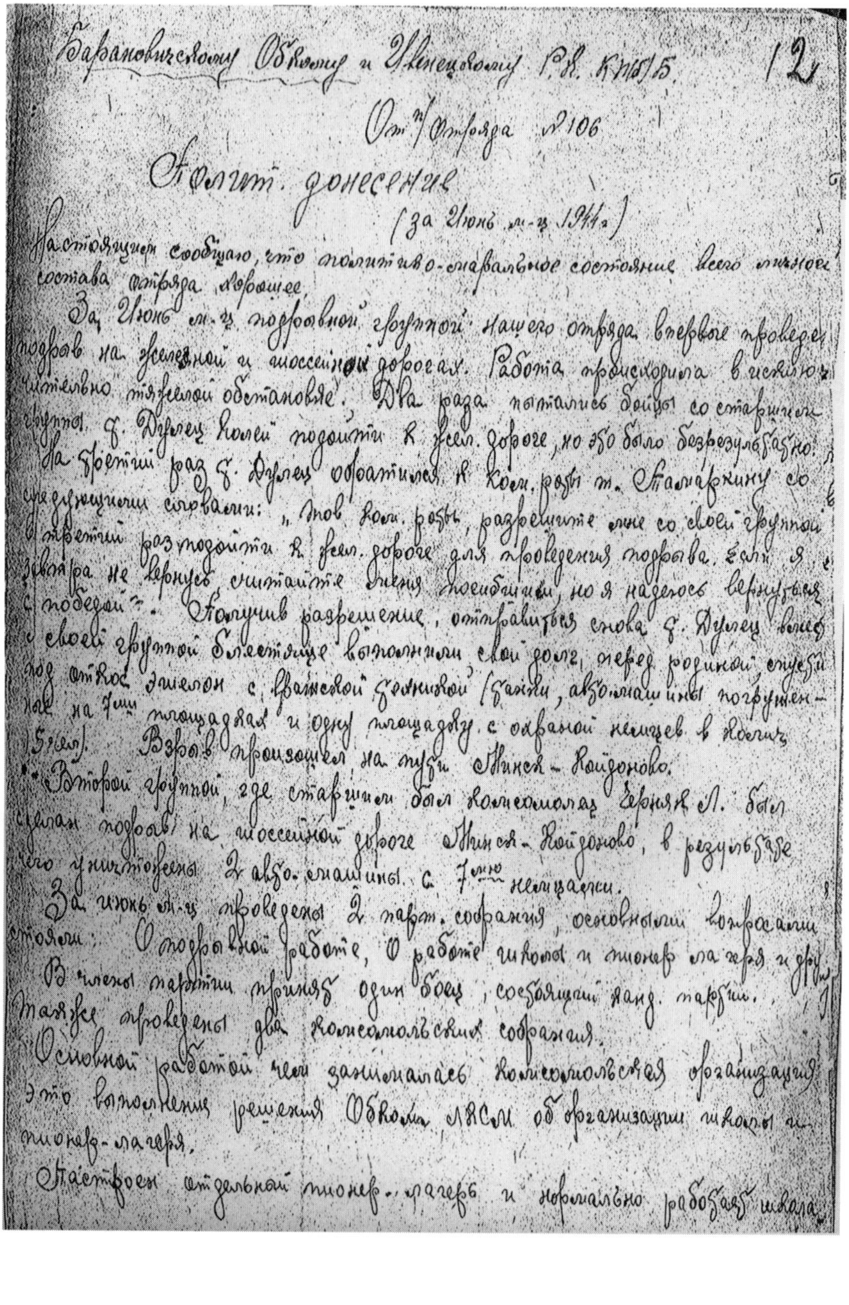

Барановичскому Обкому и Ивенецкому Р.К. КП(б)Б. 12

От п/отряда №106

Политдонесение

(за Июнь м-ц 1944 г.)

Настоящим сообщаю, что политико-моральное состояние всего личного состава отряда хорошее.

За Июнь м-ц подрывной группой нашего отряда впервые проведен подрыв на железной и шоссейной дорогах. Работа происходила в исключительно тяжелой обстановке. Два раза пытались бойцы со старшим группы т. Дулец пойти подойти к жел. дороге, но это было безрезультатно. На третий раз т. Дулец обратился к ком. роты т. Татаркину со следующими словами: „тов. ком. роты, разрешите мне со своей группой третий раз подойти к жел. дороге для проведения подрыва. Если я завтра не вернусь, считайте меня погибшим, но я надеюсь вернуться с победой". Получив разрешение, отправился снова т. Дулец вместе с своей группой блестяще выполнили свой долг перед родиной, спустили под откос эшелон с вражеской техникой (танки, автомашины погруженные на 7ми площадках и одну площадку с охраной немцев в количестве 15 чел). Взрыв произошел на пути Минск-Койданово.

Второй группой, где старшим был комсомолец Черняк Л. был сделан подрыв на шоссейной дороге Минск-Койданово, в результате чего уничтожены 2 авто-машины с 7мью немцами.

За июнь м-ц проведены 2 парт. собрания, основными вопросами стояли: О подрывной работе, О работе школы и пионер лагеря и др.

В члены партии принят один боец, состоявший канд. партии.

Также проведены два комсомольских собрания.

Основной работой чем занималась комсомольская организация это выполнение решения Обкома ЛКСМ об организации школы и пионер-лагеря.

Настроен отдельный пионер-лагерь и нормально работает школа.

стр 2

В школе имеется 5 групп охватывающих свыше 80 детей. 13

Для работы школы и пионер-лагеря подобран соответствующий педагогич. персонал, хорошо справляющиеся с своей работой.

При открытии пионер-лагеря, силами детей были подготовлены монтаж (пение, декломации и танцы). Детьми написан рапорт на имя т. Сталина. (который при сем прилагается).

В текущем си-це было выступление агит. бригады Лидского Межд. райцентра.

За это время в отряде выпущено 4 номера стенных газет т.б.з две обще-отрядных и две в пионер-лагере.

Среди всех бойцов отряда проводится систематически раз'яснительная работа, как читка сводок и газет, проведение бесед и докладов на разные темы.

Проработан материал "3 года отечественной войны на инструктивном совещании с агитаторами после чего последние данный материал прорабатали по группам.

Проведено 2 доклада о международном положении. На ряду с проведенной полит.-массовой работой наш отряд оказывает взаимопомощь другим партизанским отрядам. Так Особому Казачьему Отряду (Мирва) обмолото 150 пудов зерна. Для первомайской бригады, Райцентра и других отрядов обмолото даже большое количество зерна.

Мастерскими отряда изготовлено 100 пар белья, разная верхняя одежда и обувь. Оружейный мастер отряда т. Эльвинг прилагает все усилия к подбору и изготовлению отдельных частей для винтовок, в результате чего мы имеем пополнение до 12-ти винтовок

Комиссар о/о   /Фрейдберман/
№ 106

1/VII-1944г.

To Baranovichi Regional Committee and Ivenec DCCP/b/B

From the partisan detachment N106

Political dispatch.

(JUNE 1944)

With this I wish to inform you that the political and moral state of all the personnel of the detachment is good.

In June a group of miners from our detachment carried out explosions on the railroad and on the road for the first time. The work was done in an exceptionally difficult situation. Twice fighters under Comrade Dulec, the man in charge of the group, tried to get to the railway, but without any result.

The third time Comrade Dulec addressed the company commander Comr. Tamarkin with the following words: 'Comr. Company commander let me and my group go for the third time to the railroad to carry out the explosion. If I don't come back tomorrow consider me fallen, but I hope to return victorious! Having received permission to go again, Comr. Dulec together with his group brilliantly performed their duty before the Motherland by derailing an echelon with enemy material, tanks, lorries loaded on seven platforms and one platform with the German guard including 15 people. The explosion took place on the Minsk-Koidanovo line.

The second group, of which the Komsomol Comr. Chernyak L. was the chief carried out an explosion on the Minsk-Koidanovo road as a result of which 2 cars with 7 Germans were destroyed.

On July 2 partisan meetings were held where the main subjects of discussion were: the work of the miners, the work of the schools and a pioneer camp.
One fighter, who was a candidate for the party was accepted into the party. Two Komsomol meetings were also held.

The main work done by the Komsomol organisation was in carrying out the decision of the regional committee of the LKSM on the organisation of schools and pioneer camps.

A separate pioneer camp has been built and schools are functioning normally. There are 5 groups at school with more than 80 children. The corresponding pedagogical personnel have been chosen for the work at the school and in the pioneer camp, and are doing the work well.

For the opening of the pioneer camp the children prepared a book programme (singing, reciting and dancing). The children wrote a report addressed to Comr. Stalin (the second copy is enclosed).

This month there was a performance by the agitation brigade of Lida Inter-district centre.

During this time 4 issues of the paper including two for the pioneer camp were edited.

Explanatory work such as the reading of summaries and newspapers, the holding of discussions and reports on different topics is systematically carried out among all the fighters of the detachments.

The material 'Three Years of the Patriotic War' was examined at the instructional meeting of propagandists who later on examined this material with the group.

Two reports on the international situation were made. Along with a large amount of political work our detachment renders help to other partisan detachments.

Thus 150 lb. of grain were ground for the special Cossack detachment (Mitka's). A big amount of grain was also ground for the Pervomaiskaya brigade, for the regional Centre and other detachments.

The workshops of the detachment made 100 pairs of underpants, various items of clothing and shoes.

The gunsmith craftsman from the detachment, Comr. Elkind, does his best to find and make separate parts for rifles and as a result we have 12 additional rifles.

Commissar of the P/D   /Feigelman/

N106 1.7.1944

The Russian system was to mobilise the able-bodied, give them training and send them to the front line. By releasing the group, Bielski enabled many to find jobs that released them from the army. Berl joined the Militia and so was exempt from the army. But quite a number were mobilised, among them Asael Bielski. They were sent to the front line and few returned. Asael was killed near Königsberg.

Lots of young men from Novogrodek were killed in the battle-fields. The ones who managed to escape to Russia volunteered for the Red Army and Air Force, like Meyer who came back with lots of medals. He rose to be a Major in the Air Force, but shortly before the War was over he was shot down over Budapest. The ones that were sent to Siberia just before the outbreak of the War joined the Anders Polish army.

Long columns of German prisoners of war were led through the streets of the town; they were a scruffy lot, no longer the victorious army. I saw a high-ranking officer marching with the men, in a nice pair of boots, so I called the Russian guard and asked his permission to remove the boots. The soldier smiled with full approval 'Please help yourself!' I caught up with the officer and spoke to him in Yiddish which is similar to German. I wanted him to know that I was a Jew. I told him to stop and remove his boots, saying they were too good for him, then the Russian soldier approached and gave him a push with his rifle, whereupon he sat down and I pulled off his boots. I wore them for a long time after that; in fact I wore them on arrival in England.

Tevele Niankovski (on the right) and myself in 1944 soon after liberation. Tevele and me, 40 years later

15   *Liberation*

THE BEGINNING of the liberation was a very difficult time for me. On the first day a field kitchen was set up and food was distributed free, but after that there was no more giving away of food. In the ghetto there had been a tremendous shortage of food but I had received a ration, or charity. In the partisans as well, I was provided for but now suddenly the situation changed. Berl was eating with the Militia, but I had to start thinking how I was going to manage. During the first days I met friends like Shimon Eicher and Meyer Ginenski who were in a similar situation and we met up together in the evenings to steal potatoes.

During the day we used to cook, eat and keep the hunger at bay. Then I found a job selling lemonade in the market below the town. Mikulinski made the lemonade and I put the bottles into buckets and carried them for about one and a half kilometres to the market. I soon realised that this was not a good way of making a living.

I saved up 40 rubles. It is hard for me to know now the value of the money but even then it was not a fortune. I decided to go to Minsk to obtain invalidity documents so as to get a pension. Travelling in Russia was not easy. One needed documents and permission to travel in order to get a train ticket in the first place Since I did not have enough money I did not bother with documentation.

The journey was long and very tiring. I arrived in the partisan headquarters where they found my name on their list and gave me a document testifying that I had been a soldier in the Kalinin detachment, together with a letter to go to a medical commission in Novogrodek.

The headquarters were about three kilometres from the centre of Minsk. When I walked back to town I saw a queue and joined it, without knowing what was being sold. On reaching the counter I found that they were selling flints for lighters. The cost was one ruble each, and you could buy a maximum of 20 per person. I

Document issued by the Belorussian headquarters of the Partisan Movement to Idel Kagan certifying that he was a fighter in the Kalinin detachment from September 1943 to June 1944

bought the 20, returned to Novogrodek and sold the lot for 400 rubles in the market place. The following day I went to an invalid commission and succeeded in getting a second-class invalidity pension of 120 rubles a month.

Things were looking brighter. I started to do business by buying butter and other commodities in the market in Novogrodek and travelling with them to Minsk on trains that carried wounded soldiers from the front line. The journey was by narrow-gauge railway to Novoyelna, from there by goods train to Baranovichi and from Baranovichi by passenger train to Minsk. The first time I tried to board the train I showed my invalidity document and the military policeman at the door looked at my feet, looked at my hand and angrily asked me to move on. I went to the next compartment. As I was wearing a large army overcoat I pulled my right hand into the sleeve and showed my invalidity document with my left hand. I was immediately helped to board the train.

Idel Kagan's Invalid Card

And so I became a dealer. That was the only way I knew how to make a living. I dealt in all commodities but mainly army boots and later in anything that was wanted, like yeast for making vodka, and gold for people who wanted to leave Russia. I travelled as far as Moscow and Lvov.

One day in the market-place in Minsk I met two young men, the Caplan brothers. They worked in a shoe factory and lived in the neighbourhood. I needed a place to sleep, and they were kind enough to offer me the floor in their apartment, and that became my 'Ritz hotel' in Minsk, not only for me but also for my friends who travelled with me to Minsk.

One Sunday I arrived there at lunch time and they introduced me to their cousin Natasha. Natasha was an officer in the Red Army and very beautiful, about 22 and single. I was invited to join them at the table, and I started to ask her such questions as whether she was married, and so on, and took a liking to her. I suggested she should travel with me to Novogrodek, as I knew a most eligible bachelor there, who I was sure would like to get married.

The following day I left for Novogrodek with my general merchandise and arrived safely home. I then went immediately to see Lionke Portnoy. I told him about Natasha and said that on my next journey I would be prepared to bring her over. He thanked me, and we parted.

About a month later, I visited the Caplans again. Natasha was there on three weeks' holiday. I asked her again whether she would come with me to meet Lionke. She agreed, so after finishing my business in Minsk we left by train for Novogrodek. We arrived in the evening at Novoyelna. It was bitterly cold. The station was full of wounded soldiers, it being three days after the Russian offensive on Warsaw in January 1945. It was so cold that the little narrow-gauge train could not run. The wounded soldiers were crying with the cold.

We slept the night on the stone floor in the station. At first light we decided with some others to walk the 21 kilometres to Novogrodek as during the night there had been a snowstorm and the line was covered. The evening train had not yet moved and the wounded soldiers were still waiting on it.

We walked the best part of the day and could not see the road, but we arrived eventually. I took her to my room where Lionke met her but things obviously did not work out because a few days later she asked me when I was going back to Minsk. I knew then that it had been a wasted journey for her.

And that finished my job as a matchmaker. Looking back on it now, I think that at 16 I was too young for that profession!

Travelling back from one of the journeys I heard a farmer telling another man that my uncle Notke Sucharski had died from a stomach complaint. The man he was speaking to was familiar to me and I recognised him. It was one of the Volkin brothers. The Volkins were a large family of barbers; one of the brothers used to cut my hair. (In fact, on my first visit to New York in 1955, I surprised him in his barber's shop.) He had recently been freed from a Russian prison in Siberia, after serving four years, not knowing why he was there. He had never been officially charged with anything. He looked like a walking skeleton.

I registered to go back to school, but that was a dream. I went for two days and had to give it up, because I was hungry and there was no one to look after me. Berl was also sad, as his job was to in-

Lionke Portnoy in Munich 1946

vestigate collaborators. He drank a lot, and many times I had to put him to bed. Then, out of the blue, we heard from cousin Leizer, who was in Samarkand in Uzbekistan.

I thought about the future. I knew that if I continued dealing, sooner or later I would be caught and put in prison (dealing was a serious offence, if I was charged with that I would get five years; by comparison, if I was charged with stealing I would only get three months).

I was just 16 years old so should think perhaps about learning a trade. One day I walked along Post Street and saw a notice that one could register for a school for war orphans. I called in and explained to the man in charge that I was an orphan with very little education and would like to go to the special school advertised. He gave me a whole lecture about the country needing engineers and other good trades and that he would arrange everything, and asked me to sign the book, which I did.

The next morning Berl came back from work and started shouting that I must have gone mad. He said that outside the police station there was a notice that coal miners were wanted in Sverdlovsk and that my name was at the top of the list, that I had volunteered.

I was not worried. After a few days I received call-up papers with various documents and a mobilisation took place for people who were destined for the army of general work. I remembered seeing a mountain of rubbish near the market place, so I went there, searched, and found a torn galosh, brought it home and washed out the rubbish. The following morning I went to the Commission in the cinema with the galosh on my right foot wound round with string. The doctor asked me to remove the galosh which I did. He gave a look and thanked me a number of times for volunteering to go to the mines in the Urals but unfortunately he could not permit it and he would recommend that a special letter of thanks be sent to me. That was the first and last time that I volunteered for anything.

One morning I was in Minsk near the Dom Sovetov (Government House). A very big sailor was standing there and shouting, 'Bij zydov spasaj Rosyju' ('Beat up the Jews and save Russia'). True, he was drunk and people passed by and did not take any notice of him. But I felt terribly sad, and I made the decision then and there to leave Russia.

Document to receive medal for the victory over Germany

Jews and Poles who had lived in Poland before the War could register to leave Russia for Poland. I came home, talked to Berl and he was of the same opinion that we should leave. It would be difficult for Berl as the Militia was part of the NKVD and the penalty for desertion was shooting.

I had read somewhere that Stalin had decreed that now that the War was over men and women with ten years of education should be released from their jobs so that they could go to universities. Berl had his documents. I took them and went to Minsk University, right to the top of the queue as an invalid and a volunteer with the partisans. With these privileges I saw the Dean and explained to him that I had lost everybody, I only had my cousin and that he needed further education so that he would be able to support me. He asked many questions but I finally left with a letter to the NKVD for his release and an acceptance to the university.

We received a letter from Leizer saying that he would like to leave Samarkand for Novogrodek. I left for Baranovichi to call on a Mr Buchman who was married to a daughter of Mrs Kirsner, a good friend of ours from Novogrodek. Before the War, Buchman had been the director of a tailoring factory and a member of the Communist Party in Novogrodek. He remembered my parents and was pleased that I was still alive. I asked him if he would write a request to the authorities to release Leizer and his wife Michle from their work on the grounds that Leizer was a specialist needed in the factory in Baranovichi. He was very kind and wrote the request. When they received it in Samarkand a forger added other names to it – Michle's sister Miriam and her husband Yisrael Ganz. After a short while I travelled to Novoyelna to meet them. And soon after their arrival we talked about leaving Russia, and Leizer was in agreement with us.

Leizer had changed his name in Russia, so it was going to be very complicated for him to get official documents. To get around this, Leizer and Berl went to Zdzienciol where a forger made documents for them to leave Russia. We left in September 1945, on a special train designated for Poles and Jews to leave the Soviet Union. It took five weeks to reach Lodz in Poland.

In Lodz I thought I would do some dealing. I was arrested on the second day and then released, but felt that I was being followed, so

I decided to get out of Poland. I took a train to Stettin. There at the station I met Bakst and his wife Lola Epstein from Novogrodek. They wanted to go to Berlin. I was in a Russian army uniform. We went out of the station and I purchased a bottle of vodka. Opposite the station was an army base. I went to the officer in charge and asked him his destination. He said Berlin. I told him that we needed to see our brother in hospital there and could we get a lift. The vodka was the ticket.

We arrived in Berlin at night without any problems and I cannot remember why we separated, but we did. All I had with me were four 10-ruble gold pieces in my boots, a towel and a large piece of stale bread. I slept the night in a passageway. I took off the army overcoat which was grey like those worn by the Canadians, cut off all the army buttons as I didn't want to be stopped by the Russian Military Police and started walking towards the Brandenburg Gate. When I reached it, I found a market by Potsdamer Platz. I recognised some Jews and started talking to them and they suggested that I should leave the Russian zone of Berlin and go west. I took the S-bahn, crossed into the American zone, and walked to the Tempelhof Airport. It was full of people: Ukrainians, Poles, Yugoslavs, all nationalities from Europe, registering with the UNRRA to leave Berlin. Seeing so many people, I started to get worried. I went over to a group who were speaking Yiddish and listened to their conversation. One of them was saying that he was not going to wait, that he was going to walk to the highway and try to get a lift. I told him that I would join him. We left and walked towards the highway. There were big, heavily laden American lorries going towards Berlin, empty ones coming back. We walked towards the town and noticed a bend in the road and realised that lorries going out of town must slow down at this point. This would be the best place to jump onto one. We both jumped onto the same vehicle, and were surprised that the driver from the lorry behind did not sound his horn. We arrived at the border in the evening hidden under the tarpaulin. When we heard the Russian guard say he would check the back, we moved to the front, and thus we left the Russian zone and arrived in the British zone.

The lorry stopped outside Hanover. We started walking to the town centre when I noticed a water pump so I took out the hard piece of bread and poured water on it to soften it and shared it with my new friend. By that time I knew my destination was to be Munich. Back in Lodz I had heard about refugee camps on the American side of Germany. I also knew that I had to avoid the British military police because without documents I would have plenty of trouble.

We reached Hanover railway station and there were already lots of people there. We found that there was a Jewish soup kitchen around the corner so we had a rest and some soup. I bought a small loaf of bread, cut it in half, one piece for each pocket, and managed with my friend to get on a train to Frankfurt am Main. On the train we dodged the military police throughout the journey. Eventually we arrived at Frankfurt railway station.

Chaos! Absolute Chaos! There were thousands waiting for a train to Munich and it was hard even to find standing room on the platform. I don't know how long we stood there. Eventually, a train arrived and everybody started to push forward and in the struggle I was separated from my friend. There was no room for me on board. The train was so packed that they could hardly close the doors. But as it pulled out of the station, I decided not to stay behind, and so jumped onto the steps. The train was an express and the journey took nine hours. I soon realised that I had made a mistake. I held on like mad. It was dark, and the train was electric, so from time to time sparks flew and I would see how deep the drop was, should I fall off. I was very cold because I did not have any buttons on my overcoat and it blew up like a parachute. My hands were completely frozen. When the train came to the first stop I could not open them but somebody helped me. Some people got out and I was able to slip inside the carriage which had no seats and was completely packed. I managed to get to a corner. It was dark and I was terribly scared. I imagined that the Germans in the carriage were looking at me, recognising me as a Jew and that they would kill me.

The train arrived in Munich in the early morning. The station had been bombed. It had no roof but the building was still standing. People slept on the wet floor. I was very tired, so I took off my army overcoat, and so as not to get the coat dirty, I took off my shirt, put it on the wet ground with the overcoat on top and lay down to sleep. I was woken up by a tap on my foot from an

American MP who said I should get up. I wrung the water from my shirt, put it in my pocket and left the station.

Then all of a sudden, I saw Ishie Oppenheim. It seemed that during this period the Oppenheim family played a big role in my life and my cousin's. When my cousin escaped it was with Ishie Oppenheim. When his brother Ruvke came to the camp, I escaped with him and when I arrived in Munich, I again met Ishie. The Oppenheim family was well known in Novogrodek, dealing in bicycles and typewriters and I knew Ishie Oppenheim from the early days and, of course, from the partisans.

We were both stunned with joy for a while. He took me to the German Museum. There was a soup kitchen and Yosef Boldo was there. Boldo came from Lubcz, and I knew him from the partisan days. We joined the queue and got some soup. I ate all of three helpings. Ishie and Yosef were in partnership in a small bus company. With them I went to Fohrenwald Displaced Persons camp. The date was 31 October 1945. Ishie took me to his home and Mrs Oppenheim gave me something to eat and I had my first bath since I left Russia. Mrs Oppenheim gave me Ruvke's clothes to wear so that mine could be washed. It was the best possible time to arrive as registration of the new arrivals took place on the first day of the month.

The following day I registered and got an UNRRA parcel. I found out that Pesach Abramovitz and some of my other friends were in Landsberg am Lech. After lunch, I changed back into my own clothes, thanked the Oppenheims and left for Landsberg am Lech. I arrived in time to register and received another parcel. I was a rich man again. I met my friends Pesach and Tevele and we carried yet another bed into their overcrowded room, but nobody cared. I joined the Partisan Kibbutz.

Life in Landsberg was very boring. The Partisan Kibbutz was well organised, we had good accommodation and, best of all, we had our own kitchen. Somehow the organisers of the Kibbutz knew how to get the extras. Life revolved around food.

At this time there were about 5,000 residents in the camp, with many kibbutzim. The majority of the people only wanted to go to Palestine. And here the Partisan Kibbutz had priority, too.

A few days after my arrival, a group of 20 left on the illegal emigration route, and we heard that they arrived safely. My friend

Partisan Kibbutz in Landsberg (Kibbutz Negev)

Pesach Abramovitz and Tevele left in a second group. They were caught and held in a camp at Atlit in Palestine.

I could not get used to the life in Landsberg. The boredom was terrible. Eventually I heard that the management of the Kibbutz had been successful in acquiring a German farm on which to teach agricultural skills to kibbutzim. I decided to leave Landsberg on a temporary basis and move there instead.

The farm was in Hibshendrid, not far from Riderau by Amersee, about 50 kilometres from Munich. It was a lovely place, with a big house and plenty of food. It was nice to get up very early each morning and go to work in the fields or with the cows. We were a nice crowd of 30 young men and women, all survivors from different partisan groups.

My feet started to give me trouble. It got to the stage where I could not walk any more, and small pieces of bone were penetrating the skin. I went to the hospital in Landsberg, where the doctor examined me and kept me in. They operated the next day.

My identity card from DP camp Landsberg am Lech

While there, a friend called and told me that a parcel had arrived for me from America. I didn't believe him since I didn't know anybody there, but I gave him permission to collect it on my behalf. It was a 20-kilo parcel containing chocolate and other foodstuffs, and cigarettes – a valuable currency at this time. It had been sent by a Mrs Adell, who wrote that she used to know my parents and had heard I was still alive. This parcel gave me a big uplift; it was just what I needed. And it taught me the greatest lesson in life: the importance of giving and generosity. I was in hospital for six weeks and left it on crutches. I was in pain for many weeks.

I heard that Berl had arrived in Bad Reichenhal DP camp and got in touch with him. He visited and I told him that Leizer and Michle had managed to get an affidavit (a necessary document for travel) and were in Palestine, and that I had traced my cousin Rachel in London, where she had married and was now Mrs Konigsberg.

Most of my friends had now left Landsberg in illegal convoys to Palestine. Many were in new camps in Cyprus, after being intercepted by the British.

I started to feel much better. The operation had helped and I could walk without pain. I visited Berl in Bad Reichenhal, where he was in Hashomer Hatzair Kibbutz. I learned that the whole Kibbutz planned to go to Palestine illegally. I decided to join them, and registered. After three weeks I was asked to go to Munich to a medical commission. Unfortunately, the doctor who examined me gave a negative report, and I was told that I would not be able to go on the proposed journey.

I said goodbye to Berl and my friends and returned to Landsberg. Earlier, I had written to Rachel in London and asked if there was any chance that they could help me get to London. My plan was to reach Palestine, and I believed that the best way to get there was from London. Rachel's husband Sam wrote to the High Commissioner in Berlin, and within a short time I received permission to travel.

On 18 June 1947, while I was in bed with flu, I got notification to report the next day to the Funk Caserne in Munich, to start my journey. The Funk Caserne was the place where refugees assembled prior to being sent to other cities in Europe. Although the next day was hot, I was wrapped up in my heavy Russian military overcoat and my army boots, and felt terrible. We travelled by cattle train to the French zone, and there boarded a passenger train for Paris.

The following day we arrived in Paris. We were then under the supervision of the American Joint. They took us to a big hall near the Sacré-Coeur where we had lunch. There were about 200 of us, going on to various destinations. Only two were going to London: a Greek Jewish boy named Eli and myself. We had to wait a long time in the hall to get the documents we needed. When they finally arrived, groups of people were taken off to different hotels. Eli and I stayed near the Paris Opéra.

The flu passed and I felt better, and happy to be out of Germany. I had the address of a friend of mine, Grisha Perlman. We had been together in Hibshendrid. I sent him a note and within two hours he came to see me. He gave me a grand tour of Paris.

I left Paris early on 23 June 1947. When I arrived at Newhaven, I was interrogated for about an hour before being allowed to continue my journey. At about 6 o'clock in the evening I arrived at Victoria Station, where Sam and Rachel were waiting for me.

With Grisha Perlman in Paris, 22 June 1947

It was a very moving scene; I hadn't seen Rachel since 1938, nine years earlier. So much had happened since then; Rachel had lost all her family and my presence must have been a reminder to her of all that.

After about three weeks Sam found me a job as a 'clicker' (cutter) in a shoe factory. For four to five months I lived with Rachel and Sam, and was very grateful to them. Yet somehow the normal life in England depressed me. I could not speak the language, the job was hard, and meant standing all day, and I was sad when I found out that Berl was on the *Exodus*. I followed its progress by asking people what was happening, since I could not read the newspapers. I felt angry and upset when I heard that everyone on the *Exodus* had been sent back to Germany.

I moved out of the Konigsbergs' house and in with a young man called Bruno whom I had met at the Primrose Club. This was a club run by the Central British Fund (CBF) for the young survivors of the Holocaust.

After three months I moved again. I was only earning £3.5s. week and couldn't afford the rent. I moved to Stamford Hill. There I met others in a similar situation. I was now beginning to understand the language, and changed my job for a better paid one earning £5.15s. a week. I worked hard and started saving my money.

My life was a very sorrowful one but there was nothing I could do about this. The place where I lived in the attic had bars on the windows; in the factory there were also bars on the windows. After a day's work I was too tired to do anything. I felt I was in a prison. In September 1948 I started going to Cordwainer's College to learn the practical art of making shoes.

I was still not satisfied with my wages. I knew I was being exploited, so I left my job and searched for a new one. I found one paying £15 per week, and since I did not like living in England I made a decision to work hard, save as much as I possibly could, and start a small workshop in Israel.

By September 1949 I had over £300. I bought a special sewing machine and a finishing machine from Italy, and a very cheap ticket for Israel. It was good to see Berl again. He had married Ita in Germany, and they had set up home in Jabiliah near Jaffa. I moved in with them, but my plan went wrong. I couldn't set up a workshop because there was a terrible shortage of raw materials. Instead I went to work on a building site. The work was not difficult, but the rainy season started early. When it rained you couldn't work and you didn't get paid.

Eventually I found a job in a shoe factory not far from Jaffa. It was a good job and well paid, but at the beginning of April the company went broke. I couldn't find another job. My travel document was valid for one year and ran out on 20 April. After that date I would not be allowed back into the UK. I had no choice, I had to return.

I arrived in Dover on 19 April 1950 with very little money in my pocket. I was questioned and kept a day at the police station. Late in the evening I was allowed to take the train to London. I found lodgings in Stamford Hill. By this time I no longer had union membership, so I couldn't get a job in a shoe factory.

At this time I met 'the Boys'. This was a group of young men and some girls who had come over to England after the War with the help of the Central British Fund (CBF). Through a friend I found a job as a cutter in a handbag factory called Max Manufacturing. This job was easy compared to working in a shoe factory, and much less pressurised. The wages were good and there was plenty

Our Wedding Picture

of overtime. Within weeks I was in charge of the cutting department. After 15 months I left and started my own company, which I called Princelet Handbags Ltd. I took on a partner, because it was difficult for me to do all the buying, manufacturing and selling on my own. My partner, Harold Mack, was younger than me and a hard worker.

The business was doing well and we opened another company, Hi-speed Plastics. At a later stage we sold the company, and I started up a number of successful companies after that. I must say I enjoyed my business ventures and was dealing with some of the largest companies in the UK.

I met Barbara Steinfeld, fell in love with her and on 3 April 1955 we got married.

Our first son, Michael Leon, was born 17 July 1956, our second son, Jeffrey David, on 12 March 1959 and on 19 May 1961 we had a daughter, Deborah Judith. Between them all, we have nine grandchildren.

I settled down to a normal life, but I can never forget the past. I regret missing out on my youth and educational opportunities. I look forward to my retirement with the possibility of studying and lecturing about Jewish resistance in the Holocaust.

16   *A Visit*

U<small>NTIL</small> 1991 I had no intention of going back to Novogrodek. It
was a place of tragedy and suffering for me.

In April 1991 and on other visits to Israel, I saw Meime Isralit
who was born in Novogrodek, and had survived the war in Russia.
He told me about a visit he had made to Novogrodek. After seeing
the photographs of the graves I decided to go there later in the
year. I got in touch with Rita Ginenskaya, a school friend living in
Baranovichi.

Barbara and I arrived in Minsk from Vilnius. It was a cold day.
Rita's son Sasha came from Baranovichi to pick us up and take us
on to Novogrodek. However, on the way over from Baranovichi
he had been stopped for speeding so was late in arriving at Minsk.
We finally set off at about 10.30am, arriving at noon in
Novogrodek.

I had to move fast as a visa had not been granted for an
overnight visit, so we had to return the same day. I couldn't find
the court-house as everything looked different, which meant that
I couldn't locate the mass grave close to it.

We drove to Peresika and found the mass grave there. On the
memorial stone it was written that 5,000 Russian citizens had been
murdered there by the Nazis. I said a prayer for the dead (*kaddish*)
and went to Dr Gordin's for lunch. Gordin had been a doctor in
Novogrodek before the War. He remained in Russia until 1993,
when he went to Israel for a leg operation and died. (His son lives
in Moscow.) I told him that I couldn't find the court-house so he
rang Eli Zamoshchik to ask if he would take us over to it and to the
mass grave where the last 250 Jews were killed, including my
mother and sister. I felt so sad after saying *kaddish* on that grave.
We then went back to Minsk.

In June 1992 I got involved with Scotland Yard over war
criminals living in England, and I was notified that in Mir, some 30
kilometres from Novogrodek, there was going to he a plaque in

Shulia Rubin photographed with the three memorials in 1969. There was no mention of Jews having been killed here

Hebrew put on the Russian memorials. The ceremony would be on 8 August 1992. I immediately made plans to go there. I rang Gordin's son Ralph in Moscow and he agreed to meet me in Vilnius. I was lucky that Ralph was having his holiday in Novogrodek at that time. On 6 August I arrived in Vilnius and was met by Ralph, his wife and son. We went to Novogrodek, stayed overnight at his house and in the morning called on the Jews that remained there – that is Sonia Zabelinska, Baranchuk, Zamoshchik and Misha Troyetski (who was later murdered in Novogrodek in 1994, which reduced even further the number of Jews living in Novogrodek from six to five). It was so very sad but I was mentally prepared for it this time.

Ralph and Misha took me everywhere, to all three memorials at Skridlevo, Litovka and Horodzhilovka, and to Koldichevo. The following morning we went again to Litovka. Exactly 50 years to

This used to be Synagogue Square in Novogrodek. Now it is just a large, empty space. The Main Synagogue was so strongly built that the Russians had to bring sappers from Leningrad to blow it up in 1956

That's where the Market Place used to be in Novogrodek

That's where our home on Racelo Street was as well as the Yeshiva in Novogrodek

This was the Jewish cemetery at Novogrodek which was nearly 500 years old. In 1956 garages were built not far from the cemetery and every usable stone was torn out of the ground. A fence has recently been put up around the cemetery. The main instigator of the project was Hercl Brook from Tel Aviv.

the day had passed since the second slaughter. I cried a little, said *kaddish* and left for Mir. There I met people I knew from Mir and also Mr Lloyd and Mr Chapman from Scotland Yard. I met the Mayor of the town and after the ceremonies we left for Novo-grodek. The following day I was preparing to go back to Vilnius and, as I was walking along Grodnienski Street, noticed that where the NKVD used to be there was now a museum. It being a Monday, the museum was closed. I asked Ralph if he would visit the museum on the following day and let me know if there was anything relating to Jews.

I rang him when I got back to London and his answer was that there was nothing at all. I was very bitter. After all, Jews had lived there for 500 years and now there was no sign that we had ever done so.

I started up a correspondence with the museum and found that the curator was a sympathetic woman by the name of Tamara Vershitskaya. She put me in touch with the Mayor of the town, Mr Bako. I made up my mind that I would go to any lengths to have the Russian monuments taken down and memorial stones erected in their place. The correspondence went on until May 1993. On 7 May I was again in Novogrodek.

This time Boris Krotin and Ralph met me in Minsk, and the following day we visited the graves. I said a special prayer at my mother's and sister's graves which coincided with the 50th anniversary of their massacre, then went to see the Mayor and the principals of the town hall. Tamara was also at the meeting. I told them what I wanted to do and showed them a photograph which I had taken in Bushey cemetery of the memorial that I wanted to have put up. Their first question was: 'How do we know that what you are telling us is correct? We don't know how many Jews were killed here.'

Tamara came to the rescue, 'Mr Mayor, Mr Kagan wrote to me from England telling me what had happened during the German occupation. I put an article in the paper for witnesses and here are more than 20 replies confirming what he said.'

Then we could not agree on the wording. I wanted it to say that the Jews were killed by the Nazis and local collaborators; he wanted it to say that it was by the Nazis and mercenaries. In the end we agreed on Nazis and collaborators. On the Memorial stone at the court-house a Magen David and the words 'Holocaust Memorial' were to be engraved and the same was to be done in Litovka, the wording to be written in Belorussian and Hebrew on the front and English on the back.

The problem was that I did not know the precise location of the grave, but it turned out that the Mayor did know. He told us that he lives in Litovka village and a number of years ago, on a rainy morning on his way to work, he saw skeletons on the road. It transpired that the previous night some Lithuanians had come and robbed the mass grave. They were looking for – and found – gold teeth. They were tracked down and arrested. From what he told me, he thought that they had participated in the killing. Otherwise they would not have known the place.

The big problem was what to do about the memorial at Skridlevo. The original plaque stated that 18,000 people had been killed there, but I had come along saying that it was 5,100. That must mean that the remainder were Poles, Belorussians or Gypsies. I could not very well have the monument removed. After a very lengthy discussion, we agreed to have two monuments, one on each side of the grave, one being for the Jews and the other for the non-Jews. We were all tired and glad to reach agreement on that. I offered to pay for all the work done.

Suddenly Mr Bako said, 'Mr Kagan, how will you do all this from England? Where do you think you are now, in England? The stonemason is in Slonim and you will need to bring the memorial from there to Novogrodek. You will need a tractor, a crane and we are short of petrol.' He thought he would frighten me off. Suddenly Boris, who was sitting nearby said, 'If Mr Kagan could come from England especially to arrange it, I will do everything for him.' I felt a lot better.

The next morning Boris, Ralph and I went to Slonim and found a stonemason – luckily a very friendly one. He had had Jewish friends before the War. After hearing that I wanted four large memorials in eight weeks and that I would like everything to be ready for 8 August, his answer was that he would do his very best. He would leave for the Ukraine the next day to buy the stones. He gave me a price and deducted a 25 per cent special discount.

I left for London, and my friend Roman Halter made the drawing for the stonemason. As soon as it was ready the Mayor

Gathering, 15 August 1993

changed his mind. He decided he wanted only one stone there, which would say that 18,000 were killed here, amongst them 5,100 Jews. I agreed and after lengthy talks he gave permission for us to put the words 'Holocaust memorial' on the front.

The stonemason made a mistake and put a Magen David on the front, but they turned a blind eye to it. On 15 August 1993, about 70 people arrived from Israel, the USA, Belgium and Australia.

Two of the monuments were ready by the 14th, but the one for Skridlevo was not. Due to heavy rain, a tractor had got stuck in the mud and there was no road.

Hercl Brook arranged the Israeli group, amongst them Professor Mirski. They brought earth from Israel to put on top of the graves.

I was very worried because there were elderly people in the group and I hoped that everything would go well. I arranged for a doctor to be on site and chairs to be put in each location as a precaution. But thank God they were not needed. The ceremonies went off very well indeed, and many representatives from Minsk came along. A film crew from London made a video of the event. The municipality gave us a hall where moving speeches were

Memorial stone to the victims of the Fourth Slaughter. It is where my mother and sister were shot. Written in Belorussian and Hebrew with English on the other side

Our very good friend Hercl Brook

Memorial to the Fourth Slaughter on 7 May 1943

My cousin Rachel Konigsberg and myself at the mass grave where the Nazis and their collaborators killed 5,500 Jews on 7 August 1942. In the Second Slaughter Rachel's entire family was killed. On 4 February 1943 they liquidated the ghetto in Peresika by killing 500 more Jews

Star of David from inside the large synagogue

made. Tears were in my eyes when the partisan song was sung in Yiddish and also the *Hatikva*. We have lost so much and survived. We also went to see partisan huts in the forest that were still standing. It is worth mentioning one episode: we were sitting in the hotel, looking out through the window at the empty place where Synagogue Square had been. A man knocked at the door, with a parcel in his hand and said, 'This belongs to you. I was in the synagogue after the fire and noticed your Star of David. I decided to take it home and wait until the day somebody would return.' We unwrapped it and Hercl recognised it as the Magen David from the ark of the big synagogue. The man was a Pole by the name of Pitkewicz.

We will never forget the visit. I will always be grateful to Boris Krotin for putting so much work into the project; without him it would have been impossible. On my return to London I was back

251

Tamara Vershitskaya, with the Mayor of the town, Mr Bako, in the rear and Mr Ralph Gordin and workers of the municipality

Memorial of the First Slaughter when 5,100 innocent people were killed, amongst them Berl's family and Berele from Karelitz

During the visit we went to a Partisan camp that was preserved as a museum

Inside a dugout

253

Maria Bobrovski, being presented an award for being one of the 'Righteous Among Gentiles'

on the phone about the third monument. Boris was experiencing great difficulties and in the end the army got involved. A Jew living in Novogrodek, somebody I had never met, decided to help. He was from Kleck and was in charge of a government transport company and consequently lorries. So he supplied the lorries, the army provided labour, a road was built and the monument was erected.

In June 1994 a party of about 30 people from various parts of the world arrived in Novogrodek. *Kaddish* was said at all three graves. Tamara Vershitskaya created a permanent corner in the Museum to show that Jews had lived in the town since 1484.

I was asked to give a talk in the Belorussian school about the Jews of Novogrodek and was very surprised that the young students knew nothing about the pre-war town population. They were equally surprised that so many Jews had lived there and about what had happened to them.

Despite all the sadness, I felt pleased that I had achieved what I most wanted: memorial stones on the graves. I will always be thankful to Boris Krotin and Tamara Vershitskaya for their help.

Appendix A:
The History of the Exodus

This steamship, built at the Wilmington dockyard, was launched on the Mississippi River in February 1928. No one suspected at the time that it would one day become a symbol of the Jewish Aliyah to the Land of Israel. The *President Warefield* (named after the company's president) had 171 comfortable cabins and 80 bathrooms, intended to accommodate 300 night passengers and 500 passengers during the day. Luxurious and proud, she sailed on the waters of Chesapeake Bay, and travelled the 'love line' between Baltimore and Norfolk.

In 1932 she was turned into an oil freighter. In 1942 she was rented by the British Allies. Cannons were mounted on deck, and the ship participated in the Second World War. While escorting

A photograph of the refugee ship, Exodus, *1947*

convoys across the Atlantic, she sank a German submarine, and the captain was awarded a medal by George VI. Towards the end of the War she took part in the invasion of Normandy. In 1946 the US Navy committee put her up for sale. When no buyers came forward, she was towed to Baltimore Harbour, to be broken up. When Ilke Aharonovitz visited the harbour, he noticed the ship and signalled 'yes'. The Jews got it for practically nothing, and turned her into the flagship of the Aliyah.

What is a National Holiday?

After an exhausting journey, the three deportation ships arrived at the port of Hamburg. And even then, the spirits of the men and women of the *Exodus* remained unbroken, and the army had to drag them ashore by their hands and feet. In some cases, four or five soldiers were needed to tear a man or woman away from the ship. If anyone asks you: What is a national holiday?, do not hesitate. Take a book and read from it, thus:

> A nation celebrates on the day
> When its last stronghold faces the ultimate test
> And forces the enemy to break his teeth…
> This is a national holiday.
> That's what the dictionary says.
> And it adds: it's a day when a nation is filled
> With faith in its sons
> And contempt for its enemies.
> It's a day on which
> In its eye trembles
> That spark which may be called pride.

And it adds: a holiday is a specific day When the dawn awakens, as red as ever, And three ships come from the sea And enter a harbour in Germany. It's a certain day that demonstrates The principle of a claim for a state. It's a day that shows how five Englishmen Must grab every woman and man
If they wish to tear them away from the Jewish state.

Nathan Alterritan

Appendix B:
The History of the Ordzhonikidze Detachment, Kirov Brigade

Origin of the Detachment

The overwhelming majority of the partisans were citizens of the Novogrodek and Dyatlovo (Zdzienciol) districts, former servicemen of the Red Army hiding in the forests, and escaped prisoners of war.

The towns of Novogrodek and Dyatlovo in the Baranovichi region were occupied by Germans on 2–3 July 1941. From the first day, repressive action was taken against remaining Soviet employees, deputies, communists, intelligentsia, Jews, Belorussians and so on. At the same time there the whole population was plundered. The Germans took away everything that came into their hands: personal belongings and money, gold, bread and cattle; they imposed exorbitant taxes. For not complying in any way, people were subjected to corporal punishment, taken to prison and shot. In a short time the Germans in Novogrodek had arrested 400 people in all, including 52 Jews; the latter were taken to the centre of the town and shot.

In December 1941 the Germans organised a ghetto in Novogrodek, where they held all the Jews from the district – about 6,500 people. They were kept under very strict regime, with guards inflicting the most cruel treatment; innocent men, women, children were beaten, robbed, starved, imprisoned and shot.

In the Novogrodek ghetto the Germans shot about 10,000 Jews, servicemen and others. The first group was shot on 8 December 1941, the second on 7 August 1942, the third on 4 February 1943, the fourth on 7 May 1943.

The same situation was to be found in the Dyatlovo district. One hundred and fifty Soviet employees, deputies, communists, intelligentsia and so on were taken from there and shot. Some 4,000 Jews from the ghetto in Dyatlovo were shot.

Because of this inhuman attitude from the German-fascist authorities towards the Belorussian population, which was also manifested in the transporting of some to hard labour in Germany and burning the villages, the population had to run away from the new order to the forests. The escape of the first group from Novogrodek began in April 1942; later they increased with each day.

The runaway Jews hid in dug-outs in the forest of the Novogrodek district. The organiser of the first Jewish groups into a partisan unit was a resident of the Novogrodek district, Tuvia Davidovich Bielski from Stankiewicz. In September 1943 a large-scale escape from the ghetto in Novogrodek was organized by the Jews who still remained alive. Some 300 people dug a tunnel from the ghetto, about 195 metres long, and escaped through it to the forest, where partisan groups had already been organised by Bielski and Lieutenant Panachenko.

Disaffection and an ebullient hatred of the occupiers (and of the new order in Europe) forced the population, including the young, into the forests to begin open armed fighting against the enemy. In the fight against their sworn enemy, people showed great patriotism towards their Motherland and the Soviet people. The partisan movement grew day by day, developing from small isolated groups into a powerful armed force organised in partisan detachments.

Our first detachment, 'Oktyabrski', at the beginning of 1943 had approximately 200 armed combatants and consisted of two companies. The organisers of the last were Comrade Bielski and Lieutenant Panachenko.

The Organisation of the Detachment

According to order N26 of 19 June 1943, signed by the Representative of the Partisan Movement Central Staff CCCP(b)B in Baranovichi region, Comrade Platon, the partisan detachment 'Oktyabrski' was broken up into smaller units. The first company of the detachment became an independent unit under the command of the first organiser of the detachment Lieutenant Victor Panachenko. The second company of the detachment singled out as an independent unit was named after 'Ordzhonikidze' and was a part of the 'Kirovskaya' Brigade. From this time on all fighting activity was more coordinated.

Structure of the Detachment

According to order N2 of 8 June 1943, forming the partisan detachment named after 'Ordzhonikidze', the following structure of the detachment was introduced:

1. Commander of the detachment;
2. Commissar;
3. Chief of Staff;
4. Deputy commander on reconnaissance;
5. Deputy commissar on Komsomol work;
6. Representative on a special task;
7. Chief of food supplies;
8. Chief of medical needs and sanitation work.

The detachment consisted of two companies; each company had two platoons, and each platoon two sections. There was a senior sergeant in each company. There was a separate mounted reconnaissance platoon in the detachment, which consisted of two sections: one for troop reconnaissance and the other for secret service ('on capturing a tongue'). There was an economic section at the headquarters of the detachment.

Beginning of the Fighting Activity

Organising the reconnaissance
(a) Combat reconnaissance of a partisan detachment was headed by the deputy commander on reconnaissance who had a separate mounted platoon at his disposal, consisting of 16 people, with the task of carrying out combat and reconnaissance within a radius of

ten kilometres of the detachment's location in the district, in particular to discover the enemy's position, number, armament, direction and so on.

Reconnaissance carried out mounted patrols round the clock, reporting on the situation in the district daily at 1800 hours to the staff of the detachment. If they discovered enemy personnel on their territory they reported it immediately to the staff of the department. Reconnaissance also had in its district and beyond its borders messengers who fulfilled special tasks gathering necessary information for the headquarters of the detachment. In addition, they maintained close relations with the local population which also helped greatly in discovering enemy forces.

(b) The secret service was headed by the section commander, Comrade Yakimovich. It consisted of three people plus a staff of messengers from the civil population who would obtain necessary information. The latter were patriots of the Motherland who had connections with the German garrisons, and could find out where prisoners of war who joined partisan detachments had come from or obtain weapons and ammunition, and so on. Comrade Yakimovich personally went to the town of Novogrodek where German garrisons of police and Cossacks were situated. It is true that some messengers discredited other messengers and that as a result the enemy learned about their work with the partisans, thus threatening many lives.

Establishing contact
There were mounted and unmounted messengers to do this work when needed. There were no specially allocated people, except one messenger at the headquarters of the detachment.

Service of combat, support and ammunition supply
(a) Battle outposts were carried out by rear and side patrols, which reported about danger, the need for support and so on. While on the march, front, side and rear battle outposts were allocated and were given instructions on what distance to move, taking into consideration local conditions. In addition, mounted reconnaissance was sent forward. While in position, protection

was organised by guards or by sending patrols, depending on the place of location. While at rest, guards and patrols were organised.

(b) Barriers were constructed on routes of enemy motor vehicle movement, ditches were dug out, bridges were destroyed to delay the movement of enemy transport. Simultaneously, ambushes were set and sudden fire was opened on the enemy.

(c) At the beginning weapons came from the local population or as spoils of war obtained from the enemy. During the whole period of the detachment's activity weapons and ammunition frequently came from military garrisons. People who felt sympathy towards the partisans and were working in German garrisons sent arms to the detachment through secret service messengers.

During the skirmishes each fighter had a weapon and ammunition if they were available.

(d) Medical service in the detachment was organised under the leadership of a doctor, who was chief of the medical services of the detachment. There was a medical sister and a doctor's assistant at the chief's disposal, to provide necessary medical assistance. In cases of serious wounds or illnesses people were sent to the partisans' field ambulance base or to the 'Big Land' by plane.

Fighting Activity of the Detachment

20 April, 20, 26 and 29 September, 18 and 28 October 1943
There were seven sorties to blow up the railway in the district of Lida-Baranovichi. These activities were carried out under the guidance of Comrade Lieutenant Podkolzik, quartermaster of the IIIrd rank Peshenkov, platoon commander Zamkovy, political leader Latij, partisan Feldman. Instructions for destroying the railway were given by the staff of the Kirov brigade. Sabotage of the railway was aimed at delaying the movement of enemy echelons going to the east. In total, about one kilometre of track was destroyed. Fifty-nine people took part in the task.

17 December 1943

Groups of partisans from the detachment, under the guidance of platoon commander Yankelevich, burnt down two houses in the area of Yacuki, which were to be rebuilt as bunkers on the Lida-Baranovichi railway by the Germans. Nine partisans took part in this operation.

2–27 February 1944

A group of partisans from the detachment, under the guidance of deputy commander Bielski and Reznicki, in the area of the villages Orkevichi–Mokrec–Ugly and the Lida–Novogrodek road, burnt down five houses which the Germans had intended to use for building bunkers. The purpose of the destruction of these buildings was to delay or to stop the building of bunkers. Thirteen partisans took part.

17 September 1943

A group of partisans of the second company under the guidance of Lieutenant Podkolzik Petr constructed two obstructions on the Vsielub–Ivje road in the area of Smolyarnia. Notices saying 'Be careful! Mined! were put up. Information had been received that Germans were to move from Vsielub along this road to the partisan camp. The instructions to make an obstruction were given by the detachment's command with the aim of not allowing enemy vehicles to pass. Six people took part in fulfilling the task.

4 and 7 November 1943, 21 January 1944

Three groups of partisans blew up bridges. One iron and concrete bridge was blown up on the Vsielub–Ivje road; a second bridge was destroyed on the Vsielub–Otminovo road in the area of Berdovka. The destruction of the bridges was carried out under the guidance of major Comrade Gurchin. A bridge was taken to pieces on the Vsielub–Krivichi road in the area of Otminovo (opposite Koval). The destruction of the bridge was carried out under the leadership of Captain Lyashenko. The fourth bridge, which was burnt down, had a strategic significance on the Lida–Novogrodek road. The bridge was destroyed under the leadership of the deputy commander of the detachment, Comrade Bielski. The destruction of all the bridges was carried out according to the instructions of the Kirov brigade in order to prevent the enemy moving vehicles through the villages mentioned above. Twelve partisans took part in fulfilling the task.

22 March and 29 April 1944

Two groups of partisans of the detachment mined the Lida–Novogrodek road. As a result, three vehicles were blown to pieces and two more were damaged. Eighteen Germans were killed and two wounded. The instructions about mining the road were given by the staff of the Kirov brigade. The task was fulfilled under the leadership of the company commander, Shelyubski. Thirty partisans took part in the operation.

21 March 1944

Two groups of partisans from the detachment mined the railway in the Baranovichi–Lida area between the Yacuki–Bogdanka bunkers and Selec bunkers. As a result two enemy locomotives and 16 carriages were derailed and put out of commission. In addition, 20 motor-cycles, military ammunition and food were destroyed.

The operations were carried out under the leadership of company commander Shelyubski and 2nd company commander Grajzhevski. The instructions on blasting work were received from the staff of the brigade. The movement of enemy echelons was delayed for 25 hours. There were difficulties in mining the track, because German bunkers with guards were situated on some stretches. The mining was carried out at night and required particularly thorough camouflage. Twenty-six people took part in this operation.

27 October and 14 November 1943

Two groups of partisans of the detachment cut down 32 telegraph poles and burnt down 200 snow shields in the area of the Lida–Novogrodek road and Dyatlovo. The aim was to destroy telephone and telegraph communication between Lida and Novogrodek. The destruction of the shields, allowing the snow to drift on the road, stopped the movement of vehicles and broke telephone and telegraph communication. The instructions were given by the command of the detachment. Thirty people took part in the operation.

21 December 1943

A group of partisans from the 2nd company of the detachment under the leadership of Lieutenant Podkolzik, under instruction by the staff of the detachment, organised an ambush on the Novogrodek–Novojelnia road on passing enemy transport. As a result of the fighting one enemy motor vehicle was destroyed, and four Germans, 21 policemen and one civil worker of the gendarmerie were killed. Two people were wounded. Partisan losses: one man killed, one wounded. The plan for the ambush was worked out by Lieutenant Podkolzik. Thirty-two people took part.

5 March 1944

The detachment Ordzhonikidze took part in accomplishing a fighting mission organised by the Kirov brigade, under the leadership of the brigade's commander, Captain Vasiljev, to destroy the White Poles in the district of Lida, on the right bank of the Niemen. The staff of the brigade gave the task of checking the farmstead of Porosli to the detachment. There were no White Poles on the farmstead at 7 am. By 10 am the detachment concentrated in Dokudovo. During the fight the detachment went in the direction of Filenovcy and then moved in the direction of Petry. The detachment arrived there at 1 pm. After fulfilling the task the detachment returned to the camp. Seventy people took part in the task.

9 April 1944

The Ordzhonikidze detachment, under the leadership of the brigade's commissar, Comrade Kondiakov, fulfilled a combat task, worked out by the brigade, to destroy a group of White Poles in Lida district, on the right bank of the Niemen. The task set them to clear the White Poles from the villages of Burnosy, Milegovo and

Biskopcy and the farmstead of Biskopcy was completely achieved. Sixty people took part in the operation.

27 May 1943
A group of partisans of the 1st company, under the leadership of company commander Shelyubski, was fulfilling an economic mission 800 metres from a German post. While retreating they encountered the police. As a result they were engaged in combat. Two policemen were killed. There were no losses to the partisans. Fifteen people took part in the operation.

13 October 1943
A group of partisans from the detachment, under the leadership of company commander Shelyubski, going on a fighting mission in the area of Dyatlovo at night captured a policeman (who had a weapon and grenades) at the Rybaki farmstead. On the way to the detachment's headquarters the policeman tried to run away. He was killed. The spoils of war: one rifle and two grenades. Fourteen partisans took part.

19 December 1943
A group of partisan scouts, under the leadership of the platoon commander, Reznicki, during reconnaissance of the road in the area of Lida–Novogrodek and Leshchenka-Mokrec, sighted an enemy car. The reconnaissance group opened fire. As a result of the fire the driver was wounded and the car was put out of action. Three partisans took part.

9 April 1944
A group of partisans of the 2nd company of the detachment, under the leadership of the company commander, Groyzhevski, while fulfilling an economic mission in the district of Kamenka, clashed with the police. As a result of the exchange of fire, one German was killed and two were wounded. Nine partisans took part.

1 June 1944
A group of partisans of the detachment, under the command of deputy commander of the detachment Comrade Bielski, in the district of the village of Negremovo, attacked a group of Cossacks,

who were grazing their horses in the forest. In the course of this sudden strike, which lasted ten minutes, eight Cossacks were killed and six were wounded. Eleven people took part in the raid.

1 June 1944
The 1st and the 2nd companies of the detachment, under the leadership of the chief of staff, Lieutenant Podkolzin, in the district under the White Poles in the area of Ruda–Gancevichi–Guta, took away 34 cows belonging to the families of White Poles, the police and so on. Thirty people took part in the operation.

5 January 1944
The detachment named after Ordzhonikidze, together with the detachment 'Oktyabrski' Kirov brigade, took part in dismantling the railway in the district of Lida–Baranovichi, in front of a train moving eastward. The passing enemy train went off the railway track. Partisans ambushed the train and burnt seven carriages, three vehicles and 40 motor-cycles, together with ammunition and food. Twenty-one Germans were killed, four people were captured, and 13 were wounded. Spoils of war: 13 rifles. There were no losses on the partisan side. The plan of the combat operation was worked out by the commanders of both detachments: Captain Lyashenko and Lieutenant Panchenko. Forty-one people took part.

19 June 1944
According to an order by the Kirov brigade, a group of partisans of the Ordzhonikidze detachment was placed at the disposal of the 'Bolshevik' detachment of the 'Vperjod' brigade. They took part in a combat operation in the area of Lida–Molodechno to destroy an enemy bunker and the railway. As a result of the combat, the Germans ran away from the bunker. The task set was fulfilled. Eight people took part in it.

28 January 1944
Kirov brigade ambushed the Guta police in the district of M. Guta and Pudino. The operation was carried out according to the plan

worked out by the staff of the brigade. It was led by the brigade commander, Comrade Vasiljev. The task of the partisan detachment was to blow up the gendarmerie and police station in Guta with the help of unstable elements from the village of Vasilevichi. A group of partisans from the detachment went to Vasilevichi and pretended to be drunk. They ordered drinks and food in one house and a bath in another. The unstable elements immediately informed the gendarmerie and police in Guta about the drunk partisans in the village.

The Guta gendarmerie and police went in two motor vehicles and in carts to the village of Vasilevichi intending to attack the partisans. According to the plan of operation, the partisans laid an ambush between Guta and Pudino in difficult winter conditions, standing in water up to their knees (it was the flood season). As a result of the combat the entire force of gendarmerie and police was eliminated. Thirty-two people were killed, four were captured. All the spoils of war were taken and two vehicles were destroyed. The combat operation was fulfilled excellently. There were no losses on the partisan side. Nineteen people took part in the operation.

21 June 1944
Kirov brigade, under the leadership of the brigade's commander Comrade Vasiljev, fulfilled an especially important state task in the district of the village of Noviny. The Ordzhonikidze detachment took part. As a result of combat with the Germans near the village of Noviny, three Germans were killed and five were taken into captivity. According to additional information, in the second combat 24 Germans were killed and 13 wounded. Ten partisans from the detachment took part in the combat which had involved 70 people in all.

Life in the detachment
1. The supply of food to the detachment throughout its existence could well be regarded as satisfactory. Food supplies were obtained from the resources of the local population. However, it prevented the Germans taking deliveries of bread, cattle, milk

and other foodstuffs from areas where the partisans were located.

2. The living conditions of partisans were unsatisfactory. Partisans had to adapt to local conditions at their camp's location.

3. Morale of the detachment's personnel could be regarded as quite satisfactory. Partisans in the detachment were mainly Jews, who had already lived through especially great difficulties in saving their lives from the German-fascist fiends.

4. There were up to 30 women and girl partisans who took part in the struggle.

5. Partisans Blyachman, Sh., Buslin, E. and Kagan, A. distinguished themselves in action and died while fulfilling the task. Kudryaveev, A.A.; Jakimovich, I.S.; Tober, G.N.; Buslin, I.Z.; Rachkovski, I.M.; Gercovski, A.Z.; Grajzhevski, G.M.; Lerner, I.B. and others. All the above-mentioned comrades proved themselves in action to be the best patriots of their Motherland in the expulsion of the fascist fiends.

General conclusion

Throughout its combat activity, the partisan detachment Ordzhonikidze set itself the task of making sudden, powerful strikes on German headquarters, garrisons, military stockpiles and factories, destroying lines of communication and enemy echelons and derailing trains. Because of unsatisfactory supplies of armaments, especially ammunition, explosives and automatic weapons, the partisan detachment could not achieve better results than those shown in the section about combat activity. Partisans were largely invulnerable when the enemy organised major ambushes or raids because, recognising their lack of numbers and ammunition, they would avoid confrontations with the enemy, disperse in small groups and move along their secret partisans' routes without losses. Where they knew they could achieve success against the enemy they appeared unexpectedly and brought about its destruction.

The enemy's tactics were not successful in the fight against the partisans. Despite superiority in numbers, ammunition and technique, the German army could not break the partisan movement. In the fierce struggle the partisans grew in power with each day, smashing the enemy's rear forces and all its communications.

Commander of the partisan detachment 'Ordzhonikidze' captain /Lyashenko/

Commissar of the partisan detachment 'Ordzhonikidze' political leader /Kijan/

Chief of staff of the partisan detachment 'Ordzhonikidze' lieutenant /Podkolzin/

The above text is based on a translation by Tamara Vershitskaya, the curator of the Museum, Novogrodek, from the archives of Central National Archives, Minsk.

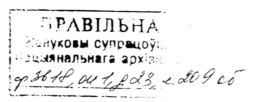

(Overleaf): The inscription on the tombstone reads:

EVERLASTING PEACE

In this cemetery, the deceased from the Nowogrudek Jewish community were laid to rest for 500 years. During the Holocaust their graves were desecrated and their tombstones were extirpated. On July 26, 1941, before the four huge massacres in which the Nazis and their henchmen murdered 11,100 Jews from the town and its surroundings, the Germans shot 52 Jewish citizens dead in the market place and they were buried in a mass grave in that same cemetery.

In memory of the martyrs of our community who perished in the Holocaust, the partizans and those who fell at the front during the war, whose last resting place is not known.

May they rest in everlasting peace

Fencing of the cemetery and setting the tombstone was performed by the Nowogrudek Jewish Association in Israel and in the Diaspora during the month of Av, July 1997.

Index